L A N D S C R I P T IS A PUBLICATION ON LANDSCAPE ÆSTHETICS INVITING AUTHORS FROM DIFFERENT DISCIPLINES TO INVEST THOUGHT ON ESTABLISHED MODES OF PERCEIVING, REPRESENTING, AND CONCEIVING NATURE. STEERED BY AN EDITORIAL BOARD COMPRISED OF INTERNATIONAL EXPERTS FROM VARIOUS FIELDS, WHICH WILL ENCOURAGE A CRITICAL AND CONTROVERSIAL DIALOGUE, ITS GOAL IS TO ACT AS A REVELATOR OF CONVENTIONAL PERCEPTIONS OF LANDSCAPE AND TO CULTIVATE THE DEBATE ON ÆSTHETICS AT A SCHOLARLY LEVEL. THIS DISCUSSION PLATFORM SEEKS TO REKINDLE A THEORETICAL DEBATE, IN THE HOPE OF FOSTERING A BETTER UNDERSTANDING OF THE IMMANENCE OF LANDSCAPE ARCHITECTURE IN OUR CULTURE, FOCUSING CRITICALLY ON THE WAY WE THINK, LOOK, AND ACT UPON SITES.

T0341757

Professor Christophe Girot, Albert Kirchengast (Editors-in-chief)
Chair of Landscape Architecture, ETH Zurich

LANDSCRIPT 6

CHRISTOPHE GIROT
ALBERT KIRCHENGAST
(EDS.)

LANDSCAPE ANALOGUE

ABOUT MATERIAL CULTURE AND IDEALISM

Foreword

Albert Kirchengast

A certain appeal lies in a collection of essays by esteemed colleagues that affords its editors the noble task of "binding" them together in the form of a publication. One might describe it as reaping someone else's harvest. The word anthology carries similar associations. Publishing texts, in turn, lends them weight and garners a readership. Positions set to paper can generate compelling friction. What counts most of all, however, is the "kaleidoscope" that comes into being. In scholarly compilations, experts' contributions respond to clearly specified research questions. This at least makes it possible to gauge the quality of such citable publications, which always remain clearly ensconced in the respective disciplines. The publication then presents itself as part of the so-called discourse. The contributions they contain are capable of influencing this or that in the respective fields of knowledge—but they always operate soberly within a framework that ensures they are "understood." They may shed light on a topic, yet often remain within standard expectations.

Is there another way? Might we devise another approach to this *genre*? How and to what extent could we succeed in "opening up" these inquiries? And especially when the future of the world we human beings shape is at stake? What if a book were to attempt to coin a term that would subsequently allow us to achieve more clarity and— this is our hope—provide a service outside the medium and at a remove from the scholarly community? And that would somehow accomplish this more freely with respect to formal constraints, simply plucking up the abundance of ideas of the many thinkers who would serendipitously come into contact with each other. An anthology would then transform into an intellectual forum. We would meet up along the way, and what we compile would become the impulse for something new. In this case, the editors would thus engage with the curiosity of the inquirers who have identified a topic. They would select authors they are confident can further develop such a concept—and contribute to a not-yet-existent, shared sense of purpose. Editors would capitalize on a chorus made up of many voices—thereby ensuring that a *single* text could not have arrived at the same result.

When we first set out to plan *Landscape Analogue*, our thoughts revolved around the role of design in our time—particularly in light of the fact that in landscape architecture, nature and culture have been intertwined since time immemorial, and its history of ideas can be traced back to a concrete Utopia. Nostalgic escapism is certainly not what the exigencies of our time would require of us. Today the shaping of our surroundings is no longer merely at risk of being assimilated by "economization," but rather of being fully subjugated to the spell of the new technologies of "ecologization." After all, having a future is being mistaken once more for enacting progress. This comparatively recent term "progress" obscures other, more intellectual dimensions of the European Enlightenment: those of the relation of the empowerment of the individual to the shared ideal. At present, for instance, in keeping with an Enlightenment 2.0, we could grasp the existential threats of our days as the chance to enact policies of limitation. This time it is not a matter of discussing what is *necessary*—a decision that might mistakenly be construed as a luxury—but rather of pointing to leeway in design and thereby to a potential that can be exploited: There is something liberating in combining the beauty of the living with an ethics of participating as a *part* in the ongoing-ness of a vibrant world and comprehending this new context as a design problem in support of day-to-day life—not pro-claiming a state of emergency. And perhaps it turns out that the amount of idealism necessary for "survival" would by no means have to be in contradiction to realism.

The sixth issue of *Landscript* is therefore oriented to the question of a possible new understanding of a "shared space of design": we are convinced that how we shape our habitats will play a central role in coming to terms with the challenges humanity faces. The decisive "how," we must concede, has yet to be outlined. We find it, however, to be out of place to want to patronizingly show the way, for example, by putting forth examples of landscape archi-tecture or architecture—this would amount to a mere presentation of results. Moreover, if we agree that the shared principles have yet to be communicated, it would not have been of much help. We propose, in contrast, to work with the conceptual pair that remained with us throughout countless debates and many moments of reflec-tion. It constitutes the title of this publication and is made up of *landscape* (a category with a long tradition of shap-ing) and *analogue* (as possible principle of our activity within it). "Analogue" is intended to address not only the mode of operation of "nature," with which our society seems to have such difficulty, but also human beings in their corporeality *and* historicity. Our appreciation of the immediacy of the concrete and the beauty of vitality causes us to have high expectations for the spaces en-hancing our daily lives—a way of communing we have found to be lacking both in the city and in the countryside.

We contacted selected authors with this—admittedly vague—sketch. Astonishingly, no one viewed it as an impediment to making a contribution to the publication. For our readers we have but one wish: that they might seek out shared themes and join us in our quest to develop ideas about what action could be taken. Therein lies the opportunity to discover the true theme of this book.

The Analogue, the Adaptive, and the New: Thinking the Grammar of Landscape

Christophe Girot

We feel that even when all possible scientific questions have been answered, the problems of life have not been put to rest.

Ludwig Wittgenstein, *Tractatus Logico-Philosophicus*

Introduction

As humans, we have the exceptional capability to apprehend our world without the need for any rational or scientific arguments. For instance, we can revel in the transcendence of a bird in flight while remaining divorced from any scientific assessment of the act itself. We can in a second's notice, through pure imagination, grasp multilayered truths from our world.

As such, a landscape is as much defined by its poetic value, its auguries and horizons, as by the asserted veracity of economy, geology, and agency. In Corsica, the people of Patrimonio learn to read and sing to their horizons; each view telling a completely different myth and story of the same place.—[1] Thus, landscape embodies myth and becomes a living partition resonating with its surroundings. By reenacting the place in the present, local beliefs trump any rational discourse about the environment and its array of imminent disasters. It is precisely this complex

1 *Sounds from Granite Island*, Acoustic Architecture in Corsica, Seminar Week Spring 2017, Ludwig Berger, editor and composer, chair of landscape architecture, Professor Christophe Girot, ETH Zurich.

mix of myths and impressions, resulting from the slow reading, the shaping of a place, that is of interest to us and gives genuine value to a landscape.

Through the relentless question of time, space, language, and culture, how can a place be experienced and read differently, whether diachronically or synchronically in the present?—[2] Be it through myths, or by analogy, adaptation, or authentication, landscapes help weave a place into the greater order of things. A greater palimpsest is interwoven, alternating seasons and meanings in a continuum in which the specific quality of a given place remains identifiable, measurable, and clear.

Landscape architecture results from a continual cultural transformation, through a series of successive acts that mark the nature of a place. It engages a subtle interaction between given site qualities of soil, water, terrain, and those visions borrowed from other regions that gradually merge and together formulate a specific *physis*.—[3]

In parallel to this landscape evolution, we have also imagined and created landscapes entirely based on the promises of science. Some of these have become iconic examples of human prowess over nature. As an example, the Ski Dome in Dubai demonstrates how humans can forge an entirely new nature on oil, completely eradicating our natural understanding of the world.—[4] Within this paradigm, landscapes are pale simulacrums of their virtual substitutes.

The young designers of today are looking squarely at these two cultures of landscape design. They find themselves confronted with the constant news feed of our ecological downfall. Students of landscape and architecture must nonetheless project, develop, and hopefully create visions of our future. If landscape is to become the crucible of more regional food and biomass production

2   In his book *The Order of Things* Michel Foucault writes about the different "epistemes" that varied according to period and produced significantly different ways of ordering thought and discourse. He hints at substrata where the questions of synchronicity of thought in a given period are juxtaposed to a diachronic reality where different periods and readings are intertwined. Here is a quote from *The Order of Things*: "In attempting to uncover the deepest strata of Western culture, I am restoring to our silent and apparently immobile soil its rifts, its instability, its flaws, and it is this same ground that is once more stirring under our feet." Foucault, Michel: *The Order of Things: An Archaeology of the Human Sciences.* London 1970, p. XXIV

3   See chapter on "Roots," Girot, Christophe: *The Course of Landscape Architecture.* London / New York 2016, pp. 15–43

4   Created in 2005 in the United Arab Emirates, the 2.5-hectare ski area is maintained year-round at minus 1°C. It includes an 85-meter-high *indoor mountain* that includes 5 slopes and is part of one of the biggest shopping malls in the world.

over time, then careful consideration in the choices of new systems and artifacts best adapted to local conditions and culture will be necessary. If this requires a capacity to merge a complex interweaving of challenges, actions, and reactions, then what are the skills needed for this new generation of designers?

The Analogue

As we try to better define the contours of a new culture that will help construct and characterize a landscape better in our age, we believe in the analogue as a foundation of learning. It is the use of these modern myths that is of critical interest here. We feel intimately bound to the analogue, because it ties us back to something that we think we already know and are able to grasp and recognize instinctively. There exists a *deep grammar* of landscape to which the analogue always refers.—[5] Depending on period, context, and religion, to name but a few factors, the grammar of design is always a matter rooted in local beliefs, practices, and materials. It has to do with how one refers to, appropriates, transforms, and articulates a given piece of land. The analogue, therefore, calls for a more substantiated explanation about the rules that drive it. Differentiated nuances between what is natural, cultural, and economic stand clearly apart from one another, yet merge together as a whole. Its grammar is thought to be more genuine because of its belonging to values of the past. Yet the analogue acts as a cultural metonym, recalling only fragments of the traits of the original. It is therefore never quite complete in its role as a landscape substitute of the past. Yet it must still strive to emanate its essence.—[6]

Let us look first into the natural world of the analogue. Old stands of elms were decimated in Britain in the nineteen-seventies by Dutch elm disease, a deadly fungal

[5] In talking about *deep grammar* "when we study human language, we are approaching what some might call the human essence, the distinctive qualities of mind that are, so far as we know, unique to man." Chomsky, Noam: *Language and Mind*. Cambridge/MA 2006, p. 88

[6] In his essay "Les Cinq Sens," Michel Serres reflects on our very sudden evolution and suggests that through this we may have lost touch with some of our senses. The analogue plays an important >

> role in this evolution-
ary transformation as it
mirrors of our own sensory
adaptation, not to say de-
generation. Serres, Michel:
Les Cinq Sens, Paris 1985

pathogen. They were replaced in the following decades by groves and alignments of hornbeam, ash, plane, linden, or maple. These trees produced a similar structure and effect in the landscape but without the same color, texture, and stature so typical of the elms. In this instance, the analogous trees played on the notion of collective memory through *mimesis*. The surrogate species planted in replacement performed well, providing ample shelter and shade. Only the elders may recall the splendid allure of the elms. The analogue here does not necessarily replicate the same shades of green, or the same rustling leaves. But it provides many of the services that the old road alignments and country groves ensured back then. In this instance, the analogue tree does not pretend to imitate the elm but rather hints back at its spirit and magnificence as best it can.

There are other cases where an analogue derails nature profoundly and becomes, to say the least, counterproductive. The California Gold Rush in the eighteen-fifties provoked widespread deforestation as coastal redwood stands were laid bare by early settlers. Eucalyptus seeds were brought from Australia to California as a good substitute for timber. To help reforest the coastal region where ancient redwoods once stood, there ensued until the eighteen-seventies a "eucalyptus boom" where hundreds of thousands of such trees were planted all along the Pacific Coast. But let us first come back to the redwood. A young redwood seedling needs to grow in the dappled shade of the low-lying California Bay under-brush for a decade before it gathers enough strength and power in its roots to propel it upwards to reach the tallest treetops. A young eucalyptus, by contrast, has no problem growing on freshly cleared ground in the blazing California sun. It adapts quickly to this new habitat to produce a full-fledged eucalyptus grove in a matter of a couple of decades. Unlike the redwoods, this species is adapted to brush fires, literally thriving on them and being able to recover faster than other species. The speed of growth and aggressiveness of eucalyptus trees has made them a dominant element in the California landscape. In addition, allelopaths located in their foliage, bark, and roots, prevent most other plant species to grow around them. This helps eucalyptus seedlings to spread and become even more established in this new habitat. It is true that both trees can attain great heights. However, on all other points, such as the quality of its shade, foliage, and wood, the eucalyptus is seriously outmatched. Despite having become widely established in California and the fact that it sometimes hosts migrant monarch butterflies, it is not really a valid analogue for the countless coastal redwood groves that have disappeared. Many other regions of the world, from the Mediterranean Basin to Southeast Asia and the entire coast of Chile, have also been deeply affected by the widespread planting of eucalyptus trees. The results, to say the least, are mitigated when it comes to the analogue restitution of original landscape traits pertaining to these regions.

What must we be cautious of when studying the analogue? One should be cautious about boundary conditions as defined by the physics of the landscape under study and the habitus of the people.—[7] Culture reverts to a broad range of seemingly unrelated topics that can result, when bundled together, in a specific set of constraints reflecting on the shaping and particular aesthetic of a given landscape. Depending on the issues at stake, the analogue often implies a cultural transgression of sorts that needs to be carefully considered in relation to context and custom. One has to study precedents carefully in order to understand the transregional migration of landscape genres. One must also learn how the contextual limitations that circumscribe a particular landscape depend as much on the capacity for new forms of habitus and acceptance in society, as they do on adaptation to climate and terrain. The limitations inherent to each place and how they

7   In his book entitled *Ecoumène*, Augustin Berque relates precisely to the culture of the natural world and the symbiotic relationship that prevails between human dwelling and landscape aesthetics. Berque, Augustin: *Ecoumène, introduction à l'étude des milieux humains.* Paris, 2009

translate into a set of ontologies and symbolic acts on a landscape help us define and secure an entirely new form of cultural context.—[8]

8   By proposing in *Politiques de la nature* to create a new collective spirit in society, Bruno Latour suggests that it is society itself that chooses what in the human and nonhuman realms really matters. Latour, Bruno: *Politiques de la nature: Comment faire entrer les sciences en démocratie*. Paris 1999

Take, for example, the King's Garden in Copenhagen, which is one of the latest, northernmost Renaissance gardens still in existence today. Designed for King Christian IV at the turn of the seventeenth century, it was originally intended to deliver fruit, flowers, and vegetables to the royal household. When it was introduced, as a Renaissance garden analogue, it represented a significant shift in scale and scope from what until then was just considered Danish medieval gardening culture. Today the King's Garden is much loved and used as a public park by the residents of Copenhagen. But upon closer observation, and beyond the exoticism of the Syrian roses and lavender beds neatly planted in geometric parterres as a direct reference to Mediterranean culture, one notes that most other plants used in this garden, such as the lime trees that frame the avenues and the trimmed quadratic hornbeam hedges, have no direct relationship to plants commonly found in the original Italian Renaissance gardens. There are no evergreen oak alignments, cypresses, or boxwood hedges to be found. The spirit of the King's Garden is indeed analogous in proportion and style to its remote French and Italian ancestors. Yet, it works also as a laboratory that refers to a more local tradition of protective garden hedges grown around ancient Danish homes. This underlines the importance of specific knowledge on the use and adaptation of local plants. For instance, the manner in which the hornbeams are trimmed to form a scaled-down orthogonal microcosm of sun niches, is foreign to the original French and Italian Renaissance garden that sought more shade than sun. It refers to much older local practices where Danes have always trimmed hornbeam hedges into elliptical sun trap palisades around their homes. This is also why the residents of Copenhagen wouldn't think twice about this

Renaissance analogue as being an integral part of their local culture.

The import of analogue landscape models in Latin America poses the difficult question of very mixed cultural practices linked to the Conquista, slavery, and the cultural transformation due to the massive immigration from Europe and Asia. The desire to forge the character of conquered cities and landscapes according to distant European references posed first and foremost a question of adaptation and economy. This probably explains why most of these analogues, belonging to another corner of the world, developed into a realm of their own with a strong identity. Buenos Aires is the perfect place to study the history of such intertwined developments. The city that came to be known as the Paris of South America touched on some fundamental questions about the cultural and economic potential of the analogue. When the Frenchman Jules Charles Thays was invited to Argentina in 1889 at the age of forty-four, upon recommendation of Jean Alphand, to design the Sarmiento Park in Cordoba, little did this student of Edouard André know that he would become the director of parks and alleys of Buenos Aires two years later.—[9] Thays began a fantastic cultural experiment in Buenos Aires by researching the local flora along the Parana and Uruguay watersheds, identifying local trees like the jacaranda and the tipuana that would adapt well to urban conditions. His research, done for the sake of economy, actually innovated and helped contribute significantly to the genuine character of the parks and alleys of Buenos Aires as we see them today. He developed a unique selection of trees and produced over 150,000 specimens, planted throughout the city under his supervision. Some critics say that Thays grossly misinterpreted the scale of Parisian avenues in his plan of Buenos Aires. But the broader avenues that he drew were better adapted to catching the breeze off the Rio de la Plata on muggy

9   Berjman, Sonia: *Carlos Thays: un jardinero francés de Buenos Aires*. Buenos Aires 2009

19

summer days. The scale of the avenues was also better suited to the taller native trees that were available. This shift in scale and proportion from the original Paris analogue contributed to an exuberant sense of generosity that is still perceptible today in places like the Palermo grove in Buenos Aires. The extraordinary blue blossoms of giant jacarandas reach out and blend with the sky in late October, leaving a lasting impression of wonder on the visitor. The variations on this landscape analogue are so strong that it would be difficult today to want to draw a comparison between the strict Hausmanian avenues of Paris designed by Alphand and those more open and generous of Buenos Aires designed by Carlos Thays that have branded the landscape identity of this city with local flora.

Most of the forementioned analogue examples, whether successful or not, are drawn from the past and play in some way or other with a reference to a long-lost original. Yet they have developed their own realm and stand now as landscapes in their own right. But with the rapid change in climatic, health, and social conditions that are now occurring everywhere, seeking an answer to the future development of landscapes through past references may be quite limited and seriously compromised. We are in the age of adaptation, where solutions will need to be carefully questioned and tested through various means of design before they are implemented. This is also where the role of new technologies and AI become central in in matters of data generation and time management, as well as monitoring.—10 These technological tools, however, will not protect us from potential failures. It is our conviction that culture must play the key role in this age of adaptation.

10 "With our move into the *digital age*—our current era that is characterized by technology or digitality—, [sic] we similarly let go of many established certainties and *way of doing things.* ... Therefore [we are] not just called upon to adapt and adjust, but more fundamentally we are given the opportunity to completely reimagine our own role in relation to what we do, the materials we work with, the works we create and the people we share our cities, our spaces and our culture with." Michael, Sebastian: "Introduction." In: *Atlas of Digital Architecture*, ed. Ludger Hovestadt. Basel 2020, p. 10

The Adaptive

It is now a fact that the change of climate occurring worldwide urgently requires that we revise and adapt the *deep grammar* underlying our approach to landscape design. We must urgently prepare and act concretely on all the foreseen circumstances to come.

Science and technology play a very important role in these models by surveying, quantifying, predicting, and proposing variants of solutions. However, these tools can significantly challenge other design processes. In some circles, the belief is that adaptive measures should be entirely determined through these tools and methods, yet there should be no such thing as environmental fatalism. Designers will need to learn how to manage and make use of the data glut that surrounds them, while maintaining clarity in the local political, scientific and societal challenges to come. One cannot deny centuries of landscape culture simply by proceeding under a banner of assumed scientific proof and truth.—11 Digital simulation tools and AI can help us model the unthinkable and adapt our landscape design approaches creatively. However, we must learn how to mix this scientific parlance with more local customs and values. Planetary emotionalism based on quantitative scientific data alone will have little or no effect on the design quality of local projects in which we will have to dwell day by day.

11 In his critique on the blind beliefs that modern science delivers, Latour points to the deep rift between cultural practices and scientific evidence. Latour, Bruno: *Politiques de la nature: Comment faire entrer les sciences en démocratie*. Paris 1999

The challenges are certainly awesome, but it is our responsibility at present to reinstate a new faith in the power of the adaptive. The adaptive implies a paradigm shift in the way we fundamentally think, conceive, and practice landscape design, but always within the framework of local culture and language. Methods and approaches to local landscape design should be repeatedly studied, debated, and tested. Our future requires fundamental changes in local landscape forms and cultivation practices. However, these changes must be made through a language and grammar of their own. Young designers must strive to extract the analogue power of a site.

Furthermore, within the disruptive environmentalist discourse that is currently trending, there remains a significant distortion between adaptive solutions, to be worked out at a more local scale, and claims on global climatic challenges, which are phenomenally beyond the range and scope of design. The distortions that occur at different scales of environmental modeling, whether planetary, continental, regional or local, will strongly affect the purpose, effect, and credibility of the landscape initiatives.—[12] As we enter the age of the adaptive, the established grammar of analogue replication will either need to be questioned and enhanced, or it will fail. New design initiatives will require that we entirely question the existing grammar of design locally and knowingly, by identifying and framing the different landscape artifacts that embody the cultural mindset specifically. Each place will define its priorities and solutions, and science will subsequently help define various possible approaches to diversity and context. One should not be mistaken: the scale at which our discipline operates is local, not global. It is precisely the knowledge of language and local lore that will be key to any successful adaptation.

Some regions will move faster and better than others. This will give the opportunity to investigate new hybrid forms of cultivation and habitat within new biomes, and that will in turn offer completely different sets of living modes and hybridized biodiversities. This approach will strongly affect the way design is taught at schools where local material culture, biodiversity, food production, urban cooling, and public health will become

12 There prevails a great degree of confusion between ambitious communication about awareness programs and the harsher reality of concrete actions and measures on the terrain. At the launch of the *European Green Deal* on December 9, 2020, Frans Timmermans, European Commission executive vice-president for the European Green Deal, said: "The European Climate Pact will bring together everyone who wants to take action for our planet. With the Pact, we want to help everyone in Europe take action in their everyday lives, and give everyone the opportunity to get involved in the green transition and inspire each other. When it comes to tackling climate change, anyone can take action, and everyone can contribute."

some of the main priorities. Students must also be able to use the tools and discourse with technological experts, in a scale of project planning that can span over decades. For any adaptive strategy to come, they must be able to parlay the rules of governance, validation, and implementation into a new aesthetic language.

New Horizons

Among the new skills to be taught, we must learn to how to actually take care of our surroundings. The problem that we face today is that we can no longer find a clear landscape as a referent to work from. When new landscape myths were created in the past, they often played with natural history and the idea of a possible return to a nature of origins. Whether as religious zealots, or the legions that founded the first colonies, new settlers always promised to better care for the land. Though the challenges of global warming and demographic pressure before us are of another order of magnitude and scope altogether, the importance of human care and attention to nature remains at the core of our concerns. This aspect cannot be stressed enough.

The etymology of the word "authentic" in ancient Greek simply means "one who does things himself."—[13] We are clearly entering an age where nature will be composed and fabricated for a variety of purposes, ranging from jungles to vineyards and town squares. There exist some striking new examples of inventive adaptive practices. One such example has taken root in countries like Sri Lanka, where current programs actually pay families to take care of just one single tree. Each year the number of leaves on the tree are counted and payment is made only when healthy growth of the tree is reported.—[14] This approach contrasts strongly with a widespread quantitative approach to programs of massive tree planting,

13 Authentic (adj.) mid-14th century, *autentik*, "authoritative, duly authorized" (a sense now obsolete), from Old French *autentique* "authentic; canonical" (13th century, Modern French *authentique*) and directly from medieval Latin *authenticus*, from Greek *authentikos* "original, genuine, principal," from *authentes* "one acting on one's own authority," from autos "self" (see auto-) + *hentes* "doer, being," from PIE root **sene-* (2) "to accomplish, achieve." >

> Sense of "real, entitled to acceptance as factual" is first recorded mid-14th century. The Online Etymology Dictionary 2021

14 "A Journey to Keep the Land Forested." In: *The Financial Times*, August 17, 2018. Interview by Frances Bulathsinghala with Dr. Ranil Senanayake, who introduced the model of analog foresting to the world.

where the survival rate of each seedling is left to its own demise—a practice that is far from optimal and limits the choice of species type to fast growing plants like eucalyptus. Could it be that nature needs more careful human attention than ever to survive and develop? Vegetation growth is being significantly impacted globally by the increased amplitude in temperature cycles, alternating extreme hot and cold spells all year round. Most currently cultivated plants will have a hard time adapting to these changes on their own and will need much more care and human attention. The burning of olive groves this summer around Corinth speaks of the incredible challenge ahead. The native olive trees cannot handle weeks of temperatures above 45° Celsius on their own. If we are to keep the most mythical tree of the Mediterranean alive, it will now need constant human care, adaptation, and water to survive. This in turn will imply very significant changes in landscape topology and cultural practices. This example, together with countless others, means that we can definitely say goodbye to the ecological cornerstone myth of a return to an original forest. We must now welcome a new age where nature will need to be invented and cared for entirely.

Forty years ago, I concluded my bachelor of science in environmental planning and management at UC Davis. There, I was fortunate enough to meet Ranil Senanayake and join him in Sri Lanka for one month as he founded his first experimental project the *Analog Forest*. Located on a hillside in Belipola, on an old eroded tea plantation exposed to the blazing equatorial sun, most of the soil had long since been washed away by the monsoon rains. The site conditions were the direct results of colonial and postcolonial mismanagement of the land that is widespread around the world. What used to be a thriving tropical jungle with an incredible biodiversity had sadly become a hillside of sunbaked rocks and drier vegetation. The *Analog Forest* was designed to develop into several accelerated seral stages, starting with the sowing of a mixed grassland to stabilize the slopes and recreate an initial humus layer. Then came the first trees, not necessarily natives like the Australian grevillea, able to provide a rapid first shade canopy under which more sun sensitive native tree species could start to grow. This was followed by regular soil microorganism transplants from adjacent forests patches. The planting and caring for shade-loving seedlings under the canopy was constant over the past four decades and allowed for a "natural selection" to occur. Once the jungle underbrush was fully created, local jungle flora and fauna gradually came back to inhabit the place. The result today is most spectacular and encouraging. The experiment has been extended to twenty other tropical countries worldwide, from Costa Rica to Cuba and Burma. Despite its name, the *Analog Forest* is in fact an act of cultural adaptation to contemporary ecological design. It is a truly a leading project that gives us hope and guidance in the path toward pragmatic ecological restoration.—[15] We can all learn and profit from this experiment, where adaptive pragmatism and local analogue culture worked hand in hand. There is no doubt that what has been created in Belipola differs from the original Sri Lankan jungle. The project, albeit synthetic and hybrid, models a new form of biodiversity and is a definite improvement from the devastating site conditions that were there in the first place. The *Analog Forest* sets an entirely new horizon in contemporary landscape design and could serve as model for further experimentations. Like some myth born from the ashes of colonial greed, neglect, and destruction, this example has grown on the faith of constant human care, attention, and monitoring. The age of the adaptive requires this high degree of human attention, dedication, and involvement. One could say that Ranil Senanayake has not only made a giant step in matters of applied ecology, but also made progress in matters of a new grammar of landscape design and intelligence that opens up a broad array of

15 Senanayake, Ranil/ Jack, John: "Analog Forestry an Introduction." In: *Monash Publications in Geography,* no. 49. Melbourne 1988, pp. 1–115

possible new horizons around the world. This experiment relates back to a genuine shift in ecological paradigms at this moment in history. We definitely need to understand how to decipher and transpose the grammar of this approach to other latitudes and contexts.

Our attention has been mostly focused on the rapid development of urban settlements over the last decades—and this to the detriment of rural areas that have been laid to waste and neglected. Could it be that our future is as much in the hands of a rural and natural revival as it is in the improvement of our urban condition? Landscapes will need to remain inhabited, to gain human support and help us find the right bearings, in order to adapt to rapidly changing conditions. In this sense, each experiment will remain true to local language and culture and be neither replicable nor transferable elsewhere. There can be no doubt that every local landscape must now reinvent itself materially and culturally. Its success will depend as much on the culture of care that is instilled as on the quality of the monitoring and maintenance techniques that will be provided. The *Analog Forest* is still in its fledgling state, but could become part of a comprehensive approach to landscape architecture in years to come. This will depend mostly on how far such human-induced projects will work as substitutes and satisfy local cultural and ecological criteria. In the best of cases, such projects will be able to revive the myth of a new analogue that has fully adapted to its changing conditions and time.

Time plays a critical role in the establishment of these experiments, and each year that passes without developing such projects is pure loss. Adapting over centuries is no longer an option today. Time to act is limited and we need to decide knowingly and act concretely with resolve. The promise of a new horizon in landscape architecture can no longer wait; local political resolve

must now be found and acted upon. City requirements
for food, cooling, and ventilation are going to change entirely the form and function of street vegetation in years
to come as they connect to their natural and agrarian
hinterlands. Our projects must be able to create hope in
a new horizon, with new forms of analogues, that will be
confirmed through successive transformations.

A migrant worker sweeps melting water at the Venice Architecture Biennale in May 2021;
Melting Landscape, a project by Kei Kaihoh with Giulia Chiatante and Kentaro Hayashi

Conclusion

We currently stand at the cusp of a widespread cultural revolution that will put all existing landscapes to the test. Jean Jacques Rousseau's firm belief in humankind's return to some original state of nature is certainly tempting and immensely liberating on an ontological level.—[16] But it will not work in the present reality and spatiotemporal complexities that we face. Landscapes should be understood as an important sphere of action within a broader evolving societal continuum. They are the expression of a given form of appropriation of the natural world, driven by the politics and economics of place, as seen through the lens of local climatic and environmental conditions.

16 See Rousseau, Jean Jacques: *Discours sur l'Origine et les Fondements de l'Inégalité parmi les Hommes*. Paris 2011

The question of the landscape necessarily passes through the subjective experience of a place as we capture its poetic uniqueness and the deeper meaning that transcends it. Landscape is as elaborate and unpredictable as it is a poetic bearer of the ethereal flight of things passing. Myths are at the basis of any culture, and these can be rekindled or reborn through attention and care. Subliminal meanings that we derive from a landscape necessarily occur through a deep act of language, memory, and cultural recognition, forming the very cornerstone of civilization. Landscape design is, now more than ever, urgent, complex, and a multifaceted and multitalented operation. It is an exercise that challenges our human intelligence as we must navigate from science and technology to hands on knowledge about a locality. It imposes constant care and thought from day-to-day action on a terrain to strategic long-term planning.

Roland Barthes always said that myths are there to be born and die, only to be born again.—[17] Similarly, the analogue as we now know it is bound to change and die, adapt, and reappear again under a different form.

17 See Barthes, Roland: *Mythologies*. New York 2013

Landscape architecture belongs to a long-standing culture of design, in which experimentation through creative design investigation, trial, and error is part of a continual form of questioning further. Rather than something prescriptive or scientifically dogmatic that can stand in the way of this lore, it is rooted in deep cultural values and in our most coveted hopes.

Toward a Theory of Contemporary Landscape Ornament

Lara Mehling

Introduction

For all the talk about architectural ornament, not once have I heard mention of the phrase "landscape ornament." Not in ornament's recent renaissance within architectural discourse and practice, not in Loos's condemnation a century ago, not during its heyday, extending from Jones and Ruskin, Riegl or Semper all the way back to Vitruvius. Is it irrelevant to the discipline? Is it taboo? Or have we simply lacked the terminology to express a series of trends that emphasize the ornamental qualities of landscape design rather than express landscape's ornamental qualities?

Before proposing a possible direction for a history and theory of landscape ornament, let us take a look at some related terms such as *natural* ornament, *floral* ornament, and *garden* ornament. Flowers, perhaps the most object-like element of a garden, have been treated as natural ornament for millennia. Before the Ruskins and Riegls of ornament, Immanuel Kant described flowers as "free beauties," elaborating on their decorative application and in particular how through stylized figures, the artist "makes the thing itself speak, as it were, in mimic language—a very common play of our fancy, that attributes to lifeless things a soul suitable to their form, and that uses them as its mouthpiece."—[1] According to

1 Kant, Immanuel: *Critique of Judgement*. Trans. James Creed Meredith. Oxford [1790] 1911, §16, p. 72 and §51, p. 188

31

Kant, a parterre of flowers and a roomful of ornaments similarly create a picture that seeks nothing other than to please the eye and engage the imagination. So flowers themselves may be considered a kind of natural ornament. And, of course, we have a long-established history of floral ornament in architecture and the applied arts. Both as stone fragments (the carved rosette medallions of Persepolis come to mind) and as mere symbols (the iconography of stitched, woven, or painted textiles is but a fraction of reference material), early records mostly in the form of representations of flowers have been preserved through the centuries and over vast regions. Floral and vegetal ornament has long been one of the fundamental modes of decorative design within Islamic ornament and beyond. Some of these patterns were later rediscovered, adapted, and disseminated across Europe in the search for a history on ornament in the mid-nineteenth century by the likes of Alois Riegl, John Ruskin, Owen Jones, and Gottfried Semper.—[2] Further reflections on floral ornament emerged in the late nineteenth century, made by botanists, artists, designers, architects, and theorists such as Karl Krumbholz, Frederick Edward Hulme, Moritz Meurer, and Christopher Dresser.

2 John Ruskin famously said: "There is material enough in a single flower for the ornament of a score of cathedrals." Ruskin, John: *The Stones of Venice*. London 1873, p. 339

The difficulty with defining landscape ornament is that for a very long time architectural ornament was largely based on botanical models. So if we are to speak of a decorative language belonging to landscape itself, then what are its models? A reciprocal gesture would suggest architectural elements. And in a way, this is true. But it is truer of garden ornament than it is of landscape ornament. In fact, adorning the landscape (*die Landschaft schmücken*) was never a foreign concept in garden design and of frequent usage in German literature on Gartenkunst: adorning the landscape with pavilions, bridges, scattered fruit trees, allées, etc. These eye-catchers in the landscape, occasionally termed garden ornaments, became so unequivocally decorative that French and English eighteenth-century landscape gardens were not complete without a folly, a word signifying either the crazy indulgence of an expensive and useless structure or else its pure "delight." What is important to note is that these classical elements, fully established in the picturesque tradition of glorifying Gothic ruins, temples, bridges, gates, etc., were never considered as separate from the garden. That is, these structures were not only often heavily adorned themselves but that they also served as ornament of and for the garden itself.

That is, of course, not to discount the vegetal forms such as tree clumps, individual trees, rows, or flower parterres, typically laid out in geometric configurations which preceded the eighteenth century trend of "beautifying the landscape" by adorning it with human-made objects. But just as furniture or art objects within a building do not define its ornament per se, garden ornaments placed in a garden as objects do not define a landscape's ornament. It is along these lines that I want to look at the question of materiality. Architectural ornament relied for many centuries on standard construction materials such as wood, stone, plaster, and metal. If these were separate from the underlying materiality of the structure, they were most frequently a painted design. In line with a parallel analysis to architecture, the logical material of choice in landscape, then, would likewise reflect the material makeup of the landscape itself—most essentially plants. But if we are to view plants not as symbols but as a landscape's *material* makeup (what it is made of), then where does the ornament come in if it is not only "natural" but also designed? Reflecting on Antoine Picon's account of how architectural ornament has gradually transitioned from being primarily "attached" (cosmetic) to structure to becoming more and more integral (cosmos) to it today—in which *kosmos* refers to a certain order that is independent of structure—it suddenly becomes evident that landscape ornament has followed a similar trajectory.—3

3   Picon, Antoine: "Ornament and Its Users: From the Vitruvian Tradition to the Digital Age." Trans. Linda Gardiner. In: *Histories of Ornament: From Global to Local*. Princeton 2016, p. 10

Moreover, architectural ornament's more recent shift away from vegetal and floral motifs and toward geometric patterns may give us another clue. In their edited volume *Histories of Ornament*, Gülru Necipoglu and Alina Payne discuss how contemporary examples "privilege geometry as the quintessential form of Islamic ornament" and "prefer to bypass other alternative genres of Islamic ornament ranging from vegetal, floral, figurative, and calligraphic to post-Mongol chinoiserie. In doing so, they respond to the current iconic emphasis on geometricism, and by extension parametricism."—4 Landscape architecture has not been immune to this fascination with parametric design, and yet, few built projects demonstrate a meaningful application which might act as a contribution to the field, for a theoretical framework is still missing. But rather than seek justification for a new geometric order in landscape, I want to point out that architectural ornament's shift away from vegetal and floral forms has opened up the opportunity for landscape ornament to reclaim its roots—to reappropriate botanical models.

The search for contemporary forms of landscape ornament began with looking for innovations in the decorative arts that may have served as models, but it soon became clear that this has more to do with landscape's own materiality and the discipline's knowledge of and interest in botany. As such—different from the categorization of ornament into vegetal, floral, geometric, and figural modes in architecture—in landscape architecture a less established (or less self-conscious) classification of decorative styles relies on mutable understandings of the natural world through botany. (Taken from *botane*, the Greek word for plant, "botany" is both a term used to describe the plant life of a particular region and "the scientific study of the physiology, structure, genetics, ecology, distribution, classification, and economic importance of plants."—5) While geometric layouts based on underlying grids have been employed as organization

4   Necipoglu, Gülru / Payne, Alina (eds.): *Histories of Ornament: From Global to Local*. Princeton 2016, p. 3

5   "Botany." Oxford Dictionary Online: Lexico.com

tools for planting patterns from antiquity to modernity, three periods stand out for not only deriving ornament *from* plant life but also achieving ornament *with* it in the landscape itself: the French formal garden (from the late Renaissance to the baroque), landscape modernism (nineteen-seventies and eighties) and contemporary landscape architecture (since 2000). Each period reveals a new expression of landscape ornament that reflects the evolving fascination with plants in the history of science—from studying, displaying, and celebrating individual rare plants, to understanding a plant's native habitat, and to acknowledging and tracing a plant's behavior, its ability to grow, adapt, and transform in response to shifting environmental and human-caused conditions. The following three sections explore what landscape ornament looks like when we view plants through *taxonomy*, *geography*, or *ecology*, respectively.

Before illustrating these points with examples, I need to mention that the designers of the selected projects have not described their own work or design approach as employing "landscape ornament." I am applying this term retrospectively to built landscapes in an attempt to find the unconscious theoretical basis of a certain line of work. I will begin by drawing on the more distant past when ornament was still more evident as such before tracing these roots to the present to find out what landscape ornament looks like, and means, today.

A Plant Motif Taxonomy: Early Modern Gardens
(Sixteenth to Seventeenth Century)

Between ornament and taxonomy, between pleasure and knowledge, between nature and artifice, the parterre makes evident the articulation between the pleasure of seeing and the construction of knowledge.—[6]

6   Transl. by the author. Guichard, Charlotte: "The Shell in the Eighteenth Century: A Boundary Object?" In: *Techniques & Culture*, no. 59, 2012, December 15, 2015, p. 156. Accessed June 15, 2021. http://journals.openedition.org/tc/6610

The element most illustrative of landscape ornament using vegetal forms, and perhaps most generally perceived as such, is the parterre as it was treated in the late Renaissance and evolved during the sixteenth and seventeenth centuries into a recognizable element of the French formal garden. Few would argue that the practice of laying out parterres at aristocratic and noble estates did not produce ornamental qualities. This is, of course, due to the fact that their formal language, namely the knots, interlacing connections, dominant scrolling arabesques, and other motifs frequently used to represent the compositions in etchings—the only true record of their form—was borrowed from a well-established discourse on ornament in architecture and the decorative arts. Their large-scale projection onto expansive terraces was, in a way, as logical as their application on *marquetry*, bed hangings, and the latest dress fashions.

Even before the celebrated *parterre de broderie*, which paid direct homage to the popular art of embroidery in the seventeenth century, the layout of parterres had evolved from regular square grids to *carreaux rompées*, as Ada Segré demonstrates with great precision in her work on the transfer of knots and other decorative modes to the ground, primarily through the work of Charles Estienne, Daniel Loris, and Jean Liébault.—[7] Notable

7   See Segré, Ada: "De la flore ornementale à l'ornement horticole." In: Farhat, Georges (ed.): *André Le Nôtre, Fragments d'un paysage culturel: Institutions, arts, sciences et techniques.* Musée de l'Île-de-France 2006, pp. 188–203

in the transition from a productive to a decorative aesthetic, however, is the increasing tendency to imitate floral motifs in an effort to achieve more organic forms. This is, of course, not unique to the art of gardening, for botanical models present the most immediate way to achieve a formal language that departs from the rigor of Cartesianism—just as botany emerged at nearly the same time as a science independent from natural history and distinct from medicine and agriculture.

Early attempts at a taxonomical order anticipating Carl Linnaeus's system of classification sought to make sense of all the newly introduced scents, colors, and forms of plant life. An interest in flowering bulbs, adapted to dry mountain slopes and arid desert climes, especially dominated the second half of the sixteenth century in Northern Europe. Adapting many of these species to a wetter and colder climate required the close observation and study of plant form. The *curieux fleuristes* filled their gardens and books with faithful copies of exotic flora, some of which had appeared in European art in early modern herbals and tapestries, yet they frequently got details such as the fruit, leaf shape, and plant's scale wrong for lack of physical models.—[8] Getting a plant's flowering, reproductive, and vegetative parts right was a veritable sign of one's learnedness.—[9] Thus, the popularity of the parterre in garden design developed in a period of not only botanical exploration but also of collecting *naturalia* along with *arteficialia* and *scientifica*, and the focus on the basic form of a plant and the details of a flower blossom reflects the emphasis on and value of individual plants at the time. While the compositions for flower parterres by French designers may first appear to demonstrate only a superficial reading of plants, in this context, it is not surprising that landscape ornament based its decorative repertoire on the taxonomy (the general form or appearance of something as described and classified) of flowering plants. In this way, flowering plants represented the material culture

8   Alexander, Edward Johnston/Woodward, Carol H.: "The Flora of the Unicorn Tapestries." In: Woodward, Carol H. (ed.): *Journal of New York Botanical Garden*. Vol. 14, no. 497, May 1940, p. 108

9   See Hyde, Elizabeth: "Flowers of Distinction: Taste, Class, and Floriculture in Seventeenth-Century France." In: Conan, Michel (ed.): *Bourgeois and Aristocratic Cultural Encounters in Garden Art, 1550–1850*. Washington, D.C. 2002

of the formal garden style in the early modern period
and a plant's floral *form* its ornamental language.

By the late eighteenth century, Antoine-Joseph
Dezallier d'Argenville distinguished between five types
of parterre: "There are divers Sorts of Parterres, which
may be all reduced to these Four that follow; namely,
Parterres of Embroidery, Parterres of Compartiment,
Parterres after the English Manner, and Parterres of
Cut-work. There are also Parterres of Water…"—[10] At
least three of these resemble ornament frequently applied
to textiles while also basing their ornamental language
on botanical motifs: the *parterre de compartiment*,
parterre de pièces coupées, and the *parterre de broderie*.
Lucie Fléjou reminds us that "Dézallier d'Argenville
insists on the essentially ornamental character of the
parterres"—[11] She describes very clearly that "compartimens & broderies" take their basic form from geometry
into which different designs are then placed.—[12] What
stands out are the many differentiated expressions for
foliage, leaflets, and florets. In fact, tracing the parterre's stylistic evolution from the 'compartment' to the
'cut work' and then the 'embroidery' through plan drawings from seventeenth to eighteenth century France (as
they became arbiters of style by this time) reflects the
increasing complexity and importance of plant taxonomy in the seventeenth century. In many ways, the
ground patterns are evidence of the growing attention
given to separate plant organs: flower, fruit, and leaf.
Beginning with the most eye-catching and colorful part
of a vascular plant (the *raison d'être* for the *curieux
fleuristes*), then its edible part (requiring the most acclimatization to yield fruit), and finally its vegetative
part (roots, stems, shoot buds, and leaves—perhaps the
least interesting but helpful in plant identification).

Flower: *parterre de compartimens*
Smaller square *parterres de compartimens*, which were
widely popular in the early seventeenth century for

10 The section on the
"parterre", in: Dezallier
d'Argenville, Antoine-
Joseph: *The Theory and
Practice of Gardening:
Wherein Is Fully Handled
All That Relates to Fine
Gardens…* Trans. John
James. London 1712

11 Trans. by the author.
Fléjou, Lucie: "Traités,
plans et dessins, modèles
et fantaisies: essai de typo-
logie". Blog: https://blog.
bibliotheque.inha.fr/fr/
posts/art-jardins.html

12 Ibid. For a full list of
terms, see Dezallier d'Argenville, Antoine-Joseph:
L'Histoire naturelle.

Detail of the plan and elevation of a "Grand Parterre de Compartiment" by Antoine-Joseph Dezallier d'Argenville, 1715

Fruit-shaped flower beds in the garden at Castle Idstein-Nassau shown in a detail of Johann Jakob Walter's *Idstein Florilegium*, ca. 1654–72

"Parterre de broderie" at Vaux-le-Vicomte as reconstructed by architects Gabriel-Hippolyte Destailleur from 1875 to 1893 and Alfred Duchêne from 1911 to 1923

displaying exotic flowers, presented fertile ground for a steady increase in the combined use of circular geometry and floral motifs in the design of parterres. Accordingly—though this has apparently gone unnoticed by past scholarship—the botanical motifs making up the formal layout of these parterres reflect details of their floristic composition hailing primarily from West Asia: some *fleurons* have three to five petals with a main central petal resembling an iris, while others have rounded petals arranged in a flat disc with a central pistil and stamen resembling a lily or the corona of a narcissus. Still others resemble the tulip and carnation—or earlier motifs of them from Ottoman decorative art. Perhaps it is the latter, the Ottoman carnation-fan motif that so closely resembles the *coquilles de gazon* (lit.:"turf shells"), which to me presents the most recognizable or fully developed floral motif implemented as landscape ornament. It appears in several parterre designs in Jacques Boyceau de la Barauderie's *Traite du Jardinage selon las raisons de la nature et de l'Art* (published posthumously in 1638), including a square parterre de broderie with beds for flowers, a cutwork parterre for flowers, and even an English parterre. Though shells certainly featured prominently in the early modern curiosity cabinets, exotic flower bulbs and dried specimen likewise filled collections. Is it so far-fetched to imagine that these fan-(or shell-)shaped compartments might have their roots in the equally popular floral Ottoman velvet and silk brocades or even the woven "tapis de Turquie"—[13] just as the scrolling arabesques of the later *parterre de broderie* derived at least in part from Islamic art?

13 Claude Mollet likens the most beautiful flower parterres to "tapis de Turquie" in *Theatre des Plans et Jardinages* (1652), p. 190.

Fruit: *parterre de pièces coupées*

A growing interest in and emphasis on the public display of flowers and their ornamental quality led to further innovations with freer forms. While flower beds had previously been largely shaped as negative or leftover space by the more dominant figures of intersecting lines cutting across the square parterre for pathways (recalling agricultural plots or the *carreaux rompeux*), the *parterre de pièces coupées* ("cut work") employed an additive method that resembles appliqué work, in which a textile ornament is achieved by applying cut fabric pieces to a larger ground fabric by needlework. Flower beds were arranged as independent motifs in space rather than within a grid, like patches of a colored carpet cut up into bite-size pieces and scattered across the terrace. In fact, a certain type of *parterre de pièces coupées* based the shape of its small compartments on various fruit shapes. A painting from ca. 1650 by Johann Jakob Walter shows such organically or "fruit-shaped" beds filled with crown imperials and tulips outlined in box hedge at the garden of Castle Nassau-Idstein in Germany. While certainly unique, this development is not entirely surprising during this period of botanical exploration, when images of exotic fruits such as pomegranates, pineapples, citrus fruits, melons, squash, and peppers began to appear in all artistic mediums. And by this time, the successful acclimatization and cultivation of exotic fruits made them ripe for harvest and consumption, both literally and figuratively. Around the same time, André le Nôtre began to arrange species in his flower parterre at Vaux-le-Vicomte (1656) according to height so that rather than reading as a low-lying flat surface decoration on the ground, flower beds now appeared as raised mounds, heaps of color served on a fruit platter, if you will.

Stem & Leaf: *parterre de broderie*

Parterres de broderie are undoubtedly the most recognizable and artful expression of landscape ornament, which is to say, they come closest to achieving pure decoration. Indeed, the ornament most commonly described as arabesques originated in the Middle East and was introduced to Europe in the sixteenth century via Italy and Spain, where it was first applied to book-bindings and

14 Osborne, Harold (ed.):
*The Oxford Companion to
the Decorative Arts*. Oxford,
1975, p. 34

15 Embroidery manuals
published in Venice in the
fifteen-thirties include
patterns of *moresques*
and *arabesques*. Fuhring,
Peter: "Renaissance Orna-
ment Prints; The French
Contribution." In: Karen
Jacobson (ed.), *The French
Renaissance in Prints*.
Grunwald Center, UCLA,
1994, p. 162

16 Selection of terms
taken from Antoine-Joseph
Dezallier d'Argenville's
L'Histoire naturelle (1742)

in embroidery—[14]—another popular form of producing
textile ornament in the early modern period that lends
itself well to fine linework—before being projected as a
surface pattern on the ground in the seventeenth century.—[15] Nonetheless, it is hard to ignore the botanical
base of the composition, even if one considers nothing
more than the abundant reference to foliage in French
gardening manuals, such as *rinceaux, palmettes, feuilles
refendues, feuilles tronquées*, etc.—[16] In the time of
Le Nôtre, parterres began taking on a more elongated
form due to being split into two mirrored plots by a
central axis. This linear form is well suited for motifs
derived from the most ubiquitous, structural, and peren-
nial element of a plant, namely its vegetative parts: its
stem and leaves. The curving figures of the *parterres de
broderie* drawn in evergreen boxwood mimic the spontaneous growth of a plant's stalk, particularly a vine or
the flexible stem of other herbaceous species, which
easily bends and curls to fit a fixed space. This is also
reflected in the longevity of some vegetal motifs such as
the acanthus and palmette, the origin of which has seen
continuous investigation. The popularity of these motifs
belies the fact that leaves are typically a plant's least
recognizable part. Whereas a flower can be more easily
associated with a region or a specific culture, the shape
of a leaf appears universal, perhaps another reason for
its global adoption.

PART II

The Phytogeography of Plant Composition:
Modernist Landscapes (Nineteen-Seventies and Eighties)

The work of distinguished scholars such as Alexander
von Humboldt, Charles Darwin, and Johann Wolfgang
von Goethe pushed botany further in the eighteenth and
nineteenth centuries by exploring new subdisciplines

such as plant geography, plant evolution, and plant morphology. An early form of ecology emerged and with it a broader view of plant communities and compositions in response to environmental factors. With this came a gradual shift away from the collection, cultivation, and display of exotics and a turn toward native plant communities. While these new trends in scientific approaches to plants did not result in any significant example of landscape ornament—during much of this time garden ornament dominated in the English landscape garden and picturesque tradition—the visionary work of Olmsted not only celebrated wilderness in equal measure as the pastoral landscape but also introduced a fiercely regional vocabulary into landscape design. The Ramble in Central Park was aimed to bring not just any wilderness into the city but that of the Northeast. Olmsted borrowed his material palette from the Adirondacks and the Catskills, just as the Hudson River School of painters took inspiration from the sublime Hudson Valley. He used glacial erratics to reveal a site's geologic history and restricted his palette to native plants.

Building on the same developments in botany but breaking radically with the status quo in design, modernist landscape architects such as Lawrence Halprin, Dan Kiley, and Garrett Eckbo rendered concepts of biogeography more visible through abstraction. A clear awareness and ethos of modern ecology is also apparent. Most evident is the direct application of the idea of terrestrial biomes (tropical rainforests, temperate forests, deserts, tundra, taiga, grasslands, and savanna), as classified by vegetation type (forest, steppe, grassland, semiarid, desert), which emerged in the nineteen-thirties. Ideas of plant succession and energy flows developed by Eugene Odum led to another subdiscipline of ecosystem ecology. Kenneth Frampton's "Towards a Critical Regionalism" (1981) called on modern architecture to work more closely with regional and cultural contexts, highlighting topographic and climatic conditions as

17 Frampton, Kenneth: "Towards a Critical Regionalism: Six Points for an Architecture of Resistance." In: Foster, Hal (ed.): *The Anti-Aesthetic: Essays on Postmodern Culture*. Seattle 1983, pp. 16–30

18 Expressed in part in their collaborative article "Landscape Design in the Urban Environment," published by *Architectural Record* (May and August 1939; February 1940).

a way of moving away from the International Style.—[17] It seems that even before Frampton's landmark publication, landscape architects were discovering the possibilities of ecological design, likewise privileging a tectonic over a scenographic approach. Three projects from the nineteen-seventies and eighties, each gleaning its "ornamental" repertoire from a specific geographic habitat type or ecosystem, lay the groundwork for contemporary landscape ornament. In each case, the ornament takes its formal language from the physical structure and organization of a natural setting seen as emblematic of the site's larger region and identity: the rugged West Cascades surrounding Portland, Oregon; the Sonoran Desert of Tucson, Arizona; and the Gulf marshes southeast of Dallas, Texas.

Inspired by modernist painters Paul Klee, Joan Miró, and Wassily Kandinsky, and modern architecture as introduced by Walter Gropius, founder of the Bauhaus, to Harvard's Design School upon his tenure as chair of the department (1938–52), landscape architects Dan Kiley and Garrett Eckbo together with James Rose defined a modernist theory for landscape design geared toward social change.—[18] Formally, however, their designs reflected abstract compositions and a rigorous attention to geometry (and an awareness of French formalism), carefully integrating the two through asymetrical figures that interrupt and cut through an underlying orthogonal grid. In fact, not entirely unlike the botanical motifs applied to landscape design in the seventeenth century, the emerging modernist landscape of the twentieth century appears to achieve ornament through abstraction, by deducing and repeating basic forms. What distinguishes the modernist examples, however, is a tendency toward imitation or emulation. Moreover, the botanical scale is greater than before and remains more recognizable as a source in the resultant ornament. A plant's *terrain* emerges as the material culture of modernist landscapes.

Urban Cascade

Lawrence Halprin & Associates' design for the Portland
Open Space Sequence, completed in 1970, narrates a
stream's progression from mountain spring to water-
fall. The sequence culminates in a massive retention wall
set between two public squares, a choreographed folding
of vertical concrete slabs, that creates a vast water-
fall with wading pools above and below on "a fractured
urban ground."—[19] This rugged aesthetic is enough to
recall images of sublime wilderness at the urban heart
of Portland—not just any wilderness but the nearby
Columbia River Gorge that cuts through the Cascade
Mountain Range, with its iconic 1000-meter cliffs
of columnar basalt on which nothing else grows except
shore pines (*Pinus contorta*). Known today as the Ira
Keller Fountain, its original name, Forecourt Fountain,
likewise evokes the grand cascades descending from the
most richly ornamented space—the forecourt—of the
French garden. In fact, "New York Times architecture
critic Ada Louise Huxtable called it 'one of the most
important urban spaces since the Renaissance.'"—[20] Why?
Because, as the Halprin Conservancy Group claims,
"Huxtable saw a civic savior, a new kind [of] 'people park'
that echoed Baroque masterpieces such as Rome's Trevi
Fountain and Piazza Navona yet with a 'geometric naturalism' befitting its region."—[21]

"Geometric naturalism" is an apt term for the landscape ornament of the modernist era. Can wilderness, the
essence of nature, really qualify as decor? By coopting
physical forms and illustrating a plant's native environs
in an artificial context, the firm creates powerful, coded
symbols. Through a stripped-down composition of an
ecosystem's main elements, they play with—even drama-
tize—familiar motifs, arranging them in a manner that
exceeds functional criteria. In Halprin's words: "My own
way has been to design the outward forms of nature but
emphasize the results of the processes of nature…This
act of transmuting the experience of the natural land-

19 "Lawrence Halprin."
Halprin Conservancy
website: https://www.
halprinconservancy.org/
lawrence-halprin

20 "The Landscape
Architecture of Lawrence
Halprin." *ArchDaily*,
Dec. 27, 2016. https://www.
archdaily.com/802422/the-
landscape-architecture-of-
lawrence-halprin (acces-
sed on June 22, 2021)

21 "History." Halprin Conservancy website: https://
www.halprinconservancy.
org/history

22 Cited by Halprin Conservancy as written by Halprin in 1995: https://www.halprinconservancy.org/history

scape into human-made experience is, for me, the essence of the art of landscape design."—22

Urban Canyon

Around the same time, Garrett Eckbo generated landscape ornament by translating the physical setting of a desert canyon into geometric form. Eckbo's design for the Tucson Community Center Landscape, completed in 1971, echoes Lawrence Halprin & Associates' technique of linking urban spaces through the narrative of flowing water. Here, too, a reference to the local environment was key. Taking inspiration from the nearby Sabino Canyon running from the edge of the Sonoran Desert into the Catalina foothills, each of the three sequential spaces abstracts a landform shaped by or for water: a wash (a shallow bed inundated only occasionally after flash flood events), an *acequia* (a small community-operated artificial irrigation canal typical of former Spanish colonies in Latin America), and a bajada (a local term derived from Spanish for alluvial fan).—23 In the large, central space aptly called Fountain Plaza, forces that appear to be natural cut through geometric circles, arcs, and rays etched into the paving, bringing an "urban canyon" into the city.—24 But while water features as the central theme, it is Eckbo's knowledge and use of plants that concretizes the landscape analog. While not all native to the Sonoran, his selection of shade trees, including Canary Island pine, eucalyptus, African sumac, Aleppo pines, and Arizona sycamores, are adapted to the extreme climate and stem from other semiarid and arid places such as the Mediterranean basin and the Australian eucalyptus forests. The ornament, as a visual language, codes the space with accurate botanical symbols.

23 Erickson, Helen: "Tucson Community Center Historic District." Society of Architectural Historians website: https://sah-archipedia.org/buildings/AZ-01-019-0088

24 Yetman, Emily: "Eckbo-Designed Tucson Convention Center Landscape." August 11, 2010, The Cultural Landscape Foundation website: https://tclf.org/landslides/eckbo-designed-tucson-convention-center-landscape-threatened

Urban Swamp

A design for a civic space in Dallas, Texas, by Kiley Walker Landscape Architects that was completed in

Sketch of "auditorium fore-court, opening day" by Lawrence Halprin, June 23, 1970

Rugged boulders and gushing water cut through concrete slabs at Garrett Eckbo's recently completed Fountain Plaza

The bald cypress grid in the Robust Cascade Area at Kiley Walker Landscape Architect's Fountain Place

25 Interestingly, Dan Kiley is purported to have conceived of a similar design for another site twenty-three years earlier (around 1973), which situates his idea in the same timeframe as Lawrence Halprin and Garrett Eckbo's fountain squares.

26 Quotation of Gary Hilderbrand from 2013 in "Fountain Place." The Landscape Architecture Legacy of Dan Kiley, The Cultural Landscape Foundation website: https://tclf.org/sites/default/files/microsites/kiley-legacy/FountainPlace.html

27 Gary Hilderbrand referred to the design as a "forested lagoon." https://tclf.org/sites/default/files/microsites/kiley-legacy/FountainPlace.html

28 Marc Treib points out the dissonance between Kiley and Jensen in Treib: "Dan Kiley and Classical Modernism: Mies in Leaf," 10, citing Kiley, Dan: *The Work of Dan Kiley: A Dialogue on Design Theory*, proceedings of the First Annual Symposium on Landscape Architecture, the University of Virginia, School of Architecture, Division of Landscape Architecture, Campbell Hall, February 6, 1982. Charlottesville: *The Division*, 1983, p. 10.

1986 brings the recurrent motif of the urban fountain to a crescendo.—[25] The firm's completed water garden, simply called Fountain Place, abstracts vegetation patterns from the cypress swamps of Southeast Texas. At the foot of the high-rise office complex there descends a grand cascade playfully evoking the Renaissance garden terraces and water spectacles of France's Loire Valley. Only here, the cascades designed by Peter Ker Walker form a hybrid with a bosquet of 200 bald cypress trees (*Taxodium distichum*) planted fifteen feet on center. Gary Hilderbrand accurately describes the space as "riddled with his maniacal order, with the smell and feel of reorganized nature."—[26] Indeed, typical of Dan Kiley's classical modernism, the formal layout of Fountain Place is a geometricization of its landscape analog. The trees of his "forested lagoon" may be standing in cylindrical concrete planters, but in their native setting, they stand in shallow water.—[27] While contemporaries such as Jens Jensen considered geometric layouts to be disdainfully unnatural, Kiley applied them strategically: "When you want to copy these dumb nature scenes, I say, If you're going to copy, copy your ancestors—the colonial gardens."—[28] To Kiley, copying a "dumb nature scene" is as simple as reducing a 'nature scene' into its most iconic elements and recreating it elsewhere as artifice using geometric order. Voilà! The grid is the firm's signature design move, the mise-en-carte of his swamp copy transferred onto the urban fabric. And the bald cypress is the main motif, marking the intersections of the grand ornamental grid.

In summary, what defines the landscape ornament of this era is the increasing awareness of plant communities and the phytogeographical limits of certain vegetation types. Moreover, an interest emerged in the role certain plants, associated with particular geological landforms, played in defining a regional *landscape* identity. The material palette of a specific ecosystem for these urban interventions, which still strived to create an "escape" to

nature or wilderness, was key in achieving a recognizable abstraction. That all three examples focused on
water is likely more the result of the dominant discourse
on the revitalization of cities in the United States at the
time—and the proved success of fountains as attractors
to public space—than a reflection of the era's defining
material culture of the modernist garden.

PART III

Ecological Plant Patterns: Contemporary Landscape
Architecture (Twenty-First Century)

If flowering plants represented the material culture of a
formal garden in the early modern period, and terrain
that of modernist landscapes, what might constitute the
material culture of designed landscapes today?
    Today's landscape ornament is not as different from
the modernist period as that was from the early modern.
While a distinct quality sets contemporary examples
apart, we still see some of the imitative approach to
"copying" familiar or regional natural settings, particularly in the early 2000s. The most distinctive element of
the very popular urban Teardrop Park in Manhattan
by Michael Van Valkenburgh Associates (MVVA), completed in 2006, is the large rock wall separating the two
sections. Inspired by the wild, dramatic landscape of
the Hudson River Valley, the wall clearly references the
iconic Palisades, a large face of basalt bluffs resulting
from igneous intrusion above the river. Not unlike
Olmsted, who had been inspired by the painters of the
Hudson School that captured those "wild" sublime landscapes, and subsequently sought to bring wilderness to
the city (most visible in Central Park's Bramble), MVVA
once again recreated a tiny slice of that place in the
courtyard of a residential complex built on sand dredged
from New York Harbor at the mouth of the Hudson

and millions of cubic yards of excavated soil and rock from infrastructure projects such as the New York City Water Tunnel, which supplies the city with upstate water. Intentional or not, the wall becomes the park's ornament; its formal and material language reveals the site's provenance and makes it speak.

By 2015 we also begin to see very graphic projections, which one could easily mistake for landscape ornament. However, imposing geometric forms with no tie to landscape heritage or direct relationship to landscape's materiality, particularly plants, falls short. While more recognizably decorative, the formal language is mute. Without lending the landscape meaning, whether through revealing a site's traces or expressing new concepts in botany, these geometric shapes appear excessive, even gimmicky. A more recent example is the 2015 Navy Yard Central Green in Philadelphia designed by James Corner Field Operations, which organizes diverse programmatic functions into circles of varying sizes within a larger circle with a toothed edge, resembling an industrial gearwheel. In their project statement, however, the office claims reference to the site's former condition ("The site was historically marked by wetlands, meadows, and bird habitat"),—[29] presumably indicating that the circular geometry should reflect pockets of open water within a stand of reeds and other wetland plants of a former freshwater marsh along the Delaware River prior to the Philadelphia Naval Shipyard's construction in 1876.

Other projects in this graphic mode include the Biblioteca degli Alberi (Library of Trees) in Milano by Petra Blaisse and her firm Inside Outside (conceived in early 2000s but only completed in 2018), as well as their design for the Walker Art Center in Minneapolis (more on this later), much of Topotek 1's work (Superkilen, Bahndeckel Theresienhöhe, Bord-Gais Networks Centre, Schlossgarten Wolfsburg), and Vogt's landscape for the SIA Hochhaus in Zurich. In some cases, despite intended references to landscape elements (such as the

29 "Navy Yards Central Green." James Corner Field Operations website: https://www.fieldoperations.net/project-details/project/navy-yards-central-green.html

single-species tree circles in the Biblioteca degli Alberi apparently recalling groves and early botanical gardens; Vogt's "urban carpet with regular patterning" and the unique tree planters "looking like gigantic pebbles lifted from a riverbed"—30), the overemphasis on *objects* appears overly decorative. Why? Because it repeats the kind of landscape ornament relevant more than three centuries earlier. The ornament is more recognizable as such because it repeats a formal approach long outdated in architecture and other design disciplines. Moreover, the primary forms in the landscape are not derived from natural settings, let alone natural processes. In this way, the result is more of a stage set than an innovative landscape design qualifying as contemporary landscape ornament. So, what is contemporary landscape ornament?

The most successful examples fall exactly between these two extremes, between the purely imitative and the overly graphic. And as with the previous periods, its decorative language borrows from the newest developments in botany. While today many aspects of botany are solved, in terms of a plant's structure (the foundation for early modern landscape ornament) and function (and that for modernist landscape ornament), the field is primarily attuned to the more urgent needs of adaptation to climate change, carbon sequestration, and ecological remediation. In short, botanical research has moved away from the static image of a plant to the *process* of natural systems: change, growth cycles, transformation. It is no longer about a park maturing as much as it is about urban landscapes adapting. With this perspective, landscape is its own agent, something to be "set in motion" or catalyzed rather than created. Landscape ornament should reflect this gradual shift from a focus on objects to one of process, just as Lydia Kallipoliti claims that the history of ecological design mimics scientific trends: "ecological design starts with the reconceptualization of the world as a complex system of flows rather than

30 "SIA Hochhaus." Vogt Landschaftsarchitekten website: https://www.vogt-la.com/sia_hochhaus

31 Kallipoliti, Lydia: "History of Ecological Design." In: *Oxford Research Encyclopedias, Environmental Science*. Online, April 26, 2018: https://doi.org/10.1093/acrefore/9780199389414.013.144

32 Kallipoliti, citing Kepes, György: "Art and Ecological Consciousness." In: Kepes, György (ed.): *Arts of the Environment*. New York 1972, p. 11. Kallipoliti: "History of Ecological Design"

33 *Design with Nature* is also the name of his most well-known publication, from 1969.

a discrete compilation of objects."—31 Kallipoliti also quotes a statement by visual artist and theorist György Kepes, which echoes the evolving discourse on botany that I have tried to outline: "What scientists considered before as substance shaped into forms, and consequently understood as tangible objects, is now recognized as energies and their dynamic organization."—32

The discourse on environment, and particularly natural systems, already forming in a period of growing ecological awareness in the seventies, entered the discipline of landscape architecture through figures such as Richard Forman and Ian McHarg. While Forman introduced principles of landscape ecology to design, McHarg developed the Geographic Information Systems (GIS), a tool for urban land use and ecological planning built on the concept of "design with nature."—33 Ideas such as species interaction, habitat structure, wildlife corridors, and edge conditions, as well as exposure, slope, aspect, and other physical parameters of digital terrain models (DTM), entered the design vocabulary of landscape architects. More recently, the work of Nina Marie-Lister, Bradley Cantrell, Kate Orff (SCAPE), and others led to the shaping of a systems approach with design strategies built on or incorporating the language of natural processes, including flows, dynamics, resilience, and adaptation. But while observations of landscape pattern led to the development of tools for land use analysis, which, in turn, can be largely credited with generating an interest in using parametricism for landscape design, these softwares (Grasshopper, Kangaroo, etc.) are primarily helpful in setting parameters and not in designing. They produce "compositions" based on simple input/output systems in order to randomize (as nature's patterns elude us) or mimic responses to certain rules (conditions of sun, exposure, soil, moisture, etc.). Contemporary architectural ornament may have been primarily preoccupied so far with scripting the distribution of geometric patterns across a big box façade; yet when it comes to contemporary landscape ornament, hand-drawn forms still appear better suited to dealing with organic materials and forms. What has, in my estimation, been detrimental to contemporary landscape design (or perhaps its discourse), is that this discourse rarely highlights the role of plants within this large spatiotemporal framework. And yet, the behavior of plants is what often renders the effects of natural and human-caused disruption, ecological degradation, climate change, etc. visible: species migration is an indicator; succession a sign; shifting species compositions a reaction; and plant morphology an adaptation.

To return to the question of *what might constitute the material culture of designed landscapes today?*—the short answer is ecologies. And if the *form of a plant* inspired landscape ornament of the early modern period, and the *physical setting of a plant community* informed that of modernist landscapes, then a plant's *behavior and ecology* underlie contemporary landscape ornament.

Succession

Large-scale patterns of colonization, growth, and succession are becoming ever more available through the proliferation of aerial imagery using drones and other digital tools that capture the vast landscape in scale images and models for a designer's use. Michel Desvigne Paysagiste (MDP) used an aerial photograph of a braided stream for the design of a rooftop garden at Keio University in Tokyo, completed in 2005, that abstracts the process of riparian succession. The garden's ground plane appears as a continuous field of circular openings in varying diameters, which Desvigne describes as "a small structure that organizes textures, porosities, densities, and transparencies—the material and the complex spaces, just as in a natural landscape."—[34] The relative diameter responds to the imagined elevation of a sand bar and thus also a particular stage of succession: out of the largest openings grow small trees while the smaller

34 Tiberghien, Gilles A.: "A Landscape Deferred." In: Desvigne, Michel: *Intermediate Natures: The Landscapes of Michel Desvigne*. Basel 2008, p. 175

53

A perforated ground pattern inspired by riparian succession at the Keio Rooftop Garden by Michel Desvigne Paysagiste

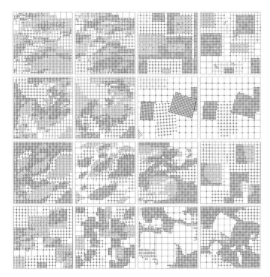

Pattern studies for Walker Art Center of mineral and vegetal surfaces, grid, and topography by Michel Desvigne Paysagiste

Sketch of three distinct fluvial landscape patterns for the Novartis Park by Vogt Landschaftsarchitekten

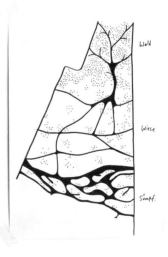

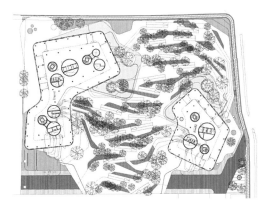

Site plan of SLA's City Dune
in Copenhagen showing
longitudinal vegetation strips
as ripple marks

Aerial photograph of
Catherine Mosbach Paysa-
gistes's Louvre-Lens
Museum Park showing an
irregular pattern of ground
perforations

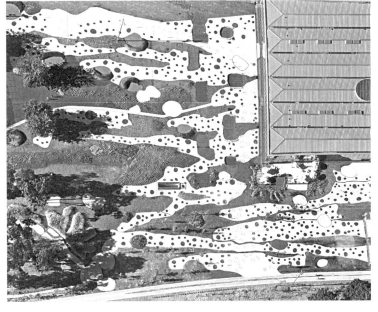

35 Ibid., p. 171

36 For one of the many attempts to recreate this pattern distribution with a Grasshopper script, see Generative Landscapes Blog: https://generative-landscapes.wordpress.com/2014/11/17/keio-university-roof-garden-michel-desvigne-case-study-02/.

37 Chris Reed's studio on "ecological mats" taught at the Harvard Graduate School of Design; Reed, Chris: *Mat Ecologies: Landscape Representations*. Oxfordshire 2012

38 Tiberghien: "A Landscape Deferred," p. 171

39 Ibid., p. 165

40 Ibid., pp. 154–55

openings contain only small shrubs, grasses, and mosses. In Michel Desvigne's recent monograph *Intermediate Natures*, French philosopher Gilles A. Tiberghien clarifies that "the idea was not to faithfully reproduce a natural setting, but rather an empirical system whose artifice is obvious."—[35] This makes sense, since the near-parametric aesthetic which many have strived to reproduce with a Grasshopper script is far from mistakable as a found landscape.—[36] However, Desvigne employs only analog tools to generate patterns based on natural processes, preempting a more widespread digital approach to designing what Chris Reed has referred to as an "ecological mat."—[37] Tiberghien nevertheless insists that even this "artificial process used to determine the texture of the microglades and forested areas … is only a device for reading and transposing" and eschews the pattern's perception as decorative: "In no way is it intended to become a motif with intrinsic interest."—[38]

In many ways, the garden at Keio is a smaller-scale version of a study MDP developed for the Walker Art Center in Minneapolis, which takes its ornamental language from the processes of erosion at the shoreline of the nearby Lake Superior and its ground pattern from the behavior of living matter.—[39] Here again Tiberghien defends Desvigne's method of transposition by "resizing the shapes found in nature" against possible claims of decoration: "The result [sic] are often drawings with striking graphics; yet at the same time, we sense that they do not fulfill any decorative concern— which Desvigne avoids like the plague!"—[40] And I agree that they are not decorative in a meaningless sense. However, the deduction of geomorphological, ecological, and historical processes, or landscapes resulting from them, into compositional elements remains explicit and even legible. "How does he transform them?" Tiberghien asks rhetorically. He replies: "By giving them legibility. How does he make them legible? By redesigning them, by rediscovering their structural frames, by trying to 'tracer les lignes principales d'un paysage, son ossature, sa physionomie' … as Baudelaire accurately said of Corot, whom he admired."—[41] The true value of aerial photographs, then, is their simplified representation of the "anatomies of landscapes."—[42] As one of the first landscape architects to celebrate the power of aerial images, James Corner claims that this approach "radically breaks with both Classical and Modernist notions of figure-ground and hierarchical spatial composition. Instead, freed from the rigid constraints of perfect objectified geometry, Desvigne's landscapes allow for a looser, more open, and porous matrix."—[43] I would argue, though, that it is not a break with geometry per se but rather a scaled-up understanding of botany that yields more flexible structures—ecological mats, porous matrix, etc. Instead of creating landscape ornament through setting flower motifs within a prescribed geometric framework, or superimposing natural elements on a geometric grid, it is more about hijacking nature's own structural frameworks, thus rendering geometric form as such superfluous.

Erosion and Deposition

Once again referencing a process rather than a fixed image of natural landscape, the 2011 City Dune project in Copenhagen by SLA is more than a copy of a dune landscape in the city. Not made to look "natural" but rather to reveal the artistic transposition, the design relies on simplification, both topographically (it rises above a tiered, underground parking garage) and in terms of the planting palette. The allusion to Copenhagen's nearby migrating coastal dunes seems apparent: a rising hill separated into numerous thin layers of white concrete to create a grand stair mimics the ripple marks of sand's aeolian deposition. The stepped ground plane that stretches across the entire site drives a pattern of longitudinal vegetation strips that ornament the space.

41 This is what Gilles A. Tiberghien says of Michel Desvigne's work in *Intermediate Natures*, citing Baudelaire, Charles: "Le Peintre de la Vie Moderne." In: *Oeuvres complètes*. Paris 1961, p. 1166. Baudelaire is referring to French landscape painter Jean-Baptiste-Camille Corot (1796–1875).

42 Tiberghien: "A Landscape Deferred," p. 177

43 Corner, James: "Agriculture, Texture, and the Unfinished." In: Desvigne, Michel: *Intermediate Landscapes*, p. 9

And yet, despite the project's acquired name for the urban square of the SEB Bank, SLA's own website claims that "the City Dune is inspired by nature's processes and built up as a Swedish hillside." It appears that the Swedish landscape firm's design intended to emulate a Swedish hillside was reinterpreted locally according to a local landscape analog. And there seems to have been a rather broad consensus that the landscape was "borrowing its big, folding movement from the sand dunes of Northern Denmark and the snow dunes of the Scandinavian winter," for the firm eventually adopted the name for its public square.—[44] SLA also states its intention to give the bank, which is also Swedish, "a strong and unique Nordic Identity" through its use of local "Nordic" vegetation. The sand or snow dune reflects somewhat of an amalgamation of dune and woodland species including pines, birches, larches, and grasses.—[45]

Another project that evades geometric order and instead bases the organization of its scheme on geomorphic processes is the Novartis Campus Park in Basel completed in 2007 by Vogt Landschaftsarchitekten. The firm's own project clearly states that "the park sequentially reconstructs the natural phenomena of the surrounding Rhine terraces on a small scale, and merges them into an atmospheric park landscape."—[46] Because the park reflects so closely the various glacial and periglacial landforms of the site's "original" landscape, one could almost put this park in the imitative group of landscape ornament. However, in a manner different from the modernist tendency to select recognizable features through objects (boulders, trees), the firm successfully abstracts various processes. Divided into three tiers, the firm captures three patterns shaped by processes of erosion and deposition using only analog methods: a forest buried in rock-fallen scree, a floodplain meadow, and eroded channels or hollow-ways (*Hohlwege*) cutting through the easily fractured sediment of periglacial loess accumulations. The resulting patterns are best

44 SLA (Stig L. Andersson): "The City Dune." In: *Landezine*: http://landezine.com/index.php/2011/10/park-by-sla-landscape-architecture/

45 "City Dune." SLA website: https://www.sla.dk/en/projects/city-dune/

46 "Novartis Campus Park." Vogt Landschaftsarchitekten website: https://www.vogt-la.com/novartis_campus_park_fr

captured in the linework of an early concept sketch, which estimates the flow of dendritic drainage channels, braided streams, and the abandoned channels of a shifting shoreline on the floodplain.—[47] The three sections labeled *Wald*, *Wiese*, *Sumpf* (forest, meadow, swamp) are further reflected in the various grains of stone, gravel, sand, and silt; the ground conditions for plant growth are highlighted through distinct tree, shrub, and herbaceous layers of vegetation following forested slope, fluvial scrubland, and wet meadow. Somewhat ironically, the landscape is largely built using "stabilised clay and Rhine gravels supplied from the excavation of the subterranean parking structure," which was laboriously redeposited above "two hectares of poured concrete that act as a new, anthropogenic geological crust."—[48]

[47] Image caption of "First Sketch" in Foxley, Alice/ Vogt, Günther: *Distance and Engagement: Walking, Thinking and Making Landscape*. Zurich 2010, p. 155

[48] Ibid., p. 206

Morphogenesis

Finally, we come to the last example: the Louvre-Lens Museum Park designed by Catherine Mosbach Paysagistes and built on the location of a former strip mine to accompany the Louvre Museum in Lens in 2014. In Mosbach's own words, the design "reflects the project site's history as a former coal mine which acts as a living memory of multiple transformation cycles: dead plant matter is buried by sediments and compressed into a combustible sedimentary rock … then, by an inverse symmetry, the abandoned coal pit is exposed to oxygen, preparing the degraded ground for the reemergence of spontaneous vegetation."—[49] Jumping fluidly between temporalities and scales, from geological and ecological processes to microbial ones, Mosbach achieves a landscape that appears both strange and familiar—with repetitive yet variegated elements, distinct spaces merged by porous boundaries on a horizontal plain. Equally subtle are the vertical depressions and incisions designed to catch water, for these "perforations, will be the favored substrate for mosses which have the ability to

[49] Mosbach, Catherine: "Delta, or the Transgression of Lines." In: Girot, Christophe/Ahn, Susann/ Fehmann, Isabelle/Mehling, Lara (eds.): *Pamphlet 20: Delta Dialogues*. Zurich 2017, p. 30

50 Mosbach, Catherine: "Louvre-Lens Museum Park." Urban Next blog: https://urbannext.net/louvre-lens-museum-park/

51 My emphasis. Mosbach: "Louvre-Lens Museum Park"

52 Mosbach: "Delta, or the Transgression of Lines," p. 33

53 Ibid.

54 Ibid., p. 32

capture and fix heavy metals to the soils."—[50] Mosbach's intervention is aimed at catalyzing organic processes, "articulating the *vegetable dynamic* through this park, which primes the attractivity of the terrain."—[51]

Pushing the envelope of ecological design to the extreme, the design seems to hint at a new direction in landscape ornament. More than any of the previous examples, this project develops its own ornamental language based on a biological process that stands at the center of all [plant] life. Mosbach cites morphogenesis—literally form's (*morpho-*) creation (*genesis*)—as a key driver in her work: "The morphogenesis of the mosses is activated … on the strips of silt excavated from the museum's foundation and explored on the façade as a significant and transformative medium."—[52] And although the term "morphogenesis" was later adopted in geology to mean "the formation of landscapes," Mosbach's usage is quite literal, or perhaps twofold: *landscapes are formed by plants* at a microscale (mosses are known to initiate ecological succession by transforming seemingly inert, bare surfaces into fertile ground), and *she generates forms in this landscape* from patterns of plant colonization and "moss proliferation typologies"—[53] at the macroscale. The striking result neither reveals a hidden layer of abstraction by which a natural setting is adapted to geometric order nor lays bare an array of vegetal motifs according to parametric rules. Rather, by a brilliant reversal of roles, she lets cyanobacteria generate an organic ground pattern that renders visible traces of *human use*. Only rather than present these traces as a past image, they are visualized in a future state subject to ecological dynamics: "In this way, the ground, at first inert, soon becomes exposed to time past and time-in-the-making through the power of spontaneous plant recolonization."—[54] And so, perhaps the most successful example of contemporary landscape ornament actually transforms artifice into nature.

Conclusion

One might have thought ornamental parterres were something of the past. But, in fact, ornament *par terre* is alive and flourishing today. Landscape ornament has demonstrated surprising resiliency through changing times, and new modes have revealed themselves in the woodwork. The early modern parterre's relation to decorative arts may have been nothing more than a fanciful display of botanical interest through the most fashionable medium of the time. But what of modernist concepts of abstract composition or contemporary tools for mapping and modeling landscape? Certainly, these frameworks lent landscape ornament further definition and unique characteristics. Much more relevant, however, is the discipline's relationship to the expanding field of botany and the subsequent modes of classification of vegetation—according to plant taxonomy, plant geography, and plant ecology.

It is the task of landscape architects, then, to find expression at the intersection of the compositional frameworks and the botanical reference points. Interestingly, site history or site specificity plays a sub-ordinate role in many of these projects. This may be due to the fact that contemporary examples of landscape ornament are almost exclusively within urban settings on heavily altered sites, as if the designer's impetus toward such landscape ornament were encoded in the *tabula rasa* that results from the concrete slabs of underground parking lids, a building's roof or land clearings, and land "reclamation" sites. In fact, these human-made surfaces are not entirely dissimilar to the terraces of Renaissance and baroque gardens. Scraped clean, the designer appears to be given permission to ornament the surface, to create a human-made design that does more than enhance the existing condition—something architects have rarely been shy to do. At the same time, this near siteless condition drives the landscape architect's desire to reveal the site's "original" landscape (real or imagined), thus also laying bare the impacts of human civilization.

Another site condition that has no doubt left its mark on landscape ornament is the dissolving frame. After the medieval *hortus conclusus*, the walled Renaissance gardens, the semi-enclosed baroque garden terraces which abutted an architectural façade on one if not three sides, and even Olmsted's iconic, rectangular Central Park, the bounds of public urban spaces designed today are less defined. Embedded in a fully established urban fabric, the edges of contemporary project sites are heterogenous, often even blurred. As such, contemporary surface ornament's use of macro or micro landscape patterns is well adapted. For while parterres designed as floral carpets replete with borders, corners, central medallions, and pendants follow an internal, centralized logic (offset shapes correspond to all four sides), ground patterns today are based on a completely different logic of natural systems. Geomorphological processes, the movement of water, wind, microbacterial growth, and the phytogeographic limits of a substrate do not require a grid, used traditionally in surface ornament, to create a boundless pattern.

Unfortunately, designers today remain hard-pressed to put words to this process of adapting a landscape analog to a project site. Just as modernist landscape architects would not have considered their work ornamental due to the fact that they borrowed their forms not from decorative arts but natural settings, many today remain allergic to the terms ornament and decoration, instead inventing such phrases as "copying," "transmuting," "articulating the vegetable dynamic," "reconstructing the natural phenomena," or putting natural settings through a process of "virtual vitrification" or "transposition."—55 And yet, many are aware of employing such a method of abstraction. Likewise, Lawrence Halprin, Dan Kiley, and Garrett Eckbo built their collages of nature and artifice on a design language intimately familiar with

55 Phrases taken from Dan Kiley, Lawrence Halprin, Catherine Mosbach, Günther Vogt, Gilles A. Tiberghien, and Michel Desvigne, respectively.

"decorative" arts by taking inspiration from Bauhaus artists who celebrated and elevated the applied arts, thus situating themselves between [phyto]geographic realism and abstraction.

Unlike our fellow architects, we have not gotten over our aversion to "ornament" in landscape. Gilles A. Tiberghien even described Michel Desvigne as avoiding decoration "like the plague!"—[56]—and possibly for good reason, since there are still plenty of attempts that go amiss. But reviewing projects from past and present, I cannot help but think that both in theoretical discourse and practice we are missing out by either avoiding or refusing to use this terminology. It has, no doubt, a complex history, but in our reluctance to use the very useful and familiar label "ornament," we are creating a headache for ourselves. Moreover, surface pattern, the dominant application of landscape ornament, should not be confused with geometric order and thus viewed as something formal or authoritative. In landscape, patterns based on natural processes reveal themselves as flexible, dynamic, and living. Echoing Kant's notion of "natural beauties," this innovative visual language, "makes the thing itself speak, as it were, in mimic language" by using the very materials of landscape. Rather than invent new names for it, we should become aware of underlying ethos driving our designs and embrace the concept of "landscape ornament" in order to become more adept at distinguishing between more and less successful examples and thus push the discipline further.

56 Tiberghien: "A Landscape Deferred," pp. 154–55

The other perspective. Mosaic of the city.
Aerial photo, Eduard Spelterini, 1907

The "Green Image of the City"
Mapping Zurich: A Case Study

Dunja Richter

"What is the mood on the streets? What can we do so that it remains peaceful? What contribution can trees make, not to mention buildings?"—[1] Today, more people live in cities than in rural areas. Worldwide, in emerging and third-world countries, the flight from the countryside has led to rapid urban growth. This is the challenge facing us today in industrialized nations, where urbanization is only slowly progressing, but above all in built-up areas that are undergoing densification. This adaptation to the existing fabric is inevitably accompanied by a loss of familiar built, environmental, and social structures, by gentrification and segregation, and by a loss of vestiges of the past and personal sites of memory. It brings with it a profound transformation of the lived environment. At the same time, the digital revolution is permeating ever more areas of our lives and fundamentally changing how we think, act, and feel.

If landscape architecture intends to position itself in a globalized, dynamic world as a design discipline and make an active contribution to improving people's standard of living, it must not only master its craft but also know its own roots. Only by examining itself in the historical context can it critically reflect on its own actions. So let's look back to the nineteenth century—which played such an important role in our discipline—when the foundations were laid for a modern landscape archi-

1   Girot, Christophe/ Freytag, Anette/ Kirchengast, Albert/ Križenecký, Suzanne/ Richter, Dunja: *Topologie/ Topology*, Pamphlet 15, Zurich 2012, p. 20

tecture and for the general availability of foreign ornamental plants.

In the context of the rapid industrialization of European cities, which in turn led to their expansive growth, the art of making gardens flourished. Not only did the conception of public space undergo a fundamental transformation; an increasingly large portion of the population also gained access to gardens and nondomestic plants, which had previously only been the province of the elite.—[2] The mapping of the "green city" takes Zurich as its case study. It demonstrates the eminent role of garden art in the transformation of the historical city into the modern city. In addition, the development depicted in this essay's five topographical portraits lends itself to drawing general conclusions: it elucidates the embeddedness of the "green sites" in Zurich's urban fabric and in the consciousness of its inhabitants; the better established the green sites became, the more they flourished. The sixth section carries this history forward to the present day.

2   The article is based on the author's dissertation: *Von der Rarität zur Alltagskultur: Der Botanische Garten Zürich und sein Beitrag zur Verbreitung neuer Pflanzen im 19. Jahrhundert.* ETH Zurich 2020

I The Lake. Appropriation of Urban Space by the Citizens

Today, who could possibly overlook that Zurich is a city located on a lake? Lake Zurich is the city's most important amenity and the most popular meeting place for residents and visitors. High-profile buildings and squares such as the Tonhalle (the concert hall), the opera, and the Sechseläutenplatz line the shore and are inviting places where people come together. The lake guides the observer's eyes past the sea of buildings and the adjoining hillside above the blue tableau into the distance—allowing the people here to breathe more freely. But this has not always been possible.

Just two centuries ago, Zurich was a self-contained city whose bastions, walls, ramparts, and moats not only separated it from its surroundings, but also nearly prevented foreigners from accessing civil rights. The liberal constitutions of the 1830s and the establishment of the Swiss federal state in 1848 finally provided the leverage to attain a civil society.—[3] The revolutionary program comprised more than political freedoms; it also included the liberation from social and economic constraints. Thanks to the resultant changes in Switzerland's society, politics, economy, and infrastructure, the country developed into a modern society and a leading industrialized nation. The new means of production attendant to industrialization led, by way of changed settlement structures, to a physical metamorphosis and a social and mental urbanization accompanied by the dissemination of urban work, living, dwelling, and social forms.—[4] Within a century, the population of Zurich grew exponentially from 10,000 (1800) to 170,000 (around 1900).—[5]

Nothing illustrates the awakening of a new era better than the 1833 decision to take down the fortifications. They not only yielded to the demographic pressure of the migration from the countryside to the city and their demolition paved the way for Zurich to become Switzerland's first modern metropolis. Their removal also freed up space so that the minor settlement on the river could develop into the urbane lakefront city it has remained to this day. The expansion of Zurich required hygienic and technical measures that led to the redesign of entire streets and districts. These new designs and the erection of striking administrative, educational, industrial, and infrastructural buildings were an expression of the new political and societal elites' economic prowess, increasing affluence, and desire to put their wealth on display.

With Europe's political restructuring, garden art evolved from a medium that was the province of the ruling class to a task whose results would serve all of society and be attuned to the city's characteristics.—[6] In the lands in which there had been monarchies, the repre-

3   Tanner, Albert: *Arbeitsame Patrioten – wohlanständige Damen: Bürgertum und Bürgerlichkeit in der Schweiz 1830–1914*. Zurich 1995, pp. 11ff.

4   Schulz, Andreas: *Lebenswelt und Kultur des Bürgertums im 19. und 20. Jahrhundert*. Munich 2005, p. 3

5   Over the centuries, the population quadrupled about every fifty years. As part of the city consolidation of 1893, the villages of Enge, Riesbach, and Wiedikon became part of the city. Behrens, Nicola: "Zürich: Sozialstruktur und sozialer Wandel." In: *HLS*, https://hls-dhs-dss.ch/de/articles/000171/2015-01-25/ (accessed on May 30, 2021)

6   For the history of urban green, see Hennebo, Dieter (ed.): *Geschichte* >

> *des Stadtgrüns*, 5 vols. Hannover 1970–1981; Hennebo, Dieter: "Städtische Baumpflanzungen in früherer Zeit." In: Meyer, Franz Hermann: *Bäume in der Stadt*. Stuttgart 1982, pp. 11–45; Schmidt, Erika: "Abwechselung im Geschmack": *Raumbildung und Pflanzenverwendung beim Stadtparkentwurf, Deutschland 19. Jahrhundert*. Hannover 1984. Hennecke, Stefanie: "Gartenkunst in der Stadt seit dem 19. Jahrhundert." In: Schweizer, Stefan / Winter, Sascha (eds.): *Gartenkunst in Deutschland: Von der Frühen Neuzeit bis zur Gegenwart*. Regensburg 2012, pp. 233–50

7   On Swiss landscape architecture of the nineteenth and early twentieth centuries, see Heyer, Hans-Rudolf: *Historische Gärten der Schweiz: Die Entwicklung vom Mittelalter bis zur Gegenwart*. Bern 1980, pp. 148–267; Burbulla, Julia / Karn, Susanne / Lerch, Gabi (eds.): *Stadtlandschaften: Schweizer Gartenkunst im Zeitalter der Industrialisierung*. Zurich 2006; Stoffler, Johannes: *Gustav Ammann: Landschaften der Moderne in der Schweiz*. Zurich 2008; Moll, Claudia: *Theodor & Otto Froebel: Gartenkultur in Zürich im 19. Jahrhundert*. Zurich 2019

8   On taking a walk as bourgeois practice, see König, Gudrun M.: *Eine Kulturgeschichte des Spaziergangs: Spuren einer bürgerlichen Praktik 1780–1850*. Vienna 1996

sentatives of the new bourgeoisie, such as merchants, industrialists, and bankers, supplanted the aristocracy, and in republican Switzerland, it was the patricians and the commercial and financial aristocracy who were the main supporters of garden art. The liberation from societal norms, in addition to a changed conception of nature and sense of aesthetics since the Enlightenment, led to adapted forms of design and to the use of parks and gardens, and to a differentiation of urban space in public and private areas. For the independent artistic gardener, an enterprise which developed in the twentieth century into the profession of landscape architect, this generated numerous new work areas related to designing and implementing.—[7]

II The Quays. Taking Walks as a Bourgeois Practice

During the Middle Ages, public green space was limited to a small number of public squares—in Zurich there was only one, the Lindenhof. Beginning in the seventeenth century, the art of designing gardens gradually found its way into the urban fabric of Europe's cities. On the one hand, princely parks were opened step by step to the public; and on the other, new promenades, esplanades, and squares accessible to the general public were created. The Platzspitz and the Hohe Promenade were established right in front of the gates to the baroque city and in the areas along the fortifications offering the best views, becoming green spaces popular among Zurich's residents. A walk along the tree-lined promenades offered relaxation, contact with nature, and a chance to socialize. At the same time, it was a political symbol. With these new amenities, the bourgeoisie unmistakably demonstrated its growing influence in the economic, societal, and political spheres.—[8]

Even in the comparatively early work of the German garden theorist Christian Cay Lorenz Hirschfeld

(1742–92), one finds reference to the aesthetic and social benefits of public parks.——[9] During the nineteenth
century, these guiding principles remained highly in-
fluential. Against the backdrop of precarious social and
hygienic living conditions, the new zoning plans, which
incorporated the systematic "greening" of the city, now
placed greater emphasis on public green spaces. With
the aid of nonprofit organizations, societies, and com-
missions, a politically knowledgeable public became
established, allowing residents to actively participate in
the development of the flourishing cities. Through civic
involvement and later through newly set up communal
administrations, new public parks and promenades were
integrated spatially and functionally in the urban context. These were the actual urban sites that bridged the
contrasts between the socially segregated and spatially
separated working-class neighborhoods and the villa
districts, and that made it possible to grasp the multi-
faceted differences in class, interests, and taste. As
spaces to spend time in, they also provided a contrast to
streets and squares that, as the city grew, gradually
evolved into places primarily meant to be passed through.

Thus, it was neither the urban Bahnhofstrasse nor the
bank-lined Paradeplatz that were to become the image
associated, calling-card like, with Zurich, but rather the
city's lower lake basin and the stately promenade flanking it, known as the Seeuferpromenade (1882–87). The
latter, implemented by Arnold Bürkli (1833–94), the
city's top municipal engineer, turned out to be a trend-
setter. The twenty-one-hectare land-reclamation project
spared the residents from the "iron ring" railroad, a
project whose promoters initially wanted to be situated
along Lake Zurich's shoreline. In striking contrast, the
promenade finally made the lake—which had previously
been inaccessible on account of property rights, storage
sites, and the natural shoreline—available to the public.
To this day, the three-kilometer-long quay grounds
between the Zürichhorn and the port of Enge, comple-

9 Hirschfeld, Christian
Cay Lorenz: *Theorie
der Gartenkunst.* Vol. 5.
Leipzig 1785, pp. 68 ff.

[I]
Enjoying freedoms. Lake Zurich as new point of reference.
Photo, Robert Breitinger, 1895

[II]
Transformation of the city. A walk along the new quay.
Photo, anonymous, around 1890

[III]
Variety of colors and forms. Dendrological collection
at the Zurich Botanical Garden.
Photo, Robert Breitinger, 1893

[IV]
Setting up connections. Zurich's Central Station.
Photo, 1907

[V]
Private idyll. Lydia (1858–91), Alfred Escher's daughter,
presumably with a governess, in front of Villa Belvoir.
Photo, around 1860

71

10 At the urging of a group of professors headed by the botanist Carl Schröter (1855–1939), the forestry scientist Elias Landolt (1821–1896), and the geologist Albert Heim (1849–1937), an arboretum, a collection of stones, and an Alpine panorama providing information about the nearby mountains were incorporated in the quay. The artistic gardeners responsible for implementing the design of the arboretum were Evariste Mertens (1846–1907) and Otto Froebel (1844–1906). See Schönauer, Roman G.: "100 Jahre Zürcher Quaianlagen: Ein Gesamtkunstwerk der Landschaftsgestaltung feiert Geburtstag." In: *Mitteilungen der Gesellschaft für Gartenkultur 5* (1987), no. 3, pp. 62–65, here pp. 62ff.

11 Most of the terrain gained by dismantling the fortifications was divided into parcels and sold to the canton, which erected public buildings such as the cantonal school, the cantonal hospital, the University of Zurich and the ETH Zurich on it. Only the bulwark Zur Katz (Alter Botanischer Garten), the Hohe Promenade, and the Bauschänzli could be retained as green spaces. In addition, smaller parks and squares such as the Stadthausanlage and the garden at the new Tonhalle (concert hall) were created. Private grounds such as the gardens of the Belvoir, Bleuler, and Wesendonck villas were also converted into public parks.

mented by an arboretum and the shade-giving trees, plant beds, and benches, invites people to take walks, see and be seen, relax, and socialize.—[10] Although, over the course of the last 150 years, tastes and leisure time activities have changed fundamentally, the city's largest contiguous green space has remained universally popular.

Unlike in Paris, Berlin, or Vienna, the liberal city council in Zurich did not guide urban development with an organized framework, but instead left it to a large extent to market forces.—[11] In contrast to these role models, thanks to its topography and water bodies Zurich never lost its proximity to nature. The implementation of the quay succeeded in setting up a new relationship to nature and the lake, and by dramatizing the Alpine panorama like a stage set, it created a place of exceptional quality for generations to come.

III The Zurich Botanical Garden. From Fortification to Place of Education

To this day, the Old Botanical Garden situated on the bulwark known as Zur Katz has remained a green oasis amid an expanding city. The site had long played a role in defending the city when, in the nineteenth century, thanks to the growing general interest in botany and garden culture, it was transformed into a botanical garden, serving also as a venue for a wide variety of official acts. This was one of the first such facilities that had been envisioned from the start as a public park, and which, thanks to its outstanding location and view of the Alps, was understood to have the potential to be an important sight.

The Zurich Botanical Garden played a key role for Switzerland as a center of science and plants and in fostering garden culture. In 1834, as part of the reorganization of the system of higher education, the administration of the garden was transferred from the

Naturforschendende Gesellschaft in Zürich (Society of Natural Sciences Zurich) to the recently established University of Zurich. Here botany—which had long been a subscience of medicine—finally received official recognition in the form of an autonomous university chair. Oswald Heer (1809–83), who held the chair and was named director of the garden, moved the botanical garden from the village of Wiedikon to the city proper. By 1839, under the direction of the head gardener Theodor Froebel (1810–93), a modern university garden had been created. This garden not only provided the material for the botany courses at the scientific institutions, that carried out experiments on new cultivars and methods of cultivation, and contributed to the improvement of horticulture and agriculture; by providing the opportunity to explore, it also gave pleasure to all societal classes and fostered general interest in the world of plants. With their pathways, lined with scientific and decorative plantings presented didactically and aesthetically to a wider audience, the grounds were consistent with the notion of general adult education. Abundant collections of annuals and perennials, trees, shrubs, roses, Alpine flora, water and bog plants, and much more demonstrated the richness of the local and foreign flora to the people of Zurich. The redesign by Eduard Regel (1815–92), who had been head gardener since 1842, lasted until 1853. During this phase, eight temperature-controlled greenhouses were already in place to assist with the cultivation, acclimatization, and breeding of plants from warmer climates such as Central America, Australia, the Cape region, and the Mediterranean region. In addition, first steps were initiated toward amassing what is now an important collection of orchids. The octagonal "palm house" with tropical plants continuously presented intriguing blossoming plants to the public. Visitors were also allowed to visit the other greenhouses when accompanied by the director or one of the other gardeners.

The Zurich Botanical Garden is both a specific place and a world unto itself. The familiar and the novel, from nearby and far off, come face to face here. As a place of education in a time in which traveling to faraway destinations required considerable effort and was not an option for the common man, it gave people the opportunity to encounter plants of foreign origin. By bringing together and arranging species that normally are located far apart, then and now "a rendering of the world" was and still is created for visitors. The garden testifies to the motivation, inquisitiveness, and openness accompanying the introduction, cultivation, and dissemination of new plants in the nineteenth century.

IV The Train Station. Gateway to the World

12 Stutz, Werner: "Der Hauptbahnhof Zürich." In: Bieri, Werner (ed.): *Schweizerische Kunstführer, vol. 774*, Gesellschaft für Schweizerische Kunstgeschichte. Bern 2005, pp. 17 ff.

Zurich's Central Station—which opened in 1871—presented itself as a gateway to the world. To make way for the new building designed by Jakob Friedrich Wanner (1830–1903), head architect of the Swiss Northeast Railways, the antecedent by Gustav Albert Wegmann (1812–58)—which had been in use for just twenty years but was considerably more modest—was demolished.—[12] Since then, as a "cathedral of mobility," it has been a microcosm of society. Here one encounters a constant coming and going under a single roof. The giant train shed, erected in stone, steel, and glass, brings to mind a modern factory. The stately main entrance gestures invitingly toward the elegant business district along Bahnhofstrasse, which connects the historical center to the lake. Since 1889, the monument to Alfred Escher (1819–82), a statesman, railroad pioneer, and bank founder—stands on an axis with the entrance. Escher's transalpine Gotthard railway, completed in 1882, transformed a disadvantage—being a landlocked country—into a forward-looking transit advantage. What had been a dead end metamorphosed into the Swiss hub.

To this day Zurich's Central Station and Alfred Escher are symbolic of an era in which acceleration became the measure of all things. In the nineteenth century, new transport corridors and means of transportation, mass media, and communication technologies were already propelling globalization. Steam boats, railway, and telegraph, connected remote regions politically, economically, and infrastructurally to the centers and incorporated in global trade; and the speed and capacity with which humans, information, raw materials, foodstuffs, and plants could be transported increased many times over. Both botanical science and commercial trade benefitted from the influx of foreign plants. When plants became desirable to wider societal circles in Europe on account of their aesthetic qualities, smaller commercial gardeners in England and Belgium such as James Veitch (1792–1863), Frederick Sander (1847–1920), and Jean Linden (1817–98) transformed into well-financed businessmen. At their behest, commercial plant hunters scoured the most promising regions looking for new ornamental plants for Europe's garden culture. Popular outdoor plants came mainly from North America, the Caucasus, Siberia, and the region stretching from Central Asia to the Far East. New greenhouse plants originated primarily in Australia, Latin America, South Africa, and the Far East.

The Zurich Botanical Garden also made use of the new technologies and the growing demand in order to conduct its domestic commercial plant and seed business—which it pursued until 1893—and to gain access to a larger marketplace in the neighboring countries. The head gardeners travelled by rail to the European centers of horticulture, nurtured customer relations, took part in exhibits and auctions, and published in renowned professional journals. Trees, bushes, shrubs, potted plants, seeds, and many other goods were transported by rail quickly and economically, including to side valleys of Graubünden which had been difficult to reach. The import and sale of exclusive ornamental plants from overseas were also part of the national and international trade. The trade network of the Zurich Botanical Garden soon spanned from San Francisco to Moscow. With considerable strategic skill, and working from his office in Zurich, Eduard Ortgies (1829–1916), the energetic head gardener, directed the transfer of plants around half the globe. The threads connecting the plant collectors, the commercial gardeners, and the private customers converged here. For many years, Benedict Roezl (1823–84), one of the most productive plant hunters of his time, supplied plants exclusively to Ortgies's agency. The agency, in turn, successfully sold its foreign imports throughout Europe. In this way, new species of plants from Mexico, Guatemala, Costa Rica, Colombia, Peru, and the United States first found their way into European garden culture.

Plants were not just one of the first products of global trade in a developing consumer society but also a status symbol for those who could afford the accompanying costs and maintenance. In particular, the exclusive novelties were in demand among the nascent bourgeoisie. The plant fashions—which were quickly adopted in gardens and parks—were a visible manifestation of the progressing globalization.

V The Belvoir. The Private Garden as Retreat

The Belvoir Park belongs to a beltway of public parks, private gardens, and urban green, which, situated in the Riesbach, Enge, and Wollishofen districts, nestles close to the hills surrounding lake Zurich and has a valuable stock of mature trees that help shape the city's character. From a distance, individual silhouettes stand out from the green ribbon; crown forms and leaf shapes distinguish the respective species and varieties. In the designated tree protection zones, the city of Zurich imposes special measures to safeguard woody plants. The oldest specimens bear witness to an era in which, for an increasingly large part of society, private gardens acquired a new, up-to-date significance and served as a countermodel to the everyday world.

As the eighteenth century came to a close, several phenomena fostered interest in foreign ornamental plants: the growth of trade and travel, the foundation of institutes dedicated to the natural sciences and of commercial nurseries, the establishment of organizations and societies, and the publication of garden literature. Gardening became a popular leisure-time activity. Even in small urban apartments, potted plants were cultivated on window sills. For those who had the financial means, a garden of one's own and a greenhouse offered a larger field of experimentation. The villa with landscape garden was part of the bourgeois lifestyle and an important status symbol. Aspects such as moral education, recalling history, arousing emotions, or striving to improve upon nature that had been integral parts of landscape gardens of the patriarchy and the aristocracy of the ancien régime took a back seat. Instead of showing idealized nature, the garden was now expected to lend itself to everyday pragmatism. As an extension of interior living spaces, it served as a place that accommodated family life and as a place to spend time with friends. But it also offered an outdoor space for self-actualization and self-expression.

More freedoms in all areas of life fostered the cultivation of individual taste, which, in turn, was reflected in the design and plantings of the gardens. Though professional garden artists such as Theodor and his son Otto Froebel (1844–1906), Evariste Mertens (1846–1907), and Conrad Löwe (1819–70) had offered their services since the midcentury, it was not uncommon for clients to become involved in the planning and design of the gardens or to take on the role of designer. One such example is Heinrich Escher-Zollikofer (1776–1853), who made his fortune in North America; in 1826, following his successful career, Escher-Zollikofer had several vineyards in Enge, a community at the gates of Zurich, transformed into a stately family seat known as the Belvoir. From then on, he dedicated a large amount of his time to the painstaking design and maintenance of this generously dimensioned landscape garden, which was one of the first of its kind in Zurich and its environs. He enthusiastically collected numerous plant genera, experimented with his own varieties, and presented them at the flower exhibitions of the cantonal Verein für Landwirtschaft und Gartenbau, where he received great acclaim in professional circles. In his time, Escher was considered one of the main supporters of flower cultivation in Zurich. Beginning in 1853, his son, the aforementioned politician Alfred Escher, was responsible for the continued development of the manor and its grounds and for the richness of its flora. The Escher family and Oswald Heer had cordial relations. For decades the Zurich Botanical Garden provided the Belvoir with trees, bushes, and climbing plants; perennials such as dahlias, hollyhocks, and peonies; bedding plants such as geraniums and petunias; plants for stone gardens and ferns; ornamental grasses; bulb plants; hothouse and cold house plants; and, last but not least, vegetable, flower, and grass seeds. In addition, there were rare costly plants such as ornamental agave from Central America sourced from the plant collectors overseas.

Today the atmosphere of the park is primarily determined by the mature trees that arrived at the Belvoir under the direction of Alfred Escher and have grown into impressive specimens. Several woody plants originating in North America such as *Sequoiadendron giganteum* (giant sequoia), *Thuja gigantea* (Western red-cedars) and *Chamaecyparis lawsoniana* (Port Orford cedar) recall the fashionable predilection for conifers that held sway in that era. With their striking habit and dark needles, they symbolize perseverance and consistency. They not only substantially contribute to the quality of today's park—which has been accessible to the public since 1901—but also bear witness to an age in which garden owners and plant lovers employed "exotic" ornamental plants to integrate what was foreign, "other" and novel in their own design for living in a world that was undergoing upheaval.—13

"The last remaining luxury of our time…"

"The garden is the last remaining luxury of our time, because it requires what is most precious in contemporary society: time, affection, and space."—14 This statement by landscape architect Dieter Kienast (1945–98) has not lost its validity—on the contrary. In the city as a functioning "organism," the public squares, parks, and promenades, as well as the private gardens—as designed spaces—are all of crucial importance on account of their aesthetic-sensual, social, ecological, and microclimatic functions. This is all the more true in the present context in which built-up areas are systematically being densified. Yet much too often landscape architecture is a mere appendage to architecture: green spaces amount to nothing more than residual space. And they are characterized by different predilections and conceptions of nature: some view landscape architecture as the design of a habitat by nature afficionados and as a discipline resting on an ecological foundation that is inclined to take a back-to-nature stance or a stance with related implications. Others see it purely as a means of "design" that lopsidedly places its focus on the discipline's artistic content. Yet in a comprehensive sense, landscape architecture must be far more than these opposing worlds would suggest, because the dis-cipline's development—as described in this essay—is rooted in traditions of aesthetics and of natural science. Landscape architecture should be

13 During the heyday of plant introduction, different foreign species were referred to as "exotics," in particular, specimens that originated oversees and had special habitat requirements.

14 Kienast, Dieter: "Sehnsucht nach dem Paradies." In: Professur für Landschaftsarchitektur ETH Zurich (ed.): *Dieter Kienast – Die Poetik des Gartens: Über Chaos und Ordnung in der Landschaftsarchitektur.* Basel 2002, pp. 71–76, here p. 76

High-quality urban space. Garden flanking EBP in Zurich.
Photo, Christian Vogt, 1996

understood as an overarching strategy that both takes into consideration the natural-science and ecological aspects and orients its design to the aesthetic and symbolic significance of a place, its heritage, and the sensual experience to be had.—[15]

In a time that was strongly marked by the natural garden movement, Dieter Kienast demonstrated that high-quality spaces that are not exclusively "green," but which also incorporate fine shades of "grey," can be created in the city under demanding conditions.—[16] In his projects he integrated design, function, and ecology, picking up on cultural traditions and, at the same time, taking a self-confident step toward the future. He influenced several generations of landscape architects with his way of working. The project for EBP in Zürich-Stadelhofen (1995–96) exemplifies his approach to planning. The engineering firm asked the landscape architects Kienast Vogt Partner to redesign the grounds of its newly acquired office building. The client's aim to allow as much rainwater as possible to percolate on-site became the point of departure of the design. Kienast transformed what had been an unsightly enclosed courtyard into a lush garden courtyard visible from the engineering firm's adjoining conference room. A chest-high concrete cone which collects the rainwater from the roof's surface is the eyecatcher. Self-sown mosses, ferns, and cranesbills inhabit a tuff wall kept moist with rainwater—the tableau that emerges is a conduit through which one can experience nature's dynamic processes. As a counterpart to the wild, spontaneous vegetation in the garden courtyard, a row of fifteen box-cut topiary linden trees in front of the building—a space that had previously been used for parking—makes reference to a gardening tradition in connection with nature in the city. A rectangular steel basin stores the surface water, which provides water when it overflows to the roots of the woody plants. The smooth reflective surface of the water basin and the dense roof created by the trees' crowns

15 When Christophe Girot assumed the professorship in landscape architecture that had been set up at the ETH Zurich in 1997 by Dieter Kienast (it was, at the time, the first university chair in this discipline in Switzerland), he initiated critical discourses on current design tendencies in landscape architecture and developed a theory and design method entitled "Topology." See Girot, Christophe / Freytag, Anette / Kirchengast, Albert / Richter, Dunja (eds.): *Topology: Topical Thoughts on the Contemporary Landscape.* Landscript 3. Series published by the Chair of Prof. Girot, Institute of Landscape Architecture ILA ETH Zurich, Berlin 2013; Girot, Christophe / Imhof, Dora (eds.): *Thinking the Contemporary Landscape.* New York 2016. See also note 1.

16 See Girot, Christophe: "Graue Landschaften." In: Professur für Landschaftsarchitektur ETH Zurich (ed.) 2002, pp. 7–10. See also note 14.

17 Erni, Andreas: "Die inszenierte Versicker-ung = Mise en scène de l'infiltration." In: *Anthos: Zeitschrift für Landschaft-sarchitektur = Une revue pour le paysage 38* (1999), pp. 4–7; Freytag, Anette: *The Landscapes of Dieter Kienast.* Zurich 2020, pp. 123–36

produce a special aesthetic quality in the otherwise highly commodified urban streetscape.——[17] Despite the limited space and the numerous planning constraints, Kienast succeeded in creating a convincing design solution through subtle yet effective interventions that to this day serves as an exemplar.

Today the garden serves as a place of refuge in a rapidly changing world and is simultaneously an alternative to the realm of digitalization. It demands a real understanding of processes und factors, a rich trove of experiences, physical action, and concrete engagement with the material. Unlike the design of a building, nothing is written in stone: even when it seems that the last turn of the shovel has been carried out, the change sets in, inexorably advancing the natural dynamics—and decay is always a threat. It is perhaps precisely this fragile momentum that turns the garden into something so true-to-life and honest, and, since time immemorial, what has been a place of longing for all of humanity. It is a vessel for memories, emotions, and experiences. The capable and the knowledgeable are rewarded with a cornucopia of colors, forms, fragrances, and sounds. It may also be the place where one's failures are unsparingly apparent, yet one can start over at will. Although styles of design, plant fashions, uses, and techniques change over the course of time, the garden as "green locus" in the proper sense of the term never loses its significance or its up-to-dateness. The garden always reminds us of the hope it holds for the future.

Távora, Siza, and Nature

Tony Fretton

We have never had any relation to nature in untouched form ... the longing for untouched nature is itself a product of culture originating in the over-artificiality of existence. In truth Nature begins to relate to us only when we indwell in it, when culture begins in it. Culture then develops and bit by bit nature is refashioned.—[1]

Romano Guardini, *Letters from Lake Como*

1   Guardini, Romano: *Letters from Lake Como: Explorations in Technology and the Human Race.* Grand Rapids MI, 1994, p. 10

In the mind of designers, nature and what it is seen to include are concepts that can be reformulated in relation to the ideas and values of their times. The two projects considered in this article, the Quinta da Conceição park by Fernando Távora (1956–60) and the Piscina das Marés swimming baths at Leça da Palmeira by Alvaro Siza (1961–66) were made close in time and with different ideas of nature but came from a similar empirical approach to that inferred by Romano Guardini from the buildings and landscape around Lake Como. That approach, Guardini wrote, "began with investigation, then noted connections, unleashed forces, realised possibilities, emphasised what is desired, and, stressing this, repressed other things. It was knowing, validating, stimulating, directing, and underlining of natural forces and relations. All that it gave form to was still in some way nature."—[2]
Guardini's commentary was based on the works and ideas

2   Ibid., p. 45

of a traditional hierarchical society. The same type of society shaped the original buildings and landscape of the Quinta da Conceição. In redesigning it as a public park for a relatively democratic society, Távora and Siza, who assisted him, freely inserted new buildings and landscape elements among those that existed and opened views to the nearby dockyard to recast it as a work of forward-looking modernity. Távora wrote: "The park was a monastery of monks who settled there in the XVth century, and later it became private property. There was the avenue, the chapel, the cloister and the pools and therefore a structure to sustain."—[3] Távora's sensibility extended backward from those elements to the Portuguese vernacular that he encountered in his contribution to the survey "Arquitectura Popular em Portugal" and forward to modernism through his presence at meetings of CIAM and Team 10.

3   Fernando Távora in: Trigueros, Luiz: *Fernando Távora*. Editorial Blau LDA, Lisbon 1993, p. 66. With contributions by Alexandre Alves Costa, Alvaro Siza, Bernardo Ferrão and Eduardo Souto de Moura and Fernando Távora.

The park is extensive, seemingly at the scale of the dockyard and highway that it faces. On the steeply sloping site that extends from the highway up to the road at the rear, Távora created a terraced lawn with a stepped pathway at one side that ascends between hedges to a landing in front of the chapel of the original estate, before continuing up to a new walled court of painted stucco.

The apparent stillness and termination of this space is dispelled by the discovery within it of a massive stair that is the rear entrance to the park. Its spatial vividness is underscored by the dullness of the back road to which it leads and the unused original gate of the estate nearby. From the left of the chapel a path leads through the hedge to a tennis pavilion by Távora, which he configured as a viewing platform above storage rooms, covered by an exotic roof resting on a low concrete beam.

Its façade materials of granite and stucco are those of the chapel that can be seen below, and the lines of white marble in the terracotta floor resemble the markings in the tennis court below.

This tiny, refined building looks out to an unscreened view of the architecturally unconsidered dockyard across the park. Moments such as these could be just coincidences, except that visual rhymes and frank acceptance of industrial buildings appear repeatedly in the work of Távora and Siza, and are essential, if unconscious aspects of their architecture.

At the back of the park among trees, the blank enclosing walls come into view of the swimming pool designed by Siza in the location of one of the pools mentioned by Távora. Inside them the pool is set into a raised terrace, which is surrounded by walls of different heights that frame views of the sky and the park below. Walls, trees and the figures of the pool and its foot bath are a studied composition of abstract and natural forms and of use and appearance. Looking back across the pool, the enclosing walls are found to be buildings with red tiled roofs that are partly buried in the land, like traditional Porto houses.

With exceptional skill Távora and Siza brought together new abstract constructions and buildings, new buildings following vernacular traditions, historical buildings and landscape elements, and views of the industrial landscape, sometimes through formal composition as I have described, and at others through sequencing, associations and contrasts. Most striking is their treatment of the trees and plants, which remain dignified, unknowable and untouched in their interior being.

The conditions for Siza's project in the Piscina das Marés swimming baths at Leça da Palmeira (1961–66) were very different. The beach on which it is located contained no traces of previous occupation and the program was for a new and unconditionally public facility. Of his architecture in this period, he said: "in the initial work I began by studying the site in order to classify it ... but now I take everything into consideration since what I am interested in is reality ... everything there is important, and nothing

should be left out … it is not only a question of making
relationships out of the real conditions but also out of
space and materials. Such relationships have to be established … the project and that which surrounds it as well as
the different parts within the project itself … the project's
internal relationships take on a completely eclectic and
hybrid nature since the external conditions of the work
must penetrate and taint it."—[4] Nature in the Piscina das
Marés includes the sky, the sea and the creatures within
it, the rocks and sand that the sea created, the minds and
experience of those who use or encounter the pool and the
nearby industrial works that shape their lives.

4   Interview with
Bernrad Huet. In: *AMC*
Magazine. Issue 44, 1978

At Leça da Palmeira a coastal boulevard runs next
to the sea wall above a beach of rocks and sand looking
out to the Atlantic. Siza placed a series of concrete buildings there at the level of the beach with copper roofs
that rest on the kerb of the boulevard. A widening quad-
rilateral space falls from the highway to the entrance
at the level of the beach.

There, in a dark room, you change into swimwear in cubicles of dark wood and hand your clothes to an attendant who rolls them away on a long rail, and then find yourself in a walled alley filled with sun but with no view yet of the beach.

It is not until you have walked along the alley and through a shallow foot bath that you enter the beach, washed, more naked and like animals in the sea. Spatial effects on the beach are created by the simplest means. A route to the children's beach starts as a path and becomes a bridge before leading to a pool with the form that parents would make for children from sand and seawater.

The main pool is formed between rocks and concrete walls at the sea's edge, where waves can break over it. In and around these parts that give the structural imagery of the project, Siza provides for an array of simple human pleasures: walking down to the beach and leaving the city and your clothes behind to become fully immersed in the beach, sun, and water. Lying low and sunbathing behind the rocks. Strolling contemplatively in the wide foot bath at the edge of the main pool. Sunbathing on the esplanade that faces away toward the next beach and putting the swimming baths and its crowds behind you. Walking and swimming there and coming back occasionally for coffee or ice cream. In the midst of all these pleasures there is a quiet acknowledgment of industrial society. The walls containing the main pool are of the same material and apparent size as the commercial shipping jetty seen across the bay, including it in the scheme as a human artifact within nature.

I have discussed Quinta da Conceição and the Piscina das Marés through their physical being and the observable experiences of people using them, to show that significant architecture can be made just from those means, and also to show that design and its way of working with physical matter, social values, and shared knowledge can be included in architectural discourse. Quinta da Conceição and the

Piscina das Marés are works of persistent value in the present time, when nature is being radically challenged by industry and consumerism. Their durability is evident in their continuous use in the half century since they were made. They persist by providing generous, collective enjoyment in a most basic and accessible form. The ideas of nature that lie in them are inclusive, consisting not only of nature and the life forms that constitute it, but human presence and consciousness and the artifacts of our societies, which if we are to survive must work within rather than against nature.

Museum Insel Hombroich: The Construction of an Alternative Natural Space

Frank Boehm

… artists have found things that seemingly destroy the worlds of those who preceded them without, of course, wanting to destroy them. They have found a practice of their own and have had an effect on others with it.—[1]

A Special Situation

When the art collector and real estate developer Karl-Heinrich Müller set out to find a suitable place for his extensive art collection, it was not foreseeable that in the nineteen-eighties and nineteen-nineties the inception of the Museum Insel Hombroich would spawn a complex and novel landscape, an immersive experience, and a natural habitat.—[2] He took a variety of locations and concepts into consideration. But it required the concerted efforts of a small group of protagonists directed toward a specific site to create this unique locale. Today this site has not only been maintained to a great degree as originally intended, but also continues to be a guidepost for other endeavors.

Art, Architecture, Labor, Landscape

An essential quality of Hombroich lies in the abundance of topics that have been tightly woven together. Müller

1   Karl-Heinrich Müller comments on the four artists—Arp, Fautrier, Klein, and Schwitters—whose works formed the basis of the collection after he and the art dealer Sami Tarica realigned it. See Kling, Thomas / Müller, Heinrich: *Energien / Synergien 3*, Kunststiftung NRW, Cologne 2004, p. 20

2   Opened to the public in 1987 as a comprehensive cultural venue, Hombroich covers an area of more than sixty hectares. In addition to Museum Insel Hombroich, the parent foundation Stiftung Insel Hombroich possesses two further parcels of land and their architectural ensembles: the Raketenstation Hombroich and the Kirkeby-Feld.

Site plan of Museum Insel Hombroich

gathered around him Gotthard Graubner, Erwin Heerich, and Anatol Herzfeld, three very different artists from Düsseldorf's art community, and involved them closely in the development of the museum. Only after the initial property purchases and the completion of the first of Heerich's buildings was Bernhard Korte asked to join the team as landscape designer. Müller commissioned these four men to each develop one aspect of the nascent institution: the consultation regarding the selection and installation of the artwork, the realization of the buildings, the embodiment of "being an artist" at this location, and the development of the landscape itself. Müller offered each of them enormous financial and artistic possibilities, and was at the same time also strongly involved in the process and in moderating the development. His role could be likened to a stage director who allows his protagonists to shape the respective parts of an imaginary script, a script which continues to be developed as the plot progresses.

A New Museum

Creating a designed landscape in Hombroich that would make a profound perceptual impression on its visitors was not a premise of the museum's conception. In fact, after the initial phase of reflection, it still could have been situated in Düsseldorf, on the outskirts of Paris, or in a woodland outside Bonn.—[3] Front and center were the collection itself, the relation of the works to one another, and the options the visitors would have to perceive these connections. The stances and practices developed in this way were to have a decisive influence on the emerging buildings and on the landscape.

Although Müller primarily collected objects and paintings and did not show particular interest in the newest forms of art, performance art and land art did have a significant influence on the development of the museum. Owing to their ephemeral nature and, above all, by means of photo documentation and other media, these forms of art reached a larger audience. Müller simply ramped up his emphasis on physical presence and unmediated perception. He brought a museum into existence with the greatest possible respect for the individual work of art, a demand that had been made at the time by artist such as Donald Judd, Daniel Buren, and Remy Zaugg.—[4] In parallel with Donald Judd and his Chianti Foundation in Marfa, Müller implemented a permanent installation of the works at Hombroich, and both of these endeavors were to undergo only minor alterations over the years—an unusual approach, particularly in the areas of contemporary art and modern art. In this way, Müller created an early countermodel to the development taking place on the international stage toward ever-larger and ever-more elaborate exhibitions. In his ideal conception of a museum, Michael Fehr names an essential aspect of this course of action: "regarding exhibitions as events with limited runs, the items which have in a particular fashion been suspended in time are placed in a time frame, the exhi-

3 Müller, Karl-Heinrich. In: ibid., p. 50, p. 24

4 It is not possible to glean from the records whether Müller was aware of the contemporaneous development of the Chinati Foundation by Judd or the texts by Zaugg or Buren. He probably intuitively developed a proximity to their ideas.

5   Fehr, Michael: *Kurze Beschreibung eines Museums, das ich mir wünsche*, www.aesthetischepraxis.de, p. 7

bition run, and thereby come under time pressure that is unknown to a museum."—[5] At the Museum Insel Hombroich, the passage of time is legible first and foremost in the changes in light and weather over the course of a day or a year. Moreover, the works of art are not loaned out. The decision to do without guards and explanatory texts further intensifies the way the art is experienced.

Sculpture as Architecture

Erwin Heerich was commissioned to design the exhibition pavilions. His conception of them could be characterized as walk-in sculptures and as variations of his earlier objects—made of cardboard or stone—and drawings. What is important is the radicality of the buildings, which, as autonomous works, do not adhere to a logic of transposing urban notions of architecture to space in the landscape.

In strong contrast to topoi such as villas or follies, reflections of which we see in the intensification and reconstruction of "images of nature" in city parks, at Museum Insel Hombroich Heerich arrived at a novel type of building. These unify aspects of architecture, sculpture, and landscape and retain great independence. They do not converse in conventional fashion with nature. After the first two pavilions—the Orangery and the Graubner Pavilion—were completed, Heerich decided, in his designs of buildings holding works of art from the collection, to forgo windows and views out to the landscape. These buildings provide enclosed spaces for art. The stark lighting—daylight being the only source—enters the space only through skylights. The changing light conditions, and the sun and the clouds, enable a play of light and shadow inside, connecting in an abstractive form to nature. The structures, reduced in this manner to geometric solids—all erected using recycled bricks—make their appearance in the landscape as quasi-geological formations, not as individual works of architecture. "Like nature, they are aids to sensual experience. The buildings are apprehended through sensual experience; they do not function as containers."—6 Tellingly, this characterization of nonarchitecture comes to us from the landscape designer Bernhard Korte.

6   Korte, Bernhard: *Insel Hombroich. Analogien zwischen Kunst und Natur.* Grevenbroich 1988, p. 5

View of the wetlands with orangery

Landscape as Nature

Müller does not succumb to the misconception that a collection of representations of nature will facilitate getting closer to nature. A rare exception is a work by Jean Fautrier which tellingly depicts a glacier and became part of the museum's collection only on account of its outstanding quality—not its content. Instead, the Museum Insel Hombroich itself develops into a unique hybrid of nature and representation of nature.

Beginning in 1984, for the second phase, Bernhard Korte was asked to join in to propose a concept for the landscape. In the previous years, three structures had already been erected in the Alter Park. During the subsequent decades, on other fields which had previously been used agriculturally, he implemented imagined, regional nature. This is often referred to as renaturation. His own definition is probably more precise: "Nature was idealized

7   Ibid., p. 7

8   Müller, Karl-Heinrich:
*Hombroich: Ein offener
Versuch*. In: Stiftung Insel
Hombroich. Neuss 1998,
p. 36

according to my ideas."—[7] Müller himself postulated:
"The island's nature is not some modified version of
a park for people, but rather a habitat for animals and
plants which people may encounter."—[8] And many people
now regard this construct as nature. A small team of
gardeners manages the flora, fauna, and water bodies
without referring to a formal handbook. Consequently,
this landscape is the only aspect of the museum that continues to develop.

An abstract site plan—a map—serves as rudimentary
orientation in the landscape; there is no signage. The
only element in this designed landscape that could not be
misunderstood as a reconstruction and is nevertheless
often overlooked deliberately disorients the individual:
the gravel paths through the three realms—park, terrace,
and wetlands—adhere to no obvious system, and visitors
are meant to stay on them. The visitors have the feeling
they are discovering the landscape and its spaces, yet are
constantly, unobtrusively being guided.

At Hombroich, at a decisive moment as the visit begins,
the landscape can be surveyed, but then, increasingly,
in contrast to picturesque landscape parks, turns into
a downright visceral experience. Guided through wooded
areas at times more open and at others more dense, the
visitor comes in close contact with a profusion of plants.
Along the way, all of the senses—not just the sense of
sight—are appealed to. Visitors smell flowers and the soil,
touch trees and masonry, hear the water burble, and taste
regional flavors in the cafeteria.

The impression this makes is all the more intense
because an overview is often lacking. Even the buildings
reinforce this effect. "[T]here's this pull of noncognizance
carrying over to the passageways between hedge and ma-

9   Korte: 1988, p. 23

sonry,"—[9] Bernhard Korte writes, commenting on the
correlation between building and landscape at the Laby-
rinth, the central exhibition building. In such instances,
Museum Insel Hombroich is at once built landscape and
built nature.

A Model

In 1998, the collector Karl-Heinrich Müller himself titled
the often-cited text accompanying the inauguration of
his foundation "Hombroich – ein offener Versuch" (Hombroich—an open experiment).—[10] In 1987, following the
opening of the museum, with additional purchases of
land—which were to become Raketenstation Hombroich
and the Kirkeby-Feld Hombroich—he had introduced
another development phase. Looking back, it can be
established that the development of these extensive spatial additions—including the new forms of landscape and
topics, as well as the inclusion of a larger number of
artists, this time from a younger generation—constituted
a turning point. Though it was still in the same spirit of
managed openness, it was increasingly marked by parallel
developments, a juxtaposition of events without relation
to one another. The spatial, thematic, and artistic intensity that to this day characterizes Museum Insel Hombroich was not achieved in the subsequent ventures.

In the past, we were more likely to encounter such intensity in metropolitan settings. For his much-noted
submission to the Parc de la Villette competition in 1982,
Rem Koolhaas applied "culture of congestion," a notion
he himself had coined. He explained that the extensive
functional program could not be accommodated on the
available surface area and in his design, the uses were
therefore stacked one atop the other. He had, in fact,
coined the term to describe an urban experience marked
by layering and interweaving a variety of functions—a
notion he had explored in great detail in his early publication *Delirious New York*.

Only at first glance does it seem far-fetched to draw
parallels to Hombroich. But the form of its landscape
arises so abruptly and intensely from the relative barrenness of the surrounding acreage—akin to Manhattan's
skyscrapers from the surrounding urban fabric. The de-
marcation is sharp and the intensity of the experience

10 Müller: 1988, p. 35

11 Korte, Bernhard:
*Insel Hombroich: Spazier-
gang zu den Bäumen.*
Grevenbroich 1989, p. 21

at the museum is high. "The Old Park is an exceptional place of irrationality … I suspect that for many people it is overtaxing"—[11] writes Bernhard Korte, referring solely to the impressions of nature, not to the works of art.

When one begins to probe the museum's landscape, one comes upon a further analogy to the city. Like urban parks, which as gaps within a metropolis heighten the impression made by the surrounding urban fabric, the museum landscape is complemented by buildings which, as we have seen, intensify how the flora is experienced. The art collection, as point of departure for Müller, next to landscape and buildings indeed the most important component, is ultimately to be experienced in separate spaces. These encounters with the art become blended with the alternating experiences of indoor and outdoor spaces and of the landscape. On a planet in which there is barely any (pristine) nature left to speak of, and the sectors that survive are maintained as "preserves," Museum Insel Hombroich is a landscape that is allowed to be nature again and a model that is both radical and subtle.

Another *Gestalt*

The site plan of the Museum Insel Hombroich does indeed bear similarities to the island depicted in the frontispiece of the first edition of Thomas More's *Utopia* (1516). In both cases, a landscape separate from the rest of the world with scattered buildings and a watercourse, not accessible by foot, but not all too far in the distance. These days the museum, whose early nucleus was indeed an isle in the river Erft, is accessible via a building that serves as a lock and an escarpment. The landscape is still characterized by bodies of water and watercourses, with individual bridges. More's island is situated near the coast, while Hombroich is located in the catchment area of several major cities. But unlike the (unfulfillable) hopes of protagonists for ideal worlds, with reference to More's *Utopia*, Alfred Kubin's *Die andere Seite*, and René Daumal's *Mount Analogue*, Müller and his team—Graubner, Heerich, Korte, and Anatol—expected from the beginning that this counterdesign would have an unresolvable relationship to the real world. Müller writes in his manifesto: "The Insel … entices and captivates," but "each person involved in the Insel has a flourishing life of his own."—12

12 Müller: 1988, pp. 35f.

Map of the island of Utopia

Hombroich is not a Utopian place of longing like the new worlds described in literature. It is a heterotopian place near us, a special element within our designed landscape, its elaborated form is both concrete and narrative. At the Museum Insel Hombroich, just as immersion in nature and landscape design are superimposed, so are the lives and episodic experiences of the visitors. What the visitors experience on this imaginary island remains separate from day-to-day life, yet reacts upon it. The arcadian model and our habitats, the "other" and the "same" reinforce each other.—13

13 In addition to the texts quoted from the Hombroich milieu, the following publications are especially noteworthy: Walter, Kerstin: *Das Pittoreske: Die Theorie des englischen Landschaftsgartens als Baustein zum Verständnis von Kunst der Gegenwart*. Worms 2006; Firebrace, William: "Museum Insel Hombroich." In: *AA Files 71*. London 2015, pp. 3–26

Ruach
Two Children

First child (large four-leaf clover):

To become aware that the language of man fails. Thus the language of
things remains untranslatable. Here, the unnamable. The onomatopoetic
Hebrew word Ruach—breath, gust, wind (consider, that god breathes
his breath into man) is what seems possible in the language of man. It
penetrates the walls: images. They (the images) coalesce in a community
that does not want to have a name; it reveals itself as sound; unreconciled
it puts us in abiding unease. Ghetto, Warsaw, Assaf—the words clatter
in the room. Where destiny, deeds, my deep, impellent desire guide me,
paradise, where language is perfectly knowing, is far. Remember: "The
translation of the language of things into that of man is not only a translation of the mute into the sonic; it is also the translation of the nameless
into name" (Walter Benjamin).

Onomatopoeia is the
process of creating a word
that phonetically imitates,
resembles, or suggests
the sound that it describes.
Third Child: rishrésh!
(to make noise, rustle).

Second child (small four-leaf clover):

In the year 5780 I met a sage. He was soul, ground, inebriation, high
spirits, and confidence: kindred in God. In his suffering, perceptiveness,
and penetration of all things have I seen light. Would I have met him
as body, would he have bathed me in holy water, and taken me with him.
Of the prayers for Assaf, of his words and mine, it is me forbidden to
speak: I have made signs.

Third child (Great Bear, constellation):

February 4, 2020:
Would here be fire, my body shall burn, and all that in it is. rishrésh!

Note, November 2019:
7 is the number of the young light.
Understand! There is no place empty of Shekinah (manifestation of the
Presence of God. Divine Presence, that which dwells).

Bambino Ebreo

Pomegranate-shaped bottles, clay, early Israelite period, Hecht Museum, Haifa, 1050–930 BCE, 2020, silver gelatin hand print, 30.5 x 40 cm

Hole-mouth cooking pot, Bir es-Safadi, 4000–3000 BCE, Eretz Israel Museum, Tel Aviv, 2020, silver gelatin print, 40 x 30.5 cm

Bambino Ebreo, plaster, wax, 1892, 2020, silver gelatin print, 40 x 30.5 cm

Untitled (Hand), Eretz Israel Museum, Tel Aviv, 2020, silver gelatin print, 40 x 30.5 cm

Incantation clay bowl, Jewish inscription in Babylonian Judeo-Aramaic language, 300–700 CE, Hecht Museum, Haifa, 2020, silver gelatin print, 30.5 x 40 cm

Ossuary, Peki'in, painted pottery, 6500–5500 BCE, Israel Museum Jerusalem, 2020, silver gelatin print, 40 x 30.5 cm

Child burial, Ghassul, Chalcolithic, 5000–4000 BCE, National Archeological Museum Amman, Jordan, 2020, silver gelatin print, 30.5 x 40 cm

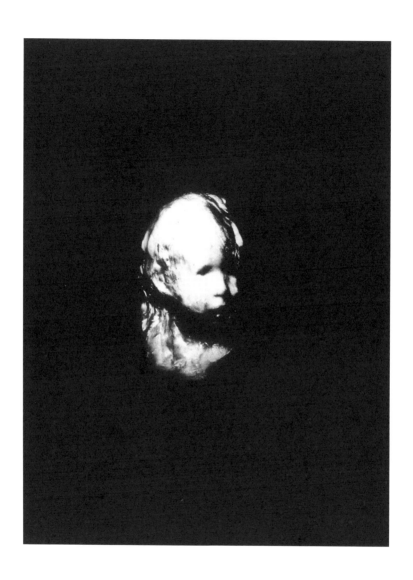

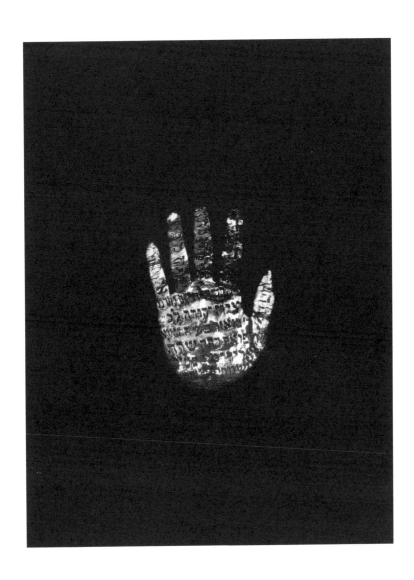

Incantation clay bowl bearing a Jewish inscription (developed from the Aramaic script), in Babylonian Judeo-Aramaic language.

Archeological Museum of Haifa

The Inscription (first part):

Geller, Markham J.: "Four Aramaic Incantation Bowls." In: *The Bible World. Essays in Honor of Cyrus H. Gordon*. Hoboken 1980, pp. 48–51

"Bound, sealed is the amulet for a sealing and binding, for the house of Metanis bar Azarmiduk through this great Name, which Rules over all evil spirits. I adjure and I decree against you, all of you, all of you—evil spirits, liliths, wizardesses, all hated dreams, all evil spirits, mighty visions, frights, and evil clingers, that you depart and go away from him and from his house, his dwelling, threshold, wife, sons, possessions, and bedroom, Metanis bar Azarmiduk and Eve his wife, that it be sealed and countersealed in the name SRSN SRYSN GYSN GYSN GYSN. They drive away male and female disturbers, they push aside bars of lead with a single twid. Suffer, MSLL. You are ruled, linded, killed, and driven away—all demons, daevas, all evil spirits, and all hated dreams. When their names are inscribed and handed down, all evil spirits and all hated dreams and liliths depart and are idle and die. All their names MSLL (magical symbols) PLYTL (magical symbols) of PTPLTS bat Ziri S S TSNYM SDYM. Banned on the authority of the Ruler of the Council and NBRWN and the Great NBWRWN who call out, and from the authority and that which is said, 'in good luck there!' You are ruled and killed and driven away, all demons, daevas, liliths, all hated dreams, and all evil spirits ... "

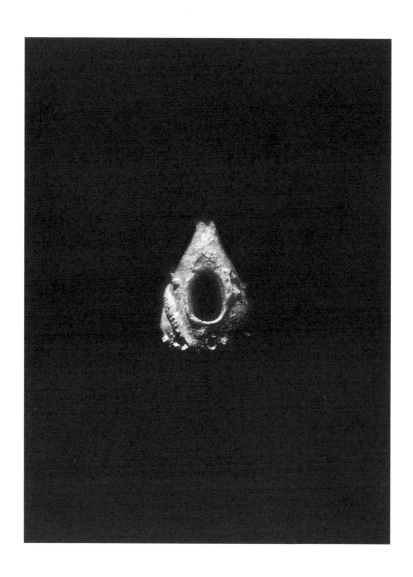

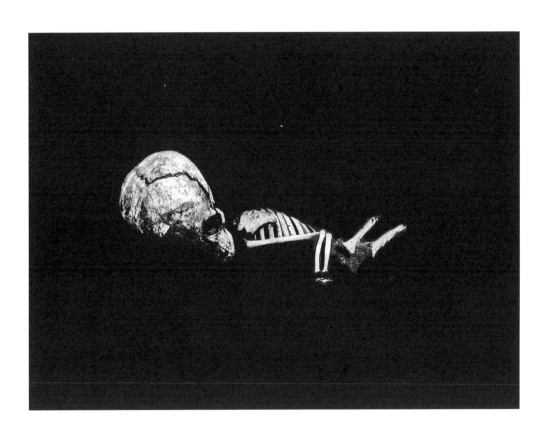

A Farewell to the Concept of Landscape?

Ludwig Fischer

Recapitulation: The "Old-School" European Conception of Landscape and Its Extensions

The notion of landscape as a viewed surrounding—whether as a more or less undisturbed natural ensemble, or a technologized shaped space—that we are all familiar with is, as is generally known, in terms of history of mentality and in its theoretical elaboration among the "achievements" of the modern era in the West. The classical conception of landscape developed when the single-point perspective became the definitive principle. The older concept/interpretation of landscape—the social and, by extension, political organization in/of a specific settlement area—[1]—has been weakened and to a great degree displaced by the new meanings of the word. An understanding of landscape as "depicted natural space" became established, according to which in effect what is portrayed is almost always what we would analytically designate "cultural landscape."—[2] From the time of Dürer's application of the term onward, landscape referred at first to pictorial scenery, a meticulously detailed backdrop. Shortly thereafter, in painting the viewed scenery, a more or less "natural" excerpt of reality, became the subject of the work.—[3]

It is evident that the principles of the single-point perspective are causally related, initially, to the artistic

1 To this day, the term continues to be used primarily in cultural-political organizations such as "Ostfriesische Landschaft" or "Oldenburgische Landschaft." See Piepmeyer, Rainer: "Das Ende der ästhetischen Kategorie 'Landschaft.'" In: *Westfälische Forschungen*, 30/1980, pp. 8–46; Müller, Gunter: "Zur Geschichte des Wortes Landschaft." In: von Wallthor, Alfred Hartlieb/Quirin, Heinz (eds.): *"Landschaft" als interdisziplinäres Forschungsproblem*. Münster 1977, pp. 13–23; Gruenter, Rainer: "Landschaft: >

113

> Bemerkungen zur Wort-
und Bedeutungsgeschich-
te." In: Ritter, Alexander
(ed.): *Landschaft und
Raum in der Erzählkunst.*
Darmstadt 1975, pp. 197–
207

2   For more on this topic, for example, in the
presentation of the bog in
the fine arts, see Fischer,
Ludwig: "Die Entdeckung
des Moors für Literatur
und Kunst." In: http://
culturmag.de/category/
litmag-specials/natur-
special August 5, 2019
(excerpts in Ludwig
Fischer: *Natur im Sinn.*
Berlin 2019, p. 251ff.).

3   For the history of land-
scape painting see Eberle,
Matthias: *Individuum und
Landschaft: Zur Entsteh-
ung und Entwicklung der
Landschaftsmalerei.* Gies-
sen 1979; Bätschmann,
Oskar: *Entfernung der Na-
tur: Landschaftsmalerei
1750–1920.* Cologne 1989;
Eschenburg, Barbara:
*Landschaft in der deutsch-
en Malerei.* Munich 1987;
Raupp, Hans-Joachim
(ed.): *Landschaften und
Seestücke.* Münster 2001

4   Simmel, Georg: "Phi-
losophie der Landschaft."
In: *Die Güldenkammer:
Eine bremische Monats-
schrift,* Gallwitz, Sophie
Dorothea/Hartlaub,
Gustav Friedrich/Smidt,
Hermann (eds.). 1913,
no. 2, pp. 635–44; Ritter,
Joachim: "Landschaft.
Zur Funktion des Ästhe-
tischen in der modernen
Gesellschaft." In: Ritter,
Joachim: *Subjektivität.*
Frankfurt am Main 1974,
pp. 141–63 and 172–90.
See also Fischer, Ludwig:
"Landschaft – überall
und nirgends? Nachden-
klichkeiten zu 'alten' und
'neuen' Vorstellungen von
Landschaft." In: Krebs,
Stefanie/Seifert, Manfred
(eds.): *Landschaft quer >*

conception of landscape, and soon thereafter spread to
the generally held conception of landscape: the notion
of landscape that is common until the late twentieth
century, readily presupposes a "subject that is viewing"
which synthesizes an excerpt of a habitat into a perceived
"composition." For the composition in this pictorial
excerpt, the horizon—projected in the pictorial mode
from a fictitious viewpoint—and the production of a
homogeneous space in which the perceived particulars
can be arranged "accurately in terms of perspective"
constitute the crucial elements of conditioned seeing.
The long-lasting conception was given a philosophical
formulation in the twentieth century by Georg Simmel
and Joachim Ritter; both emphasize the foundation
of the notion of landscape in the synthesizing behavior
of the viewing subject, which, from the diversity and
tendential boundlessness of what can be grasped visually,
effectively makes a framed excerpt a pictorial entity.—[4]

This foundation of how landscape is understood, conceived by way of theory of perception, indeed, ultimately
by way of ontology, is still valid for approaches to a
new notion of landscape, e.g., following Brinckerhoff
Jackson.—[5] Until, in a move reflecting the spirit of the
time, landscape is declared a "review of civilization's
spaces"—[6] the basic conceptual suppositions retain
their validity. This applies first and foremost to the
perspectival, carefully constructed distance between
the perceiving subject and the object being seen in the
perceived excerpt of space—and, consequently, a veritable a priori suspension of the viewing subject of every
active engagement with the "objects" of the perception,
i.e., of every form of concrete work.—[7]

This "contemplative distance"—which also holds
sway where landscape, for instance, is perceptually and
geographically analyzed in scholarly work or spatially or
ecologically mapped—is not rescinded when the landscape, preferably a largely natural ensemble, is assigned,
in aesthetic-of-nature terms, a quality which evokes in

the perceiving subject something akin to the *Anschauung* of a "life well lived."——[8] In his sketch of an aesthetics of nature, which attempts to assimilate civilization's reshaping of "nature," Martin Seel still traced the perception of the city as landscape back to the efficacy of aesthetic distance—the relation to the surroundings acquired in the landscape's nature is transferred to the urban fabric.——[9]

Consequently, the concept of landscape once again proves to be the incarnation, so to speak, of an aesthetics of nature which—framed in terms of societal and environmental theory—represents in effect the other side of an instrumental, even flagrantly exploitative appropriation of nature. This is because that distance without which there can be no contemplation of landscape, not even that of technicized spaces, must after all be made possible with respect to the lifeworld. Even the mental invocation of internalized notions of landscape presupposes that in societal practice the posture of contemplative distance can be adopted. In other words, landscape as the contingency of perception is based on the attainable or attained privilege of being at least occasionally suspended from the "metabolism of man with nature through work." But that is only possible if, within the structure of societal conditions, the privilege based on the appropriation of the work of others to secure their livelihoods presents itself. Therefore, landscape as concept originally belongs to the privileged groups who are "liberated" from manual labor. It was not by chance that Gernot Böhme identified the nascent forms of landscape perception in Plato's *Dialogues*, when Socrates visits the exo-urban, a *locus amoenus* constituting nature, to philosophize at leisure,——[12] and Lucius Burckhardt—similar to Brinckerhoff Jackson—still sings the praises of walking as the mode of fostering special scholarly knowledge.——[11] And the fact that landscape is perceived as such, also made accessible beyond societal groups as a legitimate general connection to

> *Denken: Theorien – Bilder – Formationen.* Leipzig 2012, pp. 23–36. The geomorphological determining and capturing of "landscapes(s)" later took a turn from pictorial excerpt to the physical form of the earth's surface. Regarding the problem of demarcation of landscape units and landscape, typology again encounters the seemingly vanquished authority of the "synthesizing subject." See Hard, Gerhard: *Die "Landschaft" der Sprache und die "Landschaft" der Geographen: Seminatische und forschungslogische Studien.* Bonn 1970

5   For a detailed account, see Fischer, "Landschaft" (as in note 4).

6   For a programmatic treatment, including a good survey of recent research in various disciplines, see the essay by Fischer, Norbert: "Landschaft als kulturwissenschaftliche Kategorie." In: *Zeitschrift für Volkskunde*, 2008/I, pp. 19–39. Important texts are also to be found in the anthology edited by Franzen, Brigitte/Krebs, Stefanie: *Landschaftstheorie: Texte der Cultural Landscape Studies* (Kunstwissenschaftliche Bibliothek vol. 26). Cologne 2005.

7   For more on this basis of the understanding of landscape—tellingly ignored time and again in the debates on landscape—see Fischer, Ludwig: "Reflexionen über Landschaft und Arbeit." In: Thomas Kirchhoff/Ludwig Trepl (eds.): *Vieldeutige Natur. Landschaft, Wildnis und Ökosystem als kulturgeschichtliche Phänomene.* Bielefeld 2009, pp. 101–18 >

8 For more on this, see the paradigmatic study by Seel, Martin: *Eine Ästhetik der Natur.* Frankfurt am Main 1991.

9 See Seel, *Ästhetik* (as in note 8), pp. 230ff. More at Fischer, "Landschaft" (as in note 4), pp. 27ff.

10 Böhme, Gernot: "Die Mensch-Natur-Beziehung am Beispiel Stadt." In: Böhme, Gernot: *Für eine ökologische Naturästhetik.* Frankfurt am Main 1989, pp. 56–76; here pp. 56ff.

11 Burckhardt, Lucius: *Warum ist Landschaft schön? Die Spaziergangs-wissenschaft.* Berlin 2006, in particular, p. 251ff. See Waldenfels, Bernhard: "Gänge durch die Land-schaft." In: Manfred Smuda (ed.): *Landschaft.* Frankfurt am Main 1989, pp. 29–43.

12 For an early essay on the dialectics of work and leisure, see Habermas, Jürgen: "Soziologische Notizen zum Verhältnis von Arbeit und Freizeit." In: Habermas, Jürgen: *Arbeit – Erkenntnis – Fort-schritt: Aufsätze 1954–1970.* Amsterdam 1970, pp. 56–74.

13 For a survey, see the publications named in note 6.

14 See Vince Beiser: *Sand: Wie uns eine wert-volle Ressource durch die Finger rinnt.* Munich 2021

surroundings, is crucially dependent on the separation of work and recreation: any appreciable experience of landscape is increasingly becoming part of the sphere of organized leisure activities.—[12]

Landscape and the Crisis of Humanity's Relation to Nature

We are losing the ecological innocence, or, at least, insouciance which dwells within the conventional, still dominant understanding of landscape. Anyone who considers forested areas with a large number of seriously impaired trees as landscape, who hikes across monoto-nous, agricultural acreage and considers it part of the landscape, will find it increasingly difficult to tune out the knowledge of the endangerment of natural spaces. Even the clouds are no longer the floating constructs in the celestial realm arching over the pictorial landscape that they used to be. What it is about them that possibly conveys the message of a calamity caused by man "intrudes" not only in the presence of a tornado or of torrential rain pouring down from monsoon clouds.

Nor can new theories of landscape that bid farewell to an ostensibly idealized and "beautiful" nature offer any help, as the misconception of a norm in the classical conception of landscape would have it, from the technologically fabricated surroundings by seeking to redefine "landscape" as a medial image of random spaces in "artificial worlds."—[13] The overall balance of the fabrication of these worlds—and not just with respect to the mafia-like battles to secure sand—[14] or the threat of collapse of the infrastructure and microclimates in our conurbations—becomes too problematic. The necessary norm, namely the aspect of the landscape conception relevant to good living conditions in the surroundings, cannot simply be taken care of by making reference to the glorious technologies of the future, as if the not-always incontrovertible nature as unintended side effect were to reveal itself—what is humanly attainable returns to the makers, in the meantime comprehensively as co-created natural occurrence in catastrophic events.

The relation of more-or-less natural space to appropriative work, a certain "metabolism of man with nature," can in an unforeseen manner no longer be kept at a distance—and not only in light of "damaged nature"— where landscape is at issue: the concrete reference to what is seen is "disturbed," though not because the irrefutably necessary work above which the keeping-at-a-distance seeks to elevate itself came irritatingly between, but because it is that which is seen where the problem, namely destructiveness in the societally exponentiated work, becomes manifest to the highest degree.

Landscape was to date a conception for the remote sense—the sense of sight—and to a lesser degree, of hearing, and minimally perhaps of smell. Distance as the basis for experiencing the landscape also means that there is no touching, feeling, or tasting—not to mention the senses we are barely aware of, which include, for example, perception of air pressure, homeostasis, inhalation, and exhalation of air, and the tone of the various muscles. About 90 percent of the sensations our bodies perceive are processed "autonomously"—independent of our consciousness. The classic conception of landscape and its fashionable extensions did not take this into account. The old-school European notion of landscape— including its newer guises—is not able to accept that "affectivity" to surroundings, something other than Simmel's "moods" or the new phenomenologists' "atmospheres,"—[15] itself still far from adequately understood, is based on concrete unmediated exchange processes with that which surrounds us.

It would, however, be high time to comprehend how we in our habitats are linked not only by means of "metabolism through work" to that which we call nature. Our mere existence is a constant, highly complex

15 See, for example, Böhme, Gernot: *Atmosphäre. Essays zur neuen Aesthetik.* Frankfurt am Main 1995; Martin Basfeld: "Phänomen – Element – Atmosphäre: Zur Phänomenologie der Wärme." In: Gernot Böhme/ Gregor Schliemann (eds.): *Phänomenologie der Natur.* Frankfurt am Main 1997, pp. 190–212

16 In the meantime, neu-
rologists, cognition re-
searchers, and physiolo-
gists have been investigat-
ing the "autonomous"
processing of sensations
and exchange processes
that are not perceived at
the level of the reflexive
consciousness, suggesting
that with these neuronal
processes, forms of "spontaneous consciousness"
in the most diverse areas
of bodily organization need
to be acknowledged. See
Christian Wolf's sumary:
"Embodiment-These – Nur
eine Kopfgeburt?" In: *Spek-
trum kompakt – Rätsel
Bewusstsein*. Heidelberg
2019, pp. 53–60. For a detailed account, see Fuchs,
Thomas: *Das Gehirn – ein
Beziehungsorgan*. Stuttgart
2021; Fuchs, Thomas: *Ver-
teidigung des Menschen*.
Frankfurt am Main 2020.

17 On this notion of "self-
empowerment," see Bernd
Busch: *Belichtete Welt:
Eine Wahrnehmungsge-
schichte der Fotografie*.
Munich 1989, pp. 83ff.

18 In the theory of aes-
thetics, empowerment—
which is sketched out in
the principles of landscape
Anschauung—receives its
expression in the discern-
ment of subjects most
keenly in Kant's definitive
theory of the sublime. See
Fischer, Ludwig: "Das
Erhabene und die 'feinen
Unterschiede': Zur Dia-
lektik in den sozio-kultu-
rellen Funktionen von
ästhetischen Deutungen
der Landschaft." In:
Rolf Brednich, Wilhelm /
Schneider, Annette /
Werner, Ute (eds.): *Natur –
Kultur: Volkskundliche* >

"metabolism," an exchange with nature, still inside us, where, for example, bacteria work with our bodies. We must grasp not only our bodies, the physical makeup of our very selves, as a "unified organ" of exchange with the surroundings—[16] if we want to have the chance to find our way out of the destructive dissension that passes right through us, a dissension between thinking subject and merely physical object. The conventional conception of landscape, by way of the postulate of a subject "only conceived of" in the viewpoint of the single-point perspective and the homogeneous space of the objects placed in it, participates in the dichotomy that is the basis of nearly all technology as well as indirectly of the economical imperative.

That the "disembodied" subject co-conceived in the classical notion of landscape likewise lays claim to empowerment and perception of what is viewed is usually misconstrued because the reference of the concept to principles of single-point perspective is not seen for what it is.—[17] Such empowerment corresponds to the de facto social privileging upon which the construct of the understanding of landscape rests.—[18] The social strategy becomes comprehensible in the concrete prerequisites that must be fulfilled to have a "landscape experience." Next to contemplative distance, the most important are competence and accessibility—but cannot be further elaborated upon here.—[19]

That a landscape experience can take hold of a person emotionally, even beyond a simply soothing impression had from a distance, does not contradict the principle of the disembodied subject that is contained within the conception of landscape. The affective stirring of the corporeal subject, the looking at landscape and "experiencing" of it, is sparked by the remote senses, primarily by visual perception—and a synthetization internalized in a long socialization process which makes it possible to view the surroundings as landscape, implying that the subjects do not take into consideration their bodily and experience-saturated "participation" in the environment.—[20] That is precisely what makes it possible to perceive surroundings to which we have no concrete lifeworld relation whatsoever as beautiful, sublime, pleasant, frightening landscapes and to let them have an effect on us—and, as a rule, depart from them with no "effect" on the practice of our day-to-day lives. The "reference from an aesthetic distance" that makes the landscape experience possible changes, by the way, at the moment in which the surroundings become real and existential—the ocean scenery at the beach, which also is enjoyed as landscape, is, for those present, suddenly no longer a landscape when a tsunami rolls toward the coast.

The extreme example makes it clear that genuine landscape perception requires an exceptional ability to abstract the subject from its concrete, lifeworld state in its surroundings. To remain with the abovementioned scenery: event if "just" the solar radiation at the beach is too intense, the summer heat becomes unpleasant, and the storybook panorama at the seaside loses its quality as landscape and transforms into an insalubrious environment from which one will remove oneself.

That ability to think abstractly, which is a prerequisite to this mode of perception of landscape, has a share in the abstraction principle of the technological-instrumental relation to nature.—[21] And this once again confirms that the aesthetic relation to nature, in which the perception of landscape is paradigmatically formed, only represents the noninstrumental, ostensibly "innocent" other side of the exploitative appropriation of nature.—[22]

The Transformation of Landscape into an Alliance Space

The classical, at its core, aesthetics-of-nature conception of landscape along with its novel extensions—which

> *Perspektiven auf Mensch und Umwelt*. Münster 2001, pp. 347–56, here pp. 350ff.

19 For more on this see Fischer: "Landschaft" (as in note 4), pp. 30ff.

20 For the cultural history of the ability to think abstractly in perspectival representations of reality, see the brilliant essay by Dauss, Markus: *Perspektive als Denkform der Ambivalenz: Zwischen Madame de Staël und Vilém Flusser*, Frankfurt am Main 2004. For the long history of instructing children in perspectival seeing, see Piaget, Jean / Inhelder, Bärbel: *Die Entwicklung des räumlichen Denkens beim Kinde*. Stuttgart 1979.

21 In a renowned passage in his *Harzreise*, Heinrich Heine parodied the abstractions included in the perception of landscape perception by putting words into the mouth of a "young merchant" upon seeing the sunset at the Brocken summit, he enthusiastically calls out: "How beautiful nature is, by and large!" Heinrich Heine: *Werke und Briefe in zehn Bänden*. Berlin 1972, Vol. 3, p. 63.

22 That is why a (usually pictorially manifest) >

> understanding of surroundings as "landscape" is tied to the control of nature in complex societies, both in the west and in the east. Most "premodern" ethnic groups have no conception of their lifeworld as landscape. For them, the surroundings are, as a rule, spaces of animated exchange; what appears to be the anthropomorphization of natural entities (animals, plants, stones, stars, etc.) represents the "translation" of the lived conditions of exchange in "humane" stories.

have been concisely outlined here—does not offer a "counterweight," not even a compensation for the destructive potentials that are effective in the lifeworld, which are at work in the abstraction principle and the Western relations to nature and the technicized appropriation of nature. The digital technology merely instrumentally takes away, as mentioned, the abstraction principles: it "relieves" one of the efforts to constantly consummate the abstract connection to nature, not only at work while working in the narrower sense, in principle like the "nature objects." Consequently, in "helpful" digital technology the autonomous abstraction principles can also, however, confront humans as a foreign force—this is where the real strength of the fear that machines will "take control" lies.

So the question is: how differently can humans intervene in their surroundings from the abstract relation to the technological-scientific appropriation and transformation of objects, but also differently from the perception of landscape permeated by complementary abstractions.

The already-implied thesis in which the physical and the perceptive exchange between human subjects and natural "agents" was to form the starting point, an exchange that de facto continually takes place between (societally organized) humans and their surroundings, must be elaborated upon and set forth in more detail. The notion that the point of departure is the body as a "unified organ of cognition" is not new. As one of the most important proponents of new phenomenology before the new millennium, Gernot Böhme, had already unmistakably formulated: "Earth, water, and air pass through us and we can only live in this draft ... The task is to integrate nature, which we—or, in other words, the human body—are part of in our self-consciousness."—23

23 Böhme: *Atmosphäre* (as in note 15), p. 14

A new "aisthetics" is postulated—the term refers back to the original meaning of aisthesis as "sensual perception"—which is to replace the classic aesthetics as theory of aesthetic judgement. Here, instead, the attempt is via sensual perception, which is defined as a "corporeal perception of atmospheres": "Vis-à-vis the traditional notion of sensuality as verification of data is, in full sensuality, the affective, the emotionality and imaginative are to be adopted. Sensuality is not primarily a matter of the things that one perceives, but rather the sensation one feels: the atmospheres … as one senses them in surroundings but also related to things or people are … the main subject of aesthetics."—[24] In his understanding, atmospheres form by means of perceptible "presence of people, objects, and surroundings."—[25] Thus, the atmospheres are neither something merely subjectively felt, nor an objective property of "things." Rather, they form "spaces of presence."—[26]

24 Ibid., pp. 15 ff.

25 Ibid., p. 25

26 Ibid., p. 33

Conceiving such a presence of what is perceived—which recognizing something else/other than the classical object ontology—no longer inquires into the substance, accidents, etc., but rather into the "way of appearing." This requires adopting an "articulation of the presence" on the part of the "things."—[27] To that end, Böhme chooses the expression "the ecstasies of the thing": that which is perceived is, so to speak, "taken out of itself" (*ékstasis*). *Aisthetics* devotes itself, in other words, to the "space of presence" of "things," which only through this presence are perceived in their characteristic ways of being.

27 Ibid., p. 32

Böhme's sketch has been fiercely debated and sharply criticized. In two respects, however, it constitutes a necessary step forwards in classical theory of perception. First, perception is understood as fully developed sensuality for the grasping of the respective specified presence of what is perceived. As a result, an experienceable, "occurring correspondence in the space of the appearance" supersedes the categorizing definition of properties of what has been perceived. Perception can be understood, as it were, as the subject's "coherent answer" to the presence of what has been perceived.—[28] And second, as organ of such perception, the body is acknow-

28 What is decisive here is that the "correspondence," the exchange relation- >

> ship, is not set up via impulses of the reflexive consciousness, but rather through the many "autonomous" processes of the embodied mind. For more on this, see the contributions to Fingerhut, Joerg / Hufendiek, Rebekka/Wild, Markus (eds.): *Philosophie der Verkörperung: Grundlagentexte zu einer aktuellen Debatte*. Frankfurt am Main 2013

29 See the reference in note 16.

30 Coccia, Emanuele: *Die Wurzeln der Welt: Eine Philosophie der Pflanzen*. Munich 2018

ledged with all of its sensual capabilities—including its consciousness, which is thereby, so to speak, relieved of its traditional dissociation as the only and fully immaterial instance of cognitive function.—[29]

Gernot Böhme stops, however, half way on the path to a new understanding of the connection to nature, because he holds on to the project for a "new aesthetics"—and as a result ignores the decisive dimensions of the de facto exchange between the present, active subject and the equally present, operative "counterpart." We are simply not just, as Böhme puts it, connected to nature in that "the natural media pass through us." Rather, we are situated in a continual, extremely diverse, concrete exchange with animals, plants, fungi, and microbes, as well as with other inanimate objects. Without this exchange—which is to a great extent unknown to us and uncontrolled by us—we could not live. It is not "the air" that surrounds us and enters our bodies, but we continually interact, for example, via the "medium of air," with plants and above all with trees, because we inhale the oxygen that they release, and exhale the carbon dioxide that they need to thrive.—[30] Or: above all, when we stand on "free" soil or walk, we interact constantly, without registering it, with living creatures on or in the ground—which can also mean that we injure, tread on, or, in extreme cases, are attacked by them—but also with the topsoil, dust, growths, etc. In other cultures, considerable attention is paid to precisely this reciprocal effect. Our body temperature interacts constantly with our surroundings, not only with the air, but also, as the case may be, with plants, with "vermin," with processed materials, from the fabric of our clothing to the instruments, equipment, furniture, etc. Aided by sensitive instruments, we can recognize that for the supposed inert material, this interaction is by no means insignificant. There is also exchange at the level of perception: except when we sleep, we constantly hear, smell, feel, taste, experience "something"—and we are seen, heard, and smelled,—[31] and possibly "recognized" on account of our scent or temperature. Ethnic groups who do not live in fully technicized surroundings continually take note of this—and anyone who lives in an area now populated by wolves gets an inkling of how suddenly it becomes elementally clear that one is being seen and heard and smelled without knowing when and by whom.

That means: even in artificially produced spaces and in air-conditioned rooms, surroundings are spheres in which a constant, more or less close, intense, noticeable exchange occurs. But exchange also signifies: there is at least minimal reciprocal relation, and are at least two "agents," but usually countless participants, because many of them are so miniscule. The larger part of this exchange takes place unnoticed and unknown, yet in a manner that is directed and goal-oriented. The mosquito that stings our skin "wants something," even if, as the saying goes, it "acts purely instinctively," and we ourselves "want something" when antibodies head to the site of the sting. But can we say that the tiny fungi that we have somewhere on our skin "want" an exchange with our condition? Or further still, that rocks "want" to withstand the pressure we cause when we walk on them? That wind "wants to" cool, distress, or push us along?

It is not a matter of "animating" every element in our lifeworld, of drifting off toward a new take on animism.—[32] Instead we should ask how we can take the exchange between everything that "is with us" seriously enough, how we can take seriously enough this fundamental and irrevocable reciprocal relation in which and from which we live, such that the differences and the opposition do not disappear, but indeed the autonomy of everything with which we interchange is brought to bear.—[33]

So we need options to think about and speak about the concrete exchange in which and through which we live—such that this exchanged is neither negated in an abstractive one-sidedness (for example in modern-day

31 In *Der Schneeleopard* (Hamburg 2021), Sylvain Tesson describes looking at one of the photos his companion had taken and discovering that a hidden snow leopard had been observing him (pp. 134ff.).

32 Wolfgang Riedel makes this accusation against, among others, the ethnologist Philippe Descola in *Unort der Sehnsucht: Vom Schreiben über Natur.* Berlin 2017, pp. 45ff., 74ff.

33 The important book by philosopher Jane Bennett: *Vibrant Matters: A Political Ecology of Things* (Durham 2010) discusses the possibilities of framing an "agency of matters."

Western society's fundamental, "calculable" transformation of the entire non-human nature in objects) nor violently destroyed, or caused to disappear in an ostensible "merging."—[34]

34 Weber, Andreas: *Lebendigkeit: Eine ero-tische Ökologie*. Munich 2014; see Haraway, Donna: *Das Manifest für Gefährten: Wenn Spezies sich begegnen – Hunde, Menschen und signifikante Andersartigkeit*. Berlin 2016; Haraway, Donna: *Unruhig bleiben: Die Ver-wandtschaft der Arten im Chtuluzän*. Frankfurt am Main 2018

35 Bloch., Ernst: *The Prin-ciple of Hope*. Cambridge MA 1995, p.666

36 Ibid., p.668. Here I have adopted some formu-lations from my essay on natural alliance, which is to be published in early 2022.

Landscape and Hope

In his monumental masterwork *The Principle of Hope*, the philosopher Ernst Bloch sketched a societal utopia with a relationship to nature in which "the subject is mediated with the natural object, the natural object with the subject, and both no longer relate to one another as to something alien."—[35] Following Bloch, in the theory and practice of the manifest bourgeois control of nature, for example, with respect to artisanry, in which there is still a consciousness of being dependent on the autonomy and independent activity of the natural phenomena is displaced/outed by exploitative and violent dealings with the *natural*. Hence, the conception of nature that is predominant and binding for science and technology produces a fully abstract relation to nature, because the cognizant and operative human subject is confronted with a natural entity that does not act on its own, but, if need be, functions mechanically.—[36] This is the springboard of the specifically modern-day alienation from nature. But, according to Bloch, that would also mean the loss of the forward-pointing potentials of technology for a truly humane society.

When writing his book in exile during the World War II, Bloch was not yet able to recognize the quickly escalating endangerment of ecosystems through the progressive technicization of day-to-day life and the un-checked appropriation of finite natural resources. But he did decree: "Thus the problem of a centrally mediated relation to nature becomes the most urgent: the days of the mere exploiter, of the outwitter, of the mere taker of opportunities are numbered even in technological

terms."—[37] Bloch sees the main problem of the predominant science, technology, and industry in man's "re-
ified" relation to nature. In this "abstract-mechanistic"
interpretation of nature, even nonhuman living beings—
plants, animals—become mere matter, as is still spelled
out in Germany's civil code.

Bloch contraposes this with a still-essential "utopian"
connection to nature that is also valid both for work
and technology in which "in place of the technologist as
a mere outwitter or exploiter there stands in concrete
terms the subject socially mediated with itself, which
increasingly mediates itself with the problem of the
natural subject."—[38] That is to say: the "natural object"
must become a subject in which its own "agent" dwells,
with which human development of will shall be "vividly
conveyed." To make this comprehensible, Bloch addres-
ses suppressed and forgotten philosophical traditions,
grappling first and foremost with Schelling's speculative
natural philosophy, in which an—indeed transcendental—natural subject is postulated.

Bloch dispels an animist and an idealist-speculative
understanding of the "natural subject." He is conscious
of the risks associated with his argumentation. But he
insists that, in order to turn away from the destructiveness of the predominant relation to nature, the
"subjective stimulant" in natural phenomena and natural processes should be acknowledged and included.
Therefore he deems it proper to identify and take over
the nonhuman subjectivity in the classical notion of
natura naturans, i.e., the fertile and independently active
nature, beyond the "half-mythical" original admixture.
He immediately adds: "that which is hypothetically
described as the nature-subject still" has to be "a predis-
position and latency,"—[39] and can only emerge from
such latency into societal reality through the historical
actualization of the human subject. But in his view, the
age-old—in all of its various forms—inherent notion
of the natural subject is not solely a notionally-abstract,

37 Ibid., p. 671

38 Ibid., p. 674—original text in italics

39 Ibid., p. 673

philosophical construct, but also seeks to grasp the "materially" conceived, effective driving force of the natural: "In this stratum therefore, in the materially most immanent one that exists at all, lies the truth of that which

40 Ibid., pp. 673f.

is described as the subject of nature."—[40] This thesis is eminently compatible with the sketch of a human relation to nature which comprehends the substance, the unceasingly executed "material" exchange between humans and nature as given, as mental and practical operant basis of the relationship to nature.

Acknowledging a general agent, immanent in nature, not only mentally, but also in societal reality as particularly indispensable for the work of humans and letting its cooperativeness come into play, would, following Bloch's argumentation, fundamentally change the perspective for the dealings with nature. "The will which resides in all technological-physical structures and has built them must simultaneously have both a socially grasped subject behind it: for the constituent intervention, beyond the merely abstract-external one, and a subject before it which is mediated with it: for cooperation, for the consti-

41 Ibid., p. 674

tutive contact with the intervention."—[41] Consequently, for Bloch in the utopia of a humane society, the "technology of the will and concrete alliance" is irrevocably linked to "the hearth of natural phenomena and their laws, the electron of the human subject and the mediated

42 Ibid.

co-productivity of a possible natural subject."—[42]

In the *Principle of Hope*, Bloch's main term "alliance" refers primarily to a future technology and for that reason he names it "alliance technology." His sketch proves to be thoroughly of its time: within the framework of his decidedly materialist interpretation of history he is not able to see a general "alliance relation" that goes beyond human "metabolism" with nature through a technologically potentiated work.

That, however, could be seen as one of the major challenges of our time: to comprehend, acknowledge, and incorporate into society's formation of will the constant exchange between humans and the nonhuman elements and beings as an "alliance" between nature in and of humans and nonhuman nature and subjectivity. This raises difficult philosophical-anthropological questions related to theory of nature and theory of society. But many unconventional scholarly approaches and "alternative" discourses allow us to recognize that the hitherto binding categories and constructs of our modern "Western" relation to nature move into gear.

The considerations presented here make it possible to critically examine and take up Bloch's "thinking on alliance." Transformed and expanded upon, it affords the opportunity to reframe a term from contemporary day-to-day life that is, generally speaking, irrevocable yet reformable: the "participation" of the natural, which itself is still integrated in the subject formation. Allowing such a sketch of the nonalienated transformed realization of the relation to nature in societal planning and actions to come into play remains a component of the utopian project. But the acknowledgement of the conveyed "natural basis," also regarding the notion and implementation of human subjectivity—countering its negation and diminishment in the present predominant relation to nature—is already valid.

The surroundings through which and in which the infinitely varied exchange of people with the others which we call nature is continuously carried out can be understood as alliance spaces. Their size and limits depend on the respective situation, outfitting, activity, aspiration, and "organization" of the participants—the "self-regulation" of living organisms does not by any means provide the general pattern. Alliances presuppose, as mentioned, difference, which can turn into a threat or even subjugation. Alliance thinking is in pursuit of neither identificatory empathy nor coalescence; exchange processes hold both dangers and risks. But there are examples that show that life-threatening experiences might lead to anarchical insight into that "ecological identity"

43 Plumwood, Val: "Opfer sein." In: *Dritte Natur* 1/2018, pp. 55–67

in which humans view themselves as being integrated in a comprehensive reciprocal relationship with their *Mitwelt* (literally, the "with-world").—[43]

Alliance spaces are always also a space of assertiveness, both for individuals and for groups and ultimately for genres. That means there are also destructive or—if you will—negative alliances, to the detriment of the participants. The reciprocal relation then becomes strongly imbalanced, in the most severe case, with fatal consequences for the one who is defeated. Yet—in a comprehensive ecological perspective—essential alliances still exist therein. Every self-assertion has its limits in the overall context. The main problem for *Homo sapiens* at the attained and conceivable level of societal self-assertion lies in recognizing and accepting the limits of self-assertion—which means nothing other than making the given and possible "annexation" to the forces and aspirations of the natural *Mitwelt* serve as a guide in thought and action.

If surroundings in which people are always and irrevocably interacting with the nature they encounter are understood as alliance spaces, then the predominant conception of landscape—including a modernized one—can no longer hold true. Making a guess as to whether a radically transformed notion of landscape is formed and maintained that originates in alliance thinking is not, at present, the pressing matter.

A Vision of the Rural

Albert Kirchengast

Yes, Father Leverkühn was a dreamer and a speculator, and I have already said that his taste for research—if one can speak of research instead of mere dreamy contemplation—always leaned in a certain direction: namely, the mystical or an intuitive half-mystical, into which, as it seems to me, human thinking in pursuit of Nature is almost of necessity led.—[1]

1   Mann, Thomas: *Doktor Faustus* (1947). Frankfurt am Main 1992, p. 25

I Rhythm and Ritual

To think that there is a kingdom of animals, most notably of birds—for they fly and have so many colors and songs; a kingdom of celestial light and of atmospheric conditions! A natural event that knows of no other site than where it first occurred; of no day that equals the one preceding it: harnessed to the seasonal cycle.

John Seymour, an apprentice of self-reliance—in other words, of empowerment to keep oneself alive through one's work in nature, with the soil, with the flora and the fauna, by means of a practical trove of knowledge—divided the overarching annual cycle into six time periods. He put into words the bond between nature and the human cosmos that originated in it, its basis in elementary tasks such as planting seeds and harvesting, dos and don'ts, diligence and recompense: early spring (Plough your land!),

129

late spring (Sow your seed!), early summer (Make cheese for the winter!), late summer (Harvest the wheat!), fall (Bring in the harvest, stock up!), winter (Time to rest, time to repair!). He gives his readers instructions and in the process structures day and land. The recurring annual calendar of field cultivation is active and fulfilled. Nothing is too much, so that nothing proves too little,—[2] nature in its manifestations gives the orders. The cycle of what is existential remains valid to this day, even if Seymour's instructions for an *alternative* concept for living, which he gives in *The New Complete Book of Self-Sufficiency*, date from the 1970s. In light of the shallow freedoms of today's life, a very specific prescience hovers above such texts, which call the unmediated connection between nature and culture to action in the concrete form of commandments.

Refinement was already inscribed in the elementary conduct required for survival. Breughel famously paints this most primordial, rural cultural history and seizes a bearing of diversity, which grows out of an oscillation between constants and variables. Customs, through which one expresses, informs, orients oneself—in which, of course, not only man and his fellow beings, but also nature in its manifestations are taken up; in rural spaces that are also landscapes; in paintings that provide meaning because they generalize a cyclical ferment, set at an artificial period of time, alluding to the commitment of eyewitnesses for the defense: to comprehensible senses. Human beings becoming sedentary was the beginning of this. This is not to be seen as a prehistoric occurrence, for its site-specificity is based to this day on a fragile equilibrium, the guarantors of which Werner Bätzing recognizes in his book and designates unemotionally with the term "ecological reproduction."—[3] A tacit contract had to be drawn up regarding the dealings with nature in order to stabilize the forces of nature for the time frame of human needs. Both are now inclined toward each other, nature and humankind—one would like to say: engage with each

2   Seymour, John: *The New Complete Book of Self-Sufficiency*. London 1976

3   Bätzing, Werner: *Das Landleben: Geschichte und Zukunft einer gefährdeten Lebensform*. Munich 2020, p. 39. "That is why intensifications are by no means coupled with increased ecological problems. >

other, whereby only human beings have no other option if they want to adequately shape their relation to nature. Bountiful maps of the cultural landscape come into existence, where certain achievements of conscientiousness are produced, villages grow and cities become possible, not just by means of obvious craft of traditional agriculture. Moreover, for a forward-looking agriculture, soil erosion, soil depletion, acidification in moist areas, and salination in dry areas would all have to be prevented, but bush encroachment and reforestation also become threats where humans do not carefully intervene to secure their habitats.—[4] The point of departure for further growth is this detailed mosaic of sites of the cultural landscape, where human beings make modest attempts at living with others, stabilizing themselves in nature, do not tame the weather conditions, but, to secure their survival, celebrates rites and customs as a festive accompaniment over the course of the year—giving thanks, showing humility, but not without delirious joy.

Humans incline toward the catastrophic and toward collapse where they unilaterally increase the yield. *Avant la lettre*, without much fuss, tending to the fields was once a natural form of "ecology" by means of everyday actions—where this nurturing activity stayed attuned to natural rhythms, in the orthopraxic year of cultic exaltation, which reflected the everyday tasks; it enhances them so that they take on the specialness of a gift: to be able to survive and in the process make arrangements in the societal world. Where that has been forgotten, in turn, mnemonic customs and the liturgical year set in motion by them, keep relations present for the everyday life of human and thing. One could call this preemptive activity an extraordinary-ordinary contemplation of the practice—limiting one's activeness by means of cleverness. In seeking to tend to their fields and provide themselves and others with food, farmers were nurturers out of respect for limitations that secure the cycle. Their solid experiential knowledge was characterized by a self-preservationist's

> The main issue facing traditional agriculture has always been the ecological reproduction of the cultural landscape and not whether utilizations are carried out work-intensively or work-extensively." Ibid., p. 42. Conclsions can be drawn for a forward-looking, sustainable agriculture, as this is a matter of stance, not of nostalgic living.

4   See ibid. pp. 39f.

Bernhard Fuchs, "Frau B.," Dobring 1997

sense of reality, which was directly revealed in the anonymous forms of rural culture. But to speak here of a naïve
culture, a term with which bourgeois-urbane high culture
responds to farmers' ways of life—object, house, custom—
seems itself from this perspective naïve. That is still valid
today, long after this version of the everyday has come to a
close. In industrialized agriculture, these boundaries have
only been shifted; in a remote-controlled relationship to
animals and things growing, the corporeal relationship is
interrupted. And thus the future is not only in doubt as
a challenge facing growing technology, does not come from
an everyday practice, but has long ago begun to determine it.

In his *Natural Contract*—some 300 years after
Rousseau—the French philosopher Michel Serres not only
proposes a compact for the twentieth century, he demands
it. One of the slender chapters begins with the following
comment on the astonishing connection between time
and season of the French word *temps*. Serres thereby also
touches on the newly obscured, reciprocal dependence of
culture and nature in a time of putative total control,
an urban disposition creed, in which nature (once again)
becomes dangerous, threatens to be lost as force of nature: "By chance or wisdom, the French language uses
a single word, *temps*, for the time that passes and for
the weather outside, a product of climate and of what
our ancestors called meteors."—[5] One could speak of an
intersection of time and season: in the profundity of
language, culture remains tied to the givens of a place,
the enabling-coercive, the lively-rhythmical, which the
clocks don't show. At the same time, this would only be
the point of departure through which the depth of what is
to come can be measured, the new and untested in repeti-
tions of nature's clock, without which, however, it could
not—in the pro-verbial sense—survive. Certainly, in this
intersection of imitation, refinement, and renewal lies the
origin of the term *colere*, which comprises the cultivation of the land, the *dwelling* and the cultic veneration.
Accordingly, the original cause and effect of the sedentary

5 Serres, Michel: *Der
Naturvertrag* (1990).
Frankfurt am Main 1994,
p. 51

must have been one of immediacy and nurture, along with the remembrance of culturally mastered dependence on foreign forces.

It wasn't until later that they came toward him as scenic beauty, indeed, as "painting." The senses opened up in a new way. It has taken a long time for the mythical acts to disappear from such landscape depictions, which interwove the everyday, the cultic, and nature, until the landscape with its pristine nature synonym was allowed to appear, void of people and villages—seeming as if it weren't a highly cultivated unit, a "mixed realm," in which the essential intersection of deed and celebration had been adopted aesthetically and became visible in the pleasure of the experience. Behind the beauty of such images, which are also concepts in the minds of "enlightened" people, there is danger that the work will be hidden, the day-to-day activities in the fields, in rural houses, though it is in the instant in which they are experienced that the two so emphatically belong together: contemplation and use. As if there could be "leisure" and "indulgence" without the time spent in an authentic state of being active, without depravation and barrenness. What else would beauty be than a perceptible balance, a mental consciousness of the physical in the quiet of the moment, which emerges from that cycle, in which it so steadfastly exists? Works of art can be intensifiers of that which already appears in the everyday object and in usage: the consciousness for the reemergence and, consequently, the eternal moment through the ages. Yet the physicality of the everyday also reveals itself to be special in its momentary attunement, by briefly emerging from activity—in cause and effect, as ever alert to the possibility of aesthetic experience. One would be tempted to call it "rural" because it is open to a natural vitality. It has become universal, where the experiencing of art and the everyday reaches across to the sensual presence of an unnamable vitalness.

Wine Press House with Five Leafless Trees near Hollenstein, Lower Austria

One could interpret some of these mnemonic forms of modern art and architecture as the celebration of such flaring moments by way of their terse simplicity, even abstraction, by all means corporeal immediacy, which is not nonrepresentational, but rather makes reference to the experience of materiality. The project envisioning such a culture would be influenced by anonymous building forms originating in the peasantry of the past, as well as by lessons from the Far East, in which simplicity is equated with plenty.—6 Time and again this unpretentiousness seems to be a matter of a nurturing relation to time. A time whose measure is the everyday, in which an object we encounter flares its festiveness from within: by means of its perceived weight. The base of which lies perhaps in the recognition of our reliance on the gifts emanating from it, an enigmatic pleasure.

II *Schlicht Surreal*

The German word "schlicht" [plain, unpretentious] has had a glittering career. Its etymology definitely provides a clue to the way of life whose simplicity only transformed into rich experience as time passed. To stay with the massage of language: in their dictionary, the Brothers Grimm report that in Old High German, the word was still synonymous with "schlecht" [bad]. They also, however, quote Immanuel Kant, who centuries later extols what "a great gift of heaven" it is "to possess right (or as it has recently been called, 'schlicht') common sense."—7 That certainly corresponds to everyday experience: in unpretentiousness, the lifeworld things are arranged such that they have a place of their own. And that includes not only the tangible but also the intangible matters. At times, occupying the fine line between mindfulness and casualness makes things become clear.

The motto at the beginning of a book which—like so many today—sets out in search of "new realism" presents

6   See the Heart Sutra concept, taken up in modern art, which, prominently placed, reads: "Form ist Leere, Leere ist Form" [Form is emptiness, emptiness is form] in Markus Brüderlein's introduction to *Die erfüllte Leere und der moderne Minimalismus: Japan und der Westen*. Wolfsburg 2007.

7   Grimm, Jacob and Wilhelm: *Deutsches Wörterbuch*. Digital Version of the Trier Center for Digital Humanities. In: https://www.woerterbuchnetz.de/DWB?lemid=S11557 (accessed on November 2, 2021)

the last lines of a poem by Jorge Luis Borges; in the German translation, its title is "Schlichtheit." It reads as follows: This is as high as one may reach, /what Heaven perhaps will grant us: /neither admiration nor victories / but merely to be admitted/as part of undeniable Reality/ like stones and trees."—[8] This unpretentious reality competes not only with heaven, but also with vegetation, the trees. It's odd that stones also make an appearance, inorganic nature, which, however, has a structure whose beauty seems to bring it to life. Whoever believes that such unpretentiousness is easy to achieve—constituting simply a vegetative connection—should take note of the poem's first lines. That is where it is set out: the poem is situated in a garden kept safe by a latticework gate. It was laid out—long ago—so that the trees could grow tall. The gate does not allow all to enter; once one is inside, the level of culture encountered is so high that it has been assuaged, become unpretentious again. Not every culture is so cultivated. What characterizes it? What matters to it is that it can become as matter-of-fact as growing—in seemingly effortless words and deeds: "… inside the glance/need not fix on objects/now firmly in memory./ I know each custom and soul /and that dialect of allusions/ every human aggregation weaves. /I need not speak/nor lie about privileges; /well they know me hereabouts, /my anguish and weakness." The presence of the familiar soothes our worries: the practice of repetition, the convention, or one's own ritual—that is what one believes the meaning of these lines to be. We are natural where we have such a stake in the course of affairs. A garden is one such way of a "being in time." A house can also become that: an abundance of things in the vivid form of everyday spaces.

One would not initially expect the first lines of Borges's poem to take this turn, namely, in "as high as": no longer having to pay attention to, encounter what is familiar—isn't there the threat of boredom and indifference, the negative side of the everyday, which fatigues?

8   Borges, Jorge Luis: "Llaneza". In: *Fervor de Buenos Aires*. Buenos Aires 1923, p. 34

But isn't there also an attentive inattentiveness in which the casual is allowed to become the climax, and the happening happens in order to reduce speed in the approach to the definitive, into which irritations and trivialities also flow? Borges's lines of poetry have perhaps lost their exuberance (like paintings of the landscape) and are convincingly succinct, yet are capable of being disconcerting. An image so familiar to us today: that culture is thought to have worked not toward presenting and representing itself, but instead loses itself in unpretentious-materiality as sensory delight. The garden becomes an emblem and once again a paradisical clue, timeless-present as a large growth structured by man. Those who have been around a good while recognizes themselves here in the children's voices or in the quiet beneath the branches; someone who has travelled far and wide extols the virtues of the day-by-day slowness of growth, someone who has seen a lot sees in the play of shadows the most mysterious, faraway landscape. An echo of the first cultivation of nature as rurality; a consonance of sense and sensibility, of conspicuousness of plants, animals, sounds, and scents; a state that appears to be nothing else, that doesn't appear at all, that is—that we are: right now. An order brought to phenomenonic stillness.

And yet there is nothing lulling about it, rather, at its core, even something stimulating. Originating in the cyclical-simple, transferred to the forms of culture, it has become an experience of unpretentious stillness. Such contemplative experience is an exceptional instance of stillstand, which tends to snap over into an entirely "other" reality. As Wilhelm Lehmann noted in his *Bukolisches Tagebuch* [*Bucolic diary*]: "In order to have an effect, reality becomes surreal. From the treetops of the boscage its metallic screech. It's as if solitude were suffering from itself and is airing its concerns with the call of the Euroasian jay."—[9] Lehmann, as urbanite in the landscape who had wandered into the woods. In his timeless records

9   Lehmann, Wilhelm: *Bukolisches Tagebuch und weitere Schriften zur Natur* (1948). Berlin 2017, p. 164

of time, one reads of another fall day, in this observation of nature put into words: "From the dark richness of the most beautifully formed leaves swells the abundance of acorns. What consummation of form, what effusiveness, nowhere too much, nowhere too little. The tentative fingers, which like to envelop the smooth mound, believe to have sensed that this shining egg contains a thousand-year-old life."—[10] Here, too, cultivating simplicity seems beautiful in its life-giving and life-taking equilibrium. Lehmann traces the small, day-to-day transgressions. The myth, the fantastical is now a subjective appearance of universal validity—is unpretentious presence which knows how to elevate itself into the incomprehensible, where a someone draws close to it. They are things in nature that become unsettled, symbolic—surreally transcending the moment. An attentive—cautious—attitude, not a rational-sober one, is of the essence: "over and over, the thinking falls away from the things," writes Lehmann, for "there are situations in which they explain themselves." And he warns: "the methods of the human intellect reveal themselves to be rapacious."—[11]

In the landscape one also experiences these moments of bliss in which one stands apart: a surreal event, something simple like the falling snow tinges, holds it fast like in a living tableau, which Robert Macfarlane describes, which propels him from his chamber one evening out into the streets and finally to the country paths on the city's edge. Fresh snow covers the familiar things and unifies them. They become alien, odd, stir the desire for extra-ordinary encounters with that which, each day, just passes by; a second tour in a purportedly familiar world of tasks which one could come into contact with in a different way; a field as symbol of the secret of the clarity that we can recall from experiencing the bitter cold in our noses as a moment that is inscribed in our own bodies: "The snow was overwhelmingly legible. Each print-trail seemed like a plot that could be read backwards in time; a series of allusions to events since ended. ... I chose to follow a deer's

10 Ibid., p. 163

11 Ibid., p. 162

trail, which angled tightly across a corner of the field. The slots led through a blackthorn hedge: I snagged my way after them, and emerged into a surreal landscape."—12 The world of humans and animals interlocks in the temporary emergence of the things.

12 Macfarlane, Robert: *The Old Ways*. London 2013, p. 7

III Anagogic Things

One can also speak of anonymity, of the alien nature of the more-than-just-useful things, which they are capable of changing over to, since they were in reality intended to be used. But what would such "simple" things be if they are objects of everyday use, designed first of all to serve a purpose, for example, ploughing a field?

It would be things, arranged for use, and yet something clarifying that is not forced upon them. In certain moments we come upon them like nature. That would refer not only to things, *zu-handen* [*at hand*], placing a demand on us active ones embedded in it and its material and in its form, but also to spaces and buildings that open up experiences, not "events" in the exaggerated sense. They became part of the natural history of things owing to their universality, became anonymous because within them and during moments of use every "signature" disturbed (went lost in time). "The result is buildings that provide a distinct service and at the same time represent that accomplishment in an *epic* way,"—13 according to Julius Posener in a short text about the fascination with modernity in "anonymous building." Its form originates in the sense of use which they precisely illustrate, a being operative which it itself had once created and to this day clings to its gestalt. There are types within it which are similar to landscape formations, that are comprehensible through their connection to the bodily-animate and are accompanied, where they come in contact with us, by secret bliss. Because they speak in their own

13 Posener, Julius: "Anonyme Architektur" (1978). In: Julius Posener: *Aufsätze und Schriften 1931–1980*. Wiesbaden 1981, pp. 359–61, here: p. 359

way—succinctly—they mean something and by way of their prose become poetic. Understanding is then sensual grasping.

The modern human being has begun to be interested in the immediacy of form that no longer originates in history of style or the demands of the market. The desire that incidental-practical, generally speaking, was based on self-preservation skills, would coincide with the awareness of experienceable beauty is perhaps the most absolute commission one could give a designer. What is fascinating about it at present is perhaps the opportunity to experience unpretentiousness as materiality released from function, as the "artistic" quality of fixed content and meaning situated right across from the use. Such appreciation might be connected to the moment the experienced is detached from contexts of purpose, but also to an entirely new evaluation of what is appropriate in a culture that obscures connections, that delegates and in this way contributes to the disappearance of the concrete. Materiality, conspicuousness, immediacy, inscribed therein is as "enigmatic" forms from which everything unnecessary has fallen away; they are the counterprogram to the everyday and material culture of the present day that only seldom traces its world of objects back to reasons that are "tangible": in the flesh. Wherein today more would be expressed than at the onset of industrialization with its critique of the fragmentation of all references to life. This feeling had accompanied Western society for more than one hundred years, has intensified, because the everyday is "programmed" by faraway, foreign notions of desire and a variety of purchase options that overtaxes consumers.

How could the things that accompany us today take on a beauty that achieves a union of being operative and experiencing, of the presence and cyclicality of the old cultural landscape? How would it have to be designed, produced, used, preserved, and cared for—in a program running counter to predominant notions. These thoughts are, nevertheless, neither a matter of laying out one's own "rural" world of objects, nor or an examination of art and architecture, but rather a quest for a possible life and material culture of the simple, whose track, however, has already been laid by modernity. Back in 1926, Soetsu Yanagi wrote his renowned praise of the "mixed things," in reference to Japanese folk art, to the simple useful things, whose beauty surpasses the Western boundary between arts and crafts, because these items are capable of transcending reality on a daily basis: "What an amazing thing it is that objects made for use in real life should possess a beauty that transcends reality."—[14] By comparing the potter's deft, practiced use of their hands at the wheel with nature's cycles, its variance within the seemingly same, to the unavailability of the small co-incidence in artisanal expertise, it becomes apparent that the potter introduces a freedom into this occurrence that is a special sort of production: "It is this freedom that is the mother of all creativity. The great variety and variation found in miscellaneous things is an accurate reflection of this fact. ... The moment everything is left in the hands of nature is the astonishing moment when creativity begins. ... This is not a meaningless cycle, not mere duplication. Each piece is the beginning of a new world, fresh and vivid."—[15] By way of these objects of day-to-day use a correspondence is now set up between the becoming of form, closely intertwined with nature, in which everything is in its place, and at the same time, is voluptuous and gushing. This would only succeed where "natural environment, raw materials, and production"—[16] remained, like in in anonymous traditions around the globe, inseparably linked. The seemingly unpretentious comes at a cost, demands a certain way of living and of experiencing.

Likewise, at the beginning of the twentieth century, Yanagi looked back to the Meiji era, when the memories of it were being lost. Accordingly, in the period in which the nineteenth century drew to a close, in which protagonists in Europe were also in search of the expression of mean-

14 Yanagi, Soetsu: "The Beauty of Miscellaneous Things." In: Yanagi, Soetsu: *The Beauty of Everyday Things.* London 2017, pp. 27–57, here: p. 54

15 Ibid., p. 48

16 Ibid., p. 40

ing for forms of urban mass culture. Bernard Leach intellectually and actually "wandered" from England to Asia and back again, and in the ceramics of China's Song Dynasty he found the formal potential for a modern presence. At the time, a synthesis of spirit and craft was achieved in them: Until the beginning of the industrial era, analogous processes of synthesis had always been at work amongst ourselves, but since that time the cultural background has lost much of its assimilating force, and the ideas we have adopted and used have been molded into conformity with a conception of life in which imagination has been subordinated to invention and beauty to the re- quirements of trade. In our time technique, the means to an end, has become an end in itself, and has thus justified Chinese criticism of us as a civilization 'outside in.'"—17 This is how in the 1940s, Leach's *A Potter's Book* estab- lished the history of modern European ceramics, and not without making a point for today's era of upheaval.

17 Leach, Bernard: *A Potter's Book*. London 1940, p. 14

The productive consequences of his new tradition could be traced to Leach's student and biographer Edmund de Waal. One could also find stimuli there as designer: simplicity and terseness arising from the repetitive move- ments of a wheel and the materiality of the earth; forms that are suitable for use and yet have already crossed over into the special realm of art; the anonymity of vessels that have expression and character in their own right, linked to the fascination with different grades of white porcelain, enigmatic-naturally-occurring material that only appears in nature in such rigor in the form of bare bones. De Waal manages to break loose from traditions and yet remain within them; his oeuvre establishes a new history in mea- ningful contexts. He too uses the language of poetry for a seemingly prosaic work. For instance, in one of his exhibitions, Paul Celan's poem "Lichtzwang" [Light- duress] stimulates the imagination: "What's required as stars/pours itself out, / your hands' leafgreen shadow/ gathers it in." Below the barrel vault of Vienna's Temple of Theseus—an island in a sea of green—the contrasting

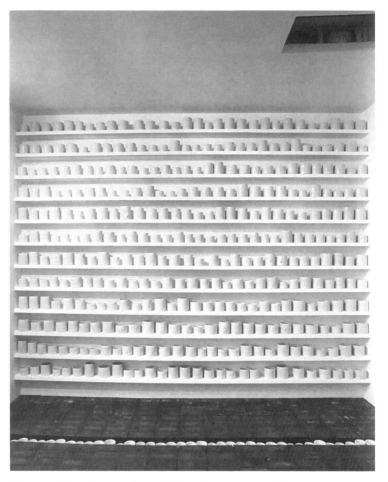

Edmund de Waal, "Porcelain Room," Geffrye Museum, London 2001

light befalls the hand-formed surfaces, infinitely simple yet characteristic cups in porcelain. Not only the variable appearance of nature's cyclic time makes reference through the sensual-symbolic light to the thus transformed small-scale world of objects, but also the spatial configuration of a cult site, which has long shed its function yet spatially conveys it to observant visitors. Regarding the original, anonymous culture of pottery and the mixture with the artistic, Yanagi however writes in his short treatise: "What is the art of the kiln? The artisan knows nothing of that. Still, without knowing all that there is to know, his hands continue working swiftly in the process of creation ... the hand of the artisan is no longer his or her own hand, but the hand of nature. The craftsman does not aim to create beauty, but nature assures that it is done."—[18]

Julius Posener, who critically accompanied the development of modern architecture, looks back in his aforementioned short text to the past anonymous culture of building and finds that even back then, not everything could be explained by the relation to its use, which, however, would contain everything if only one were to change the vantage point.—[19] The perceived "naturalness" of rural culture corresponds to cultural traditions that have been incorporated in typologies. Yet they could not be adopted so simply, but instead would have to be engaged in vibrant use; otherwise there is a risk that one simply "copies."—[20] His "anagogic culture" would, in other words, be an analogue action, which accepts the resistance that is inscribed in these things, which grow on their own terms in nature-culture, or have been revoked over the course of the long history of the complete availability of the individual. This is now also valid for the kind of activity these potters have shown for a world of objects situated between the everyday and cult. In both cases time inscribes an impersonal foreignness in them in an interplay of types of conduct. They are things whose production and materiality become clear to the active senses in the moment

[18] Yanagi, p. 30

[19] See Posener, p. 360

[20] See ibid., p. 361

145

in which they are used, and which now and then open another door: to the unavailable residue within.

IV *Unverfügbarkeit*

It may be that time is in fact the major binding puzzle. That is the status of the human being in nature: situating the culture time in nature as desire for permanence. In Martin Heidegger's work, temporality is the reason to grasp humans as caring beings who care with, about, and for each other, and about themselves. Care becomes existential when acts of survival change into rituals, transparent to the attention to the plain things, in which nature's vitality can come back in the form of culture. A contemplation which would come from the pausing while using the simple things, a stillstand in the time as cele- bration of the day-to-day. Here the rural-nurturing dealings become simplicity, which is at once "reflecting surface" and "receptacle."

One way to achieve this lies in the act of doing it, in the bond between production and use that long ago retreated to the background of consumption. Where the production from the use and the use from the conditions of production: where both activities, which were once one, remain linked by caring attentiveness. If namely the production preserves the relation to the particularities of materiality and to the efforts and knowledge of work, and in this way the raw transforms into the thing without excess and superfluity, which one could not allow oneself; if, in other words, the usage is not to be ashamed and at any time can become a celebration in the usage of things, thus as a grateful memory of their becoming and of their subservience, such a unity can again be conceived of. Then, however, one emerges from the state of solely using something. To express this, Heidegger came upon the term *Gelassenheit* [*releasement*]. It denotes being engaged in a practicable nature; a lane of life, trodden by others through their work, but which one can also traverse again while speaking and thinking, attentive, dwelling, to identify oneself with the proximity of the fields and the seasons manifest in them. Yet one would not only be guided by the paths of others, but by the quiet decisions of one's own conversations, which one in fact holds not just with oneself but also with companions. The horizon is always present. Here and yet far away, never reached: "Yet releasement toward things and openness to the mystery never happen by themselves. They do not befall us accidentally. Both flourish only through persistent, courageous thinking."—[21] Rudolf Bultmann, a theologian who corresponded with the philosopher coined the term "Unverfügbarkeit" [unavailability] for this form of presence—a "vitality" of the things, inherently elusive puzzles, because they express precisely that gift that comes to the surface in them, where they are nothing other than what they must be, and make this perceptible. It occurs in a life that has recognized beauty in the unconditional simplicity of the nonconditional. The puzzle of a space experienced this way, which opens to the daylight changing within it over the course of a day, a year; in rooms facing north, south, east, west, without names, a defined space for the people, into which nature enters, its prepossessing appearance unavailable in time, its vitality. There can be objects of great simplicity which are pervaded by it and grow brighter from the oscillating experiences of a uselessness for the moment of forgotten purpose; moments that consist of nothing other than the possibility to experience what simply "is." And *what is*: that which is not available precisely in the moment, pleasantly alien right across from us.

There is obviously a path from the basic use of things to the moment of contemplation as a chance to pause and become aware of beauty which is not present, but has a place here. Such that everything must be a certain way, even if it could be otherwise: contentment, in other words, peace for the moment. Its proximity to the surreal does

21 Heidegger, Martin: *Gelassenheit* (German orig. documenting 1955 speech). Stuttgart 2004, p. 25

not necessarily assign it a spot in the dreams and utopias, but rather in the concrete world of objects that would have to be relieved of nonmaterial aims—if architecture and its spaces have a share in allowing the adventure that something is, that a cloud can enchant us: for example, a rain cloud, as long as a bit of the day remains; then it becomes greyer and darker while the sound of the drops, that in the night—which has now come—yields a different, darker spectacle. And if we were to wish to live a day entirely experientially, or even a year: in all of our years, we will not experience such a duration, because that is not available to us, nor is the bliss of sensation at our disposal.

"And our immemorial rites are in Time what the dwelling is in Space. For it is well that the years should not seem to wear us away and disperse us like a handful of sand; rather they should fulfill us. It is meet that Time should be a building-up. Thus I go from one feast day to another, anniversary to anniversary, from harvesttide to harvesttide,"—[22] writes Antoine de Saint-Exupéry on the union of thing and time in ritual, in the space of architecture as defined by time. Contemplation and use—two sorts of implementation as scale for the things, to what extent they can be capable of establishing a connection from their immediacy. Contemplation, that is, of course, the coming into view of a whole at the moment of the experience; release from the everyday, without constraints, and yet sought out from it and in reference to it. It is with such experiences in such conditions, the untranslatability of one language into another, or also the uniqueness of literary expression whose beauty pleases by way of its freshness—far surpassing the clear aim of the message, and through it applies simple words. One such sentence is found in Thomas Mann's *Doktor Faustus*, a book written in an uncertain time, because a culture was drawing to a close, and a new one was not yet in sight: "Es ging der Oktober zu Ende, das Wetter, noch trocken, war rauh schon und düster. Die Blätter fielen." [It was late October, the weather was still dry, though already raw

22 Saint-Exupéry, Antoine de: *The Wisdom of the Sands*. New York 1950, p. 16

and gloomy. Leaves were falling.]—[23] The musicality of these words lies in their constellation, in the surprising consonance of their unpretentiousness, by the stored, unmediated experiential knowledge of natural rhythms— that, in other words, a possible, changing language specific to you or to me remains within the conventions of communication and needs not invent enigma in order to sparkle, but instead preserves it, for it was already present, in the nature of the things.

23 Mann, p. 342

The Ethical Relevance of Simple Things
Art, Crafts, Design, and Modern Life

Günter Figal

1.

Likely no one would seriously deny the importance of
things for human life. As middle-sized stable entities,
things can easily be referred to, and thus they are the
most distinctive correlates of perception and cognition.—[1]
Moreover, many human activities cannot be performed
without things. For production and for action in general,
utensils or tools are needed very often, and some activities and customs would not even exist without particular
things. One could not ride a bicycle without bicycles
and would even have no idea what bicycling is; sitting
on chairs is by no means natural to human beings, but
enabled by the production of chairs. And finally, there
are things that effect particular pleasure and insight as
objects of contemplation. Such things, artworks, stand
separate among things, and are often regarded as unap-
proachable for use and handling. In any case, artworks
are not defined as related to something else—like utensils
that are defined by their relation to use. Artworks just
are what they are: they are things in themselves. Not
being relational, their determinateness is not twofold, but
simple. Artworks are simple things.

Very likely because of their specific character, artworks
normally are treated with esteem and special care. Accordingly, people mostly are shocked whenever artworks

1 Figal, Günter: *Un-
scheinbarkeit: Der Raum
der Phänomenologie*.
Tübingen 2015, pp. 89–138

are wantonly destroyed or damaged, as Taliban fighters did with Buddha statues of Bamiyan, or a person with a mental illness did with Barnett Newman's painting *Cathedra* in the Stedelijk Museum in Amsterdam. If the Taliban fighters had blown up an aircraft without thereby killing someone, or if the person who damaged Newman's painting instead had damaged a luxury car, this would very likely have appeared strange or reprehensible, but not deeply shocking. Harming or killing human individuals is certainly worse than damaging or destroying an artwork. Yet the loss of an artwork can, like the loss of a person, elicit feelings of a distressing loss, because a true artwork, like an individual, is irreplaceable.

In line with such considerations, one could suppose a kind of moral commitment to artworks and, if artworks as mere things were somehow to represent things in general, also to things as such. Examined more closely, however, this supposition proves to be problematic.

There is good reason to regard moral commitment as basically confined to living beings that are in principle "like us." These are beings with which we can share a space and thus "live together," in such a way that whenever such beings are present, we do not feel "alone," either in a positive or in a negative way.—[2] Not being alone, we have to coordinate our intentions and activities with those of other living beings, to recognize their needs, desires, and expectations, and to decide how to react to them. In this context the basic moral or ethical question would arise: What, in consideration of other living beings, "should" we do or are we even obligated to do in order to live together as well as possible? Such morally determined living together includes primarily all human beings, regardless of their age and physical or mental state, as well as some other living beings, such as domestic animals. As to animals, it may be difficult to decide which of them can or even should be included and which not. However, morally determined life definitely does not include things, because things, despite their importance for human life,

2   Ibid., pp. 170–90

make no difference as to whether humans are alone or not. On the other hand, however, esteeming artworks in the way exemplified above is undoubtedly a normative attitude. Though different from ethical commitments, this attitude is similar to ethical normativity, and perhaps even in some decisive respects. Like ethical normativity, the normative attitude toward artworks cannot be reduced to hedonistic or profit-oriented motives. Understanding the very character of artworks, we would not exclusively esteem artworks we personally like and would even less so deny the artistic character of works because we do not like them; rather, we would admit that, irrespective of our preferences, all artworks deserve the same esteem and care. Identifying the artistic significance of a work with its market value would also be inadequate and implausible; true artworks may be reasonably priced, whereas extremely high-priced works are not necessarily artworks, but can also be a kind of ephemeral luxury kitsch.

If the normative attitude to artworks thus cannot be reduced to extrinsic reasons, such an attitude must be founded in the artistic character of artworks as such. Artworks, then, would be esteemed just because they are artworks; recognizing something as an artwork would go along with esteem, and accordingly someone voluntarily damaging or destroying an artwork would more or less explicitly oppose the esteem appropriate to artworks However, what precisely makes artworks estimable? What it is that makes a thing an artwork? And, if artworks are adequately regarded as simple things, how precisely is the simplicity of an artwork to be understood?

2.

In order to respond to these questions, it may be helpful to examine in more detail the attitude characteristic of the experience of artworks. This attitude, as already mentioned, is contemplation, which, again, can be described as an attentive, more or less continuous and more or less reflective perceptional experience. Such experience is without any aim. Contemplating a picture or a sculpture, one has no intention to effectuate something, not even to investigate the object to which experience refers. Contemplation is not motivated by any result, and thus it is without inherent temporal limitation. One may contemplate something for a longer or shorter time, but contemplation as such would not cease in an end. Therefore, contemplation could infinitely be continued, or it could also begin again and again.

However, contemplation would not be continued or repeated if the objects contemplated did not encourage this by reappearing anew, again and again. Though, for instance, a painting is something of limited size and stable in its qualities, firmly fixed once it has been painted, one will never assume to have seen the painting once and for all, assuming the painting is an artwork. In this case, whenever contemplated, its compositional elements would correspond to each other in ways not seen before, and the picture's color very likely each time would show new tones, nuances, and surface effects. Admittedly such variety is dependent on different situations of light, and to some degree also on a contemplator's particular disposition. However, a picture can only be experienced differently if it has—or is—a potential of appearing differently. Its composition must be "open" instead of being strictly and schematically organized, and its color, instead of being merely plain, must have ambiguity and depth.

Compositions of the kind just sketched can be called "decentered."—[3] They are not organized by a central meaning determining the significance and function of all details so that the whole structure could be decoded and reconstructed. Decentered orders cannot be decoded at all; they are combinations of elements more or less irregular, ordered without any commensurability. This is so not least because the decentered order of an artwork cannot be abstracted from a work's material character. A pictorial

3   Figal, Günter: *Erscheinungsdinge: Ästhetik als Phänomenologie*. Tübingen 2010, pp. 72–76; 95–98. English translation: *Aesthetics as Phenomenology.* Translated by Jerome Veith. Bloomington, Indiana, pp. 56–60; 75–78

composition, for instance, is embedded in painted color, so that its appearance and the color's appearance form the same incommensurable appearance, an appearance not "of something," but simply appearance, reducible to nothing, evident as what it is—thus simple, and it its simplicity beautiful. It is beauty as appearing simplicity that makes something into an artwork.

Since artworks thus are primarily material appearances they are made for perception; contemplating a picture means looking at it, for instance. It is no accident that the experience of artworks is commonly called "aesthetic," based on the Greek word for perception, aisthesis. This signification indicates that perception is not just an aspect of such experience, but its essential character. Accordingly, an experience of artworks is truly aesthetic only if reflections and interpretations do not presuppose how to look at a picture. Rather, reflection and interpretation should be led by perception. Interpretations not based on what is perceived could not be convincing.

Due to this priority of perception, aesthetic experience is devoted to a perceptible individual thing that is just what it is. If taken as "a case of … " or as "an example for … ," artworks are not regarded as artworks. Their aesthetic character, their beauty, is incommensurable with conceptual knowledge, be it practical or theoretical. This is because the beauty of artworks does not fit into conceptual contexts, whether practical nor scientific, technological or historical, and because it cannot fulfill or relieve practical or theoretical expectations. Being beautiful, artworks are of an irreducible and thus simple objectivity.

Following these considerations, the normative attitude to artworks, which we can call "aesthetic normativity," should no longer be difficult to determine. Contemplation of an artwork in the way described is not possible without recognizing the artwork's perceptible objectivity—its beauty. Such recognition is not additional to aesthetic contemplation; it neither precedes, and thus enables, nor complements the contemplative experience of an artwork, but belongs essentially to it. For instance, viewing a picture as an irreducible and incommensurable appearance, and thus in its beauty, is independent from any epistemic or practical presuppositions; one immediately recognizes the picture as objective or, what is the same, as a thing in itself. Aesthetic recognition has consequences. Recognizing artworks aesthetically, one would not exploit them in favor of personal advantage or gain. However, one should not only see to an artwork's safety and conservation and avoid everything that could impair or destroy it, but also foster cultural conditions that favor artworks and their appearing objectivity.

Aesthetic normativity has some analogy to ethical normativity. In both cases we would not make decisions and act exclusively on our personal interests or desires, but instead regard the existence of someone respectively something with respect, as something that binds us. Bound by ethical or aesthetic normativity, we would consider what would be adequate to someone or something for their sake. Thus, ethical and aesthetic normativity could be regarded as complementary. Both impede or even avert a merely self-centered life and support a sense of the exterior as irreducible to one's own ideas, beliefs, and intentions.

Despite such complementarity, ethical and aesthetic normativity are not symmetrical; whereas ethical normativity, as an essential condition of human life and even more so of a good life, is as such binding for everyone, the general obligatory character of aesthetic normativity is confined to recognizing artworks as objects destined *for the very possibility* of contemplation. Accordingly, damaging or destroying an artwork is clearly reprehensible and thus not incidentally defined in some countries as a crime. However, no one is committed to taking a positive attitude to artworks, recognizing artworks from the perspective of a contemplator, whereas at least some positive attitudes to other human beings like considerateness, helpfulness, or solidarity are ethically obligatory.

One can only argue in favor of aesthetic contemplation; possibly the most convincing argument would be ethical in character, saying that aesthetic contemplation essentially contributes to a better life and thus is of ethical relevance.

3.

Considering the previous discussion on its own, one could perhaps take this argument for an exaggeration. So far one could regard artworks as exceptions among things and suspect the normative attitude they demand as irrelevant for reference to things in general. However, one should not prematurely restrict the scope of aesthetic objects. Thinking of aesthetic objects, one first of all should not limit oneself to examples typical for what could be called "the Western canon" and thus, as to visual art, only consider pictures and sculptures. Moreover, one should not draw the line between artworks and other things too rigidly. There are many things experienced and designated as beautiful that are not artworks and accordingly do not demand contemplation in the same way as artworks. However, if we take the meaning of "beautiful" as it refers to artworks and apply it to other things, we do find that there are aesthetic objects besides artworks—things that appear as how they are with aesthetic experience only. As a consequence, aesthetic experience would be of a much broader range than commonly supposed.

As to restrictions going along with the "Western canon" of art, one may mainly recall that in East Asian cultures ceramic vessels are recognized as artworks, and, as such, are much more important than in the West. In Japanese tea culture, artworks—such as masterly made tea bowls (*chawan*)—even exceed pictures in significance.—4 The artistic character of vessels may become evident in comparison to things more familiar as artworks, even if this is not immediately noticed. Such a correspondence is that of bowls and a vase made by Young-Jae Lee with a

4   Figal, Günter: *Gefäße als Kunst: Erfahrungen mit japanischer Keramik.* Freiburg im Breisgau 2019, pp. 8–15

painting by Rudolf de Crignis as it was to be seen at the Paul Ege Art Collection (PEAC), Freiburg, in 2019. Lee's vessels and de Crignis's painting correspond to each other so harmoniously that they must be the same kind of things, namely artworks. Both vessels and painting have no message. They do not express anything, but are simply what they are—the vessels individually changing in form between elegance and solidity, with glazes in delicate variations and shades; the painting, though "monochrome," of indescribable depth in color, deep blue as well as bright blue. These works are as self-evident as they are wondrous, intense in their quiet appearance, converging in beauty, and to be contemplated timelessly, again and again.

So, when compared with de Crignis's painting, Lee's vessels undoubtedly appear as true artworks; they are in principle not different from paintings and other "canonical" works of visual arts. However, Young-Jae Lee has not only created what she calls her "masterworks," but also designed a collection of tableware—plates, bowls, jars, pitchers, mugs, cups, and teapots—resembling her masterworks in style. These works also are handcrafted, though not by herself, and standardized in form and color. However, Lee's tableware is also worth looking at. Though standardized, the glaze is not uniform. It is lively, spotted with irregularities caused by mineral inclusions in the used clay, and the forms are clear and harmonious— simple forms that are reminiscent of traditional Korean ceramics, and of the reduced, geometrical forms developed in the Bauhaus workshops.

Though meant for everyday use and thus commensurable with practical knowledge, one very likely would not use these pieces without particular attention. They are beautiful—not wondrous like the masterworks, but evidently beautiful in their appearing simplicity. Though one very likely would not repeatedly and intensely contemplate a tableware piece, one nevertheless would recognize it as an object that is beautiful in itself, and look at it with particular approval. As distinguished from contemplation of artworks, such recognition and approval normally would be more incidental, more implicit, and thus seldom reflective.

Nevertheless, it would be a contemplative attitude, like the contemplation of artworks relating to the perceptible appearance of something objective. Admittedly Young-Jae Lee's tableware pieces are not as individual as her masterworks. Looking, for instance, at a bowl from the tableware collection, and knowing that it is from this collection, one would understand the bowl as "an example of" a certain type of bowl. However, a bowl, recognized aesthetically while looked at, would not be reduced to being just one example among many of the same kind. Though one would know that many other examples of the same shape and color exist, one would aesthetically recognize the bowl as a particular thing that is beautiful in itself. Accordingly, one would handle it carefully in order to conserve it as an individual piece and also in practical recognition of its beauty.

Young-Jae Lee's tableware is a good example for illustrating how beautiful things that are different from artworks nevertheless can be akin to them. As products of craft, ceramic artworks are produced in basically the same way as such vessels, and necessarily so, because no ceramic artist could make artistic vessels without craftsmanship. Ceramic art is a modification of craft; it is a craft more attentive to the appearance character of its works and thus more reflective. However, works of craft can also have an aesthetic quality that is not inferior to that of artworks, but rather is able to attain what artistic production can reach.

Soetsu Yanagi, philosopher and founder of the Japanese "folk art" movement (*mingei*), has argued to this effect. He holds that a traditional Korean or Japanese potter throwing the same type of vessel again and again, without reflection and rational control, could produce vessels of great beauty without ever having intended this.—5 Even if one is convinced by this, one can nevertheless

5   Yanagi, Soetsu: "The Beauty of Miscellaneous Things." In: Yanagi, Soetsu. *The Beauty of Everyday Things*. New York 2018, pp. 27–57

reasonably doubt that ceramic artisans really have no sense of the beauty they produce, and also that such beauty of involuntariness is out of reach for artists. Ceramic artists are quite able to produce true, incommensurable artworks that take involuntariness into account; they can even develop "strategies of involuntariness" and thus confirm the reflective character of art without subordinating art to conceptual rationality.—6

However, not all beautiful things are of the kind just discussed. There are also beautiful things whose beauty is not an immediate result of manual production, but of a conception that predetermines production, be it manual or mechanical. Such things are, to introduce the common term for this procedure, products of design: for instance, many pieces of furniture, cars, and technical devices like laptops and smartphones, as well as tableware pieces not thrown on a potter's wheel, but produced in a factory.

The term "design" is not restricted to, but especially significant for, the period of modernity. For the sake of liberation from nineteenth-century historicism, attempts were made to establish new criteria for the quality and appearance of things necessary for human life and to create such things from a new point of departure. Though many—if not most—representatives of modern design have stressed functionality as a criterion, an understanding of beauty has been established that has brought simplicity to special prominence. Speaking not only for himself, but also for the Bauhaus tradition he represents, the designer Dieter Rams has claimed going "back to purity, back to simplicity," by making design products "honest," "unobtrusive," with "as little design as possible," and, not least of all, "aesthetic."

Explaining the latter, Rams adds that "aesthetic quality deals with nuanced and precise shades, with the harmony and subtle equilibrium of a whole variety of visual elements" or, to put it differently, with the specific quality of simple, decentered orders.—7 As curators of an exhibition entitled *Super Normal*, designers Naoto

6   Figal, Günter: *Unwill-kürlichkeit: Essays über Kunst und Leben*. Freiburg im Breisgau 2016, pp. 64–69; Figal: *Gefäße* (as in note 4), pp. 51–56

7   Rams, Dieter: *Weniger, aber besser / Less But Better*. Hamburg 1995, pp. 6–7

Fukasawa and Jasper Morrison were completely in line with Rams's criteria. For their exhibition they chose everyday simple objects whose character cannot be reduced to functionality, but which have a beauty of their own—as Morrison says, a "beauty which takes time to be noticed,"—[8] the beauty of the simple, which is just what it is, far from what Dieter Rams calls "'purchase stimu-lation' aesthetic."—[9]

8   Fukasawa, Naoto/ Morrison, Jasper: *Super Normal: Sensations of the Ordinary*. Zurich 2007, p. 103

9   Rams: *Weniger, aber besser* (as in note 7), p. 149

4.

Widening the scope of beautiful things in the way argued for so far, one has to cope with an issue challenging the traditional Western understanding of art; almost all beautiful things that have been introduced are things to be used. This holds even true for some artworks. Whereas pictures and sculptures, indeed, can only be contemplated, tea bowls, the most precious vessels in Japanese tea culture and undoubtedly artworks, are for use and not only to be looked at. However, use in this case must be different from the everyday use of utensils, tools, and furniture as of things that have a particular function, and could easily be replaced by something else serving the same purpose. Everyday use of such things can be called "subjective"; it is centered on users with their particular intentions, and what counts as to things used is nothing except their usefulness. In contrast, the use of something recognized as beautiful like a tea bowl is "objective"; it would allow a thing used to appear as itself, and thus be contemplative or at least have a contemplative dimension.

The idea of contemplation in use could seem paradoxical only as long as one would identify contemplation with mere viewing and thus take objects to be contemplated like pictures. However, for adequately contemplating a ceramic vessel like a tea bowl, one would have to hold it in one's hands and feel its shape and surface. Also preparing tea in such a bowl and drinking from it would be led by attentively perceiving the bowl, visually as well as by touching the object, and thus be contemplative. Use thus determined by a contemplative attitude primarily would be an experience of the bowl's beauty. Accordingly, using such a bowl would by no means impair it as an artwork. Rather, traces of use even may contribute to its beauty and thus improve the pleasure of contemplation. When damaged or broken, precious tea bowls are mostly repaired artificially with lacquer and a thin layer of gold. Such repair, the Japanese word for which is *kintsugi*, is regarded as an augmentation of beauty.

Certainly not every use of something beautiful is of that kind. For instance, one could use a teacup from Young-Jae Lee's tableware collection primarily to have tea. However, if the cup is experienced as a beautiful thing, its use will be determined by the contemplative attitude of recognition and esteem. One will not just fill such a cup with tea and drink, but also view and touch it as a thing in itself. Basically, the same holds true for the use of all beautiful things. Using things that are aesthetically esteemed, one does not just subordinate them to one's own intentions; rather, such use can confirm and augment one's sense of the objective and thus possibly change one's practical life. One will—perhaps gradually—realize that things, even if produced manually or mechanically, and even if showing traces of use, do not owe their appearance and significance to us. Rather, things, simple things without any message or pretention, without "flattery" as Fukasawa says,—[10] appear in themselves. Thus they allow us to approach them freely, without presuppositions and ambitions, and thereby, together with a sense of the objective, enhance a sense of freedom. This holds true for all simple things, but admittedly most of all for artworks. Being mainly objects of contemplation—contemplation in use included—they allow experiencing most clearly what contemplation is and thus make explicit the contemplative attitude we would take in reference to other beautiful things.

10 Fukasawa/Morrison: *Super Normal* (as in note 8), p. 107

5.

Being things in themselves, beautiful things, besides the
aspects mentioned so far, also allow for a better understanding of things in general. They represent things as
things, and thus can draw attention to properties characteristic of all things. Since beautiful things primarily
appear as perceptible, their most significant character
of materiality is that in which structural elements are
embedded—canvas and paint, paper and the marks of
charcoal, pencil and ink, stone and wood, clay, porcelain
and the different materials of glaze, metal, glass and
others. Being simple, beautiful things do not hide their
materiality. Their surface is not concealed by decoration
and it is not showy, but moderate, even if bright. It is a
plain surface, allowing plain material to appear. So, with
simple, beautiful things, the particular materiality of
their textures can be discovered, and with materiality, the
structures and forms, too, that are embedded in it. With
their perceptibility, free from superfluous meaning or
expressive gestures, beautiful, simple things show how
one could perceive things in general and thereby discover
their objectivity. Thus, one may find the whole world of
things condensed in beautiful, simple things.

My shed

Other Ways We Could Build

Florian Nagler

I planned and built my first building while still at university: a shed for a farmer. After I completed my apprenticeship as a carpenter, the summer break always provided a welcome opportunity to earn money for college by working on a construction site. The client had requested that we forego elaborate connection solutions—because they are costly—and limit the size of the building components, which made it possible to set the shed up with a tractor and a few assistants. The shed was to be built using the lumber from a dismantled threshing floor that had been stored for several years. The floor plan was to measure seven by ten meters (the maximum size allowed without a building permit). So I developed a structure based on the available cross-sections of the wood salvaged from the threshing floor. The connections were carried out with carpenter's joinery techniques; the use of equipment was kept to a minimum (circular saw, chain mortiser, chisel, axe, hammer).

Though *green building* had not been given a thought, this project was to become the implementation of an—admittedly very simple—exemplary, sustainable concept that had been based solely on the client's specifications: wood that had been harvested centuries ago and had already been used in a building, that had then been stored for decades, and which still held a large amount of carbon dioxide, was employed again as a building material.

165

Its processing consumed very little energy, and it only had to be transported a very short distance.

Today's slogans are *low-tech*, *reuse*, and *recycling*. But perhaps one could also call such an approach a form of construction informed by reasoning, appropriateness, and—a quality seemingly completely lacking at present—thrift. For millennia, there was no alternative to resourcefulness, because obtaining construction materials required a great effort. It was also a matter of course—at least in the countryside—for buildings to be erected with the materials that were available locally. Buildings were also, of course, informed by centuries of experience, built in a way that made them well-suited to dealing with the respective climate conditions. This aspect, in combination with economies that were largely agricultural, led all around the globe to the development of regional building types and characteristic built landscapes, which have in this way become integral parts of their surroundings and well-integrated in the respective context.

Industrialization and, at the very latest, the advent of the modern age have obliterated these principles. The rapid technological advancement since the early nineteenth century, with its exponential growth, has—in addition to negative repercussions—brought about considerable welcome change and enabled breathtaking achievements. But parallel to the technological possibilities, our demands have also grown. At present we—by which I mean all of the residents of the rich industrialized nations—take much for granted and consider many things a necessity that not long ago were great luxuries.

Some years ago, my friend, the artist Peter Lang, asked me to design for him a mobile atelier. The intention of the atelier was to allow him to travel to remote locations where he would stay for several months to paint "in the wilderness." The equipment would have to fit in a standard twenty-foot container unit. He wanted to take some 300 square meters of canvas with him, and

Peter's travel container, 2010

an atelier with a floor area of about sixty square meters would let him work on formats measuring up to two by six meters. In addition, we decided to equip the atelier in such fashion that it would allow for subsistence living, in other words, only provide what is necessary to survive in an undeveloped part of the world. We designed a light-weight structure made of wood, aluminum, and sailcloth that could be attached like a large tent to the container— which in turn served not only as the trunk, but was also integrated in the spatial concept. All building components were scaled so that one person could assemble and disassemble the structure on his own. The atelier was equipped with a wood stove for cooking and heating; a sleeping berth; a large cabinet for provisions, paint, pigments, etc.; and a small kitchen with sink and foldout table. The water that collected on the roof was guided to a small cistern and supplied the camping shower. Last but not least, it included a composting toilet.

On his first trip, Lang travelled to Patagonia. The incredible paintings he brought home were inspired by the grandiose landscape. After he returned, we spoke about his experiences on-site. Everything functioned wonderfully, as planned. But there was one thing that we had deluded ourselves about, namely, our estimation of what "subsistence level" is. What we had determined to be a necessity differed starkly from that with which other people on this planet must make do: his were the most luxurious lodgings for miles around. At the time, this fact made a big impression on me and has influenced my thinking in the long term: a project that I had developed and which, in my opinion, had been pared down to an absolute minimum made me realize that we—with our Central European and North American lifestyles—are the ones who are wasting the greatest portion of the world's resources, and this still holds true, it turns out, even when we think we are being modest. It should, however, become clear to all logically thinking individuals that our planet cannot sustain this lifestyle for all of humankind. We must therefore urgently consider whether we need everything with which we surround ourselves and whether we might manage with less and perhaps as a result even become more content.

We still succumb to the notion that without growth we cannot exist. And the statement "Our children should be better off than we are" demonstrates this attitude. But what does it mean to be better off? With respect to building: What should buildings be capable of in the future? Should they offer even more comforts? Function as completely digitalized realms? Be carbon neutral during construction and in operation? Be better looking? Over the course of more than twenty years of practice, we have always made it a point of developing projects that are mindful of energy consumption and that use natural resources responsibly. More recently, however, that has involved an ever-greater utilization of technology as well as increasingly elaborate structural and tectonic solutions, resulting in far greater complexity in the building sector.

The highly ambitious initiative to build a secondary school in Diedorf, Germany, which we developed and built with Hermann Kaufmann Architekten, once again made me aware of this increasing complexity and the attendant problems. On the one hand, the prize-winning school is constructed in wood, produces a surplus of energy, and boasts an innovative pedagogical concept that had been developed as part of a research project funded by the district of Augsburg. On the other hand, the fact that, following completion of the school in 2015, it took a three-year monitoring process to finetune the building services—or, put more plainly, get the systems up and running—was truly cause for concern. Not to mention the amount of planning required to develop the highly complex—in the most literal sense of the word multi-faceted—building, optimized with respect to a variety of functional requirements. On the whole, following completion of the project and some self-critical reflection, I felt like I had reached a dead end.

Ventilation control room at the Schmuttertal Secondary School in Diedorf, 2016

Research house in Bad Aibling, 2020

I didn't want to continue working this way and did not want to erect any more buildings that demand so much of the planners, the contractors, and the users. Inspired by examples by colleagues who had had similar experiences and who had sought alternatives—e.g., the 2226 Building in Lustenau by Baumschlager Eberle—we felt that the time had come to initiate a research project at the Technische Universität Munich (TUM) that would look into whether it would be possible to erect less complex buildings again: "simple building." We were especially interested in examining whether it is only possible to respond to today's requirements with ever-more complex technology. The aim of the research project was to create a foundation upon which a simple, robust building could be developed and to reduce the complexity, e.g., by only using monolithic or single-ply construction methods.

Because our aim was to arrive at findings with greatest possible relevance for practical application, we selected the three most common materials used in today's construction and made them the focus of our explorations: wood, concrete, and brick. For a publicly funded research project on "future building" we joined forces with our colleagues at the TUM and started out at the spatial level by carrying out a series of simulations with the aim of optimizing an eighteen-square-meter living room—the standard size. This involved examining the three different materials, different geometries, ceiling heights, window sizes, and types of glass, as well as the orientation to the cardinal points. By running 2,605 separate simulations we studied the behavior with respect to thermal protection in summer and energy load in winter in each room over the course of a year—though in all variants we decided to do without external sun-shading, while nevertheless taking into account the different storage capacities of the chosen materials for the walls enclosing the respective room.

The result did not really surprise us but confirmed that we should continue along the same path: considering the materiality of the structure enclosing the room and of the room's orientation, with respect to the heat load, as well as the number of hours in which the room overheats in summer, those rooms functioned best that had a width of three to six meters, a ceiling height greater than three meters, and a window whose size is calibrated to guarantee a daylight quotient of at least two percent at the room's center. In other words, the type of rooms we find in prewar apartment buildings...

Our research also investigated the "grey energy" that our buildings consume during a hundred-year life span. The buildings we conceived—robust and requiring minimal technological investment (standard heating implements, ventilation via slits integrated in windows, and fans for windowless bathrooms) that is not compromised when residents occasionally leave the window open longer than is strictly speaking necessary—have a better grey energy balance than today's conventionally constructed buildings and better than ones erected in low-energy standard, even though our buildings just manage to stay within the guidelines of the EnEV, Germany's energy saving ordinance.

We didn't want to conclude the study on a purely theoretical note, and therefore we set out in search of a client. B & O-Gruppe, located in the German city of Bad Aibling, specializes in repairing buildings in the residential sector and carries out about one million such repairs annually. Consequently, it had great interest in erecting three case study apartment buildings with us on their grounds, formerly the site of military barracks.

For the construction of the wood version, we selected a three-ply, cross-laminated timber whose inner layer contains additional air pockets (wall thickness 30 cm, U-value 0.22 W/m^{2}K, bulk density 410 kg/m^3, compressive strength 17 N/mm^2). The wood construction is protected by a spruce façade with ventilated cavity.

The insulating concrete, which is implemented without steel reinforcement (wall thickness 50 cm, U-value 0.35 W/m^{2}K, bulk density 750 kg/m^3, compressive strength 12 N/mm^2), gets its insulating properties from lightweight expanded clay aggregate and expanded-glass-granulate, which replace gravel and sand, respectively. The masonry building is erected using vertical coring brick (wallthickness 42.5 cm, U-value 0.25 W/m^{2}K, bulk density 850 kg/m^3, compressive strength 3.4 N/mm^2) and has just a single coat of stucco inside and outside. In all three versions the floor assembly has a simplified stratification: we employed a thirty-centimeter-thick reinforced-concrete deck covered with carpet (noise reduction). With regard both to the insulating concrete version and the brick version, the question arose of how to find a solution that would make it possible to construct the door openings without requiring special lintels. In this case we drew on traditional architectural structures—semicircular arches for the insulating concrete and segmental arches for the brick masonry.

One component of the architectural conception seeking to simplify the structural means could also be described as harking back to architecture's authentic means, its structural and constitutive elements: walls, ceilings, doors, and windows, deep reveals, marquee roofs, etc., which have proven themselves for centuries and make it possible to build in synchrony with the regional climate, but also with the regional tradition. And, it is in this "harking back" to the elements that are necessary structurally, and the resulting basic formal vocabulary derived from the extremely simple structures and materials, that we see the potential to arrive at a contemporary architectural expression—the expression of an architecture that grapples with the questions of our time! Therefore, we view our case study buildings as motivation to continue to reflect on whether, if we adjust our expectations slightly and employ simpler yet more robust means, we might be able to arrive at attractive, well-functioning buildings, while still, thanks to a fine-tuned consumption of energy and resources, staking out a responsible stance toward the built environment.

I am under the impression that with the findings from this research project we have only cracked the door open toward a vast expanse that must be elaborated upon. This will involve instituting a reduction of land use in all construction measures in the city and in the countryside; making use of the building stock as a resource both with respect to floor area and material; and using materials that consume the smallest possible amount of grey energy, are easy to recycle, and can be returned to nature's cycle! We will only succeed at this if all of these aspects are taken into consideration from the very beginning of the design process. As architects we are, of course, inter-ested—aside from the structural and technological aspects of our buildings—in their architectural potential. The derivation, for example, of the form of a window from the structural exigencies of the material is something that not only makes sense, but also brings pleasure—and can yield an autonomous aesthetic along the way.

In the meantime, we have begun to incorporate the ex-perience we gained in the research project in nearly every project we design. And this has, in turn, helped us learn even more—for example, that there are many different interpretations of what "simple building" means. Some craftspeople find it easier to adhere to the standard oper-ating procedure rather than use their critical faculties to find out if there might be a simpler approach. And for the employees of an architecture firm, the tendency is to rely on the "catalogue," which contains details for every imaginable application approved by construction super-vision agencies rather than develop one's own "simple" details. But perhaps the most important realization of all is that one must simply design to be in a position to build simply. And to me, such a proposition is not at all limiting. On the contrary, it offers an opportunity to con-tinue to develop.

Sustainable, Dense, Simple:
A Manifesto

My colleague Roger Boltshauser has long grappled with similar questions. In 2020, we joined forces to prepare a contribution to the exhibition entitled "urbanaible – stadthaltig" at the Akademie der Künste in Berlin. We showed projects by our students at the ETH Zurich and the TU Munich, as well as projects from our respective offices. In our text for exhibition catalogue, we did not want to limit ourselves to descriptions of our projects but instead wrote a manifesto that illustrates how buildings could and should be erected:

The building industry currently accounts for more than a third of the global resource consumption. Due to its unbridled growth, the energy expenditure needed to operate the building stock is ever increasing. Almost three-quarters of the primary energy requirement is still covered by conventional fossil fuels. Like most building materials, these are finite in their availability. The same is true of land. Every day, natural and cultivated landscapes are losing valuable acreage to the construction of buildings and infrastructure. However, the long-term disposal of many building materials that are used—and approved by the building authorities—remains unresolved. Constantly increasing requirements, along with ever more demanding legal provisions, lead to overcomplicated structural solutions and buildings that are overburdened with technical equipment, which overtaxes residents and users thus renders the buildings' adaptability and service life insufficient.

We can only meet our responsibility to future generations if we manage to use raw materials, energy, and land as sparingly as possibly in the future.

From this, the following requirements for contemporary building can be derived:

—Reduce land consumption for all construction projects in both town and countryside! Implement appropriate density within existing settlement structures; develop living and working forms that allow a reduction of available area per person; reduce the energy consumption arising from building site–induced user mobility.

—Use the building stock as a resource of space and material! Recycle, in the uppermost quality, building materials when demolishing buildings; give more attention to converting existing buildings.

—Use materials that consume as little grey energy as possible, are easy to recycle, or can be returned into the natural cycle! Whenever feasible, use renewable materials or materials with a good CO_2 balance; increase the use of regionally or locally available building materials.

—Construct buildings with the lowest possible energy consumption during operation! Use renewable (preferably regional) energy sources; consider the regional climate; reduce the technology required to the absolute minimum; use architectural instead of technical elements.

—Develop durable, robust buildings that are easy to use! Question exaggerated demands; concentrate on the essentials—on what we as a society, but also as individuals, really need in order to live.

These demands can only be met if climate aspects are considered from the very start of the design process. Dealing with these issues not only contributes to the responsible use of available resources but also allows us to find a new contemporary architectural expression.

The Simple's Strength
Rethinking Vernacular Form

Klaus Zwerger

For decades, ways of thinking about "the vernacular" have oscillated between two poles: at one end, a romantic idealization, and at the other, the critique that architectural, sociological, and cultural realities have been naïvely disregarded. The entire spectrum can be found both in poorly substantiated statements and in scholarly articles. The equation *vernacular architecture = traditional building forms = good* is naïve. It is based on the false premise that our predecessors have already found perfect solutions to all pertinent questions and problems. More specifically, the equation obscures our view of the continuously changing interdependency of architecture, building process, material, time, usage, and user. Architecture derives its identity from its users. The choices made regarding the material, its procurement, the construction process, and the furnishings reflect social, economic, cultural, and material processes embedded in cultural traditions. We must rethink these traditions in light of contemporary needs. The climate crisis hanging over us like a sword of Damocles and the reckless exploitation of our planet at the expense of those whose voices are not heard provided the impetus for my essay "Vernacular Architecture."—[1] There are "only" few who question the urgency of a fundamental change in our thinking, of a profound reorientation, particularly in architectural practice.

[1] See Zwerger, Klaus: "Vernacular Architecture: A Term Denoting and Transporting Diverse Content." In: *Built Heritage*, no. 3, 2019, pp. 14–25

Tradition inherent to vernacular architecture is expressed in continuous adaptation to changing conditions. The changes were based primarily on the efforts of an individual or on the reflection about making desired modifications. Knowledge and experience gained from such efforts goes hand in hand with appreciation—or at least respect—for our built surroundings.—[2] Who among us views slums as models for our inhabitation? Yet there are lessons to be learned from such housing. If our aim is to manage natural resources equitably and without depleting nature, then we must look, for example, to the settlements of the poorest people and to the detailing of centuries-old farmhouses for new ideas. Sustainability has many faces.

Taking themes such as identity and an individual's efforts into consideration brings us to manual work. Manual work is not the opposite of brainwork. Nor is it an imprecise, slow alternative to machine work. If manual work is seen as an expression of experience and accumulated knowledge that grows over time as the skill is put into practice, it is an asset. It allows a flexible response to contingencies at any time. Ideally this process is accompanied by constant dialogical exchange between practical action and reflection.

If *vernacular* is understood as usage in everyday life by ordinary people in a particular region that brings about dependence and embeddedness, it stands in opposition to individualism. In its extreme form, individualism causes people to act recklessly, lack consideration for others, and neglect the responsibility they have for their neighbors' well-being. Not until the individual acquires a sense of collective responsibility can a place become imbued with the vitality that allows people to identify with it. Gion A. Caminada recognizes a basic human need in the "sense of belonging" that appears to be missing in the eyes of so many despite the considerable improvements to the standard of contemporary housing.—[3]

2   See Strasser, Susan: *Waste and Want: A Social History of Trash*. New York 2000, pp. 10–11

3   See Caminada, Gion A.: "Faith in a Community." In: Girot, Christophe et al. (eds.): *Topology*. Zurich 2013, p. 56

Perhaps examples of vernacular architecture from the past can help generate ideas for a vernacular architecture of the present. Experience does not lend itself to generalization. Experience thrives on being challenged anew. It craves perpetual development. Verbal expression might be too limiting to transport the variety and nuance of impressions comparably in-depth to images.—[4] Images should spur innovation—not imitation. The examples' simplicity underscores their intrinsic strength. Rethinking vernacular architecture will require a realm free of profit-oriented pursuits. We must find contextualized parameters for specific functions. In the future, architecture must again be beneficial enough to be appreciated and preserved for generations to come because it provides us with places to identify with.

4   See Cooper, Nigel et al.: "Aesthetic and Spiritual Values of Ecosystems: Recognising the Ontological and Axiological Plurality of Cultural Ecosystem 'Services.'" In: *Ecosystem Services*, no. 21, 2016, pp. 218–29

The passage of time becomes inscribed in architecture as a site-specific alteration of an earlier state. Time will tell how a material ages and develops a patina. If architecture is to be sustainable, it must anticipate the aging process.
Krzemienica, Poland

What appeals to us about walking through an allée? The rhythmic interplay of the trees—or, more precisely, of the tree trunks—defining the
space triggers a cascade of emotions: a sense of security, safety, structure,
guidance. Conversely, which mental processes are involved when we let
hard-driving engineers convince us to eliminate columns at all costs?

St. Cyr-sur-Nenthon, France; Lucijani, Croatia; Villeron, France;
Holzkirchen, Germany

A carefully arranged pile of firewood is no better ventilated and no more stable than a pile cast off a cart. Properly stacked logs do, however, dry faster. Beyond such practical considerations, these assembled "architectures" depict the notion of spatial organization. The architectural forms communicate solidity and appreciation. The amount of time spent on the work signals this esteem. Such a pile records the actions of someone "dedicated to good work for its own sake," writes Richard Sennett in his book the *The Craftsman*. These archaic architectures have fascinated the photographer Pekka Turunen as well as the designer Michele de Lucchi, who focused his attention on them in his Cataste models.

Unterwart; Krakauhintermühlen; Oberhöflein; Gössl-Wienern, all Austria

Shakes demonstrate the vitality of natural materials. Because they are
small in size, they can be used to cover hips and valleys as well as ridges.
Grooved shakes must be thicker than face-nailed shakes, as grooves can
only be cut if the material's cross section permits it. Face-nailed shakes
may be split as thin as is practicable. Although they are typically small,
shakes require the highest-grade material. Such a categorization does
not, however, signify flawlessness. Irregularities that occur within a cell
complex are visible in the adjacent shakes as well. They continually
come to the surface and subside again. Laid next to each other, shakes
only seal a roof surface tightly when they are installed in the same order
in which they were split. The roof covering can be read like statistics
on a cell complex's regularity or irregularity within a log section.

Greschitz, Austria; Zakrzów Turawski, Poland

Hola, Poland; Teichalm; Maria Saal, both Austria; Bardejowske Kupele, Slovakia

Farmers apply their knowledge of wood's elasticity to their fences. The more loosely defined the usage was, the greater the scope for the design. Wood lintels are strongest if "prestressed." If installed correctly, a slightly crooked ridge beam will resist sagging as time goes by.

In the case of wattle walls, the fence was not the sole source of inspiration. The branches of hornbeam hedges are grown interwoven so tightly that they serve the same purpose. Yet they don't need any maintenance. Gardeners have long understood how branches can be trained to become intertwined. The future will show whether attempts to harness natural growth properties, in combination with the material's elasticity, will fulfill our expectations, or whether this is yet another short-lived idea aiming at quick economic success. The living root bridges in the Indian state of Meghalaya demonstrate that nature offers such options.

Pernat, Croatia

Wheel guards serve both a psychological and a practical purpose. Wood can easily be split with a strong, swift motion along the line of its fibers to cleave open the cell structure in the direction of the cells' linear growth. Using an axe to chop down a tree in the forest requires application of force crosswise to the fibers' structure. If the door post's base had been carved from straight timber, it would not be able withstand the impact of a cartwheel. The post's broad base—intended to repel wheels—would simply be chipped away. A well-selected piece of wood causes damage to the wheel and can wait confidently for the next attack. It was the carriage driver who had to be on his guard.

Cloppenburg, Germany

"It is only the design that reveals the function and enables the use" declares Hermann Czech in conversation with Tom Schoper. Curved supports can prove to be ideal if chance would have it: seeing the supports in the forest, having a suitable use for them, and coming up with the idea that brings the two together. The supports—the lower ends not in contact with moisture in the ground—hold up the protective roof shielding the hay poles (which are used just once or twice a year) from rain, need no maintenance, and are free of cost: a stroke of genius!

Gössl, Austria

Triangular bracing in Norwegian stave churches demonstrates the structural superiority of root flares; the eaves brackets of Finnish churches are, in turn, made of branch attachments. Many trees grow pyramidally. On account of climate and topography, some trees form especially strong root flares to provide stability to tall trunks. The outer contour of a tree corresponds to the cellular structure, reflecting the tree's transition from horizontal roots to the vertical trunk, and from the trunk to the branches. When the tree trunk transitions from its verticality to the horizontality of the roots concealed beneath the soil, the cellular structure follows it. This can be clearly seen in the wood grain.

Petäjevesi, Finland; Torpo, Norway

Thatched roofs and grass roofs have impressive advantages, but also weaknesses. Considerable effort is required to maintain them. The ridge covering demands special attention. It must be crafted to withstand gusts of wind. Heavy crossed rods were the most widespread measure employed to keep the ridge cover in place. One distinctive version secures the grass sod ridge with "hat pins." Both of these examples share the usage of smaller pieces of wood collected in the forest. An experienced farmer seeks out material that needs little or no treatment.

Saliencia; La Pornacal; Saliencia, all Spain

Neither a machine nor the most experienced craftsman is able to connect a post to the beam above it more effectively than this construction technique employing three forked timbers does. The forked timber is an eye-catching feature in numerous genre paintings depicting the lowland plains of Hungary. The support holds the hinge of the lever that draws water from the well. The fork directs the load into the support. The material is used optimally: the wood cells in the prongs are aligned with those in the vertical support.

Cloppenburg, Germany; Böhönje, Hungary

Licht im Norden

Vor längerer Zeit habe ich einige Jahre an der Stockholmer Universität
Dienst getan, als ausländischer Lektor. Ich wohnte außerhalb der Kom-
mune Stockholm, in einer angrenzenden Vorstadt, deren zum größten
Teil lockere Bebauung sich in den Kiefernbeständen bis nahe an die Klippen verteilte, die das breite Fahrwasser von der Innenstadt hinaus in
den Schärengürtel und zum offenen Meer hin säumen. Von dem Holz-
haus aus, dessen Dachgeschoss ich gemietet hatte, konnte ich über ein
unbebautes Nachbargrundstück, auf dem die Granitbuckel fleckenweise
nackt zwischen Moosen und Heidelbeersträuchern zu Tage lagen, bis an
die steile Kante der abgerundeten Klippen gehen. Dort hockte ich mich
immer wieder hin oder blieb auch einfach nur stehen, sah auf das Wasser
hinunter und zu den Inseln gegenüber – Djurgården, das parkartige
frühere Jagdgebiet der Könige, mit Villen aus der Gründerzeit und dem
Mini-Schloss des malenden Prinzen Bertil, das längst Museum ist,
dahinter Lidingö mit Hochhäusern und großen Wohnblocks, den Hafen-
anlagen – und vor mir die vielen kleinen und kleinsten Inselchen im
und am Fahrwasser, Schärendampfer, Segelboote, ab und zu eines der
Kreuzfahrtschiffe oder der riesenhaften Fähren, die an den Kais nahe
der Altstadtinsel anlegen, bei Slussen, dem mit einer Schleuse versehenen,
engsten Durchgang des Wassers, das vom riesenhaften Mälarsee zur
Ostsee hinaus strömt. An schönen Sommertagen wurde der dunkle
Granit der Klippen warm, und wenn gegen Abend hin das flache Licht
von Westen, über die Stadt hinweg, das Wasser und die Ufer vor mir mit
einem abgemilderten, gelblichen Schein beleuchtete, blieb ich ab und zu
lange sitzen. Die Sonne geht sommers erst gegen zehn, im Juni noch
später unter, und bei klarem Himmel bleibt bis fast zu Mitternacht eine
glasklare, über dem Horizont leicht orange gefärbte Helligkeit stehen,
die mich immer wieder buchstäblich gebannt hat. Der Himmel erscheint
im Westen völlig durchsichtig, man blickt in eine unergründliche Tiefe
aus nichts als Licht, die Augen sind gefangen vom Sog des Unendlichen,
das anschaulich geworden ist, und ich mochte mir andauernd einreden
„es ist nur der Widerschein der Sonne, die auch mitten in der Nacht bloß
ganz flach hinter die Kimm absinkt und die Lufthülle um die Erde
sozusagen von unten durchstrahlt", ich mochte mich mit Erklärungen
und verfügbarem Wissen von dem Eindruck loszumachen versuchen –
ich konnte mich lange, manchmal sehr lange nicht abwenden.

Stockholm, das mir heute noch als die schönste Stadt der Welt erscheint, auf Inseln in dem Durchfluss gelegen, den der Strom vom Mälar
auf dem Weg in den Schärengürtel durch die Felsen gesägt hat, der süd-
liche Stadtteil ist an die Kante eines steilen Granitabbruchs gerückt,
der vierzig, fünfzig Meter zum Wasser abfällt, altes Arbeiterviertel, das
heute der Bohème und den Jungreichen gehört: Kneipen, Cafés, Galerien,
Boutiquen, und an der Promenade entlang dem großbürgerlichen Grün-
derzeitviertel nördlich liegen umgebaute Segelschiffe und Kutter vertäut,
schwimmende Wohnungen, die Altstadt auf der Mittelinsel, mit Schloss,
Dom, Börse, Schwedischer Akademie, ist von engen Gassen durchzogen,
die alle an die Kais zum Mälarstrom hin führen, damals legten dort
noch die großen Fährschiffe nach Åland und Finnland an, Touristen-
gedränge fast das ganz Jahr über, hohe, alte Häuser, edel renoviert, in
Ocker- und Rottönen gestrichen, die Szenerie, mit kleinen Plätzen, wo
sommers die Stühle vor die Restaurants gestellt werden, lässt eher an
Mittelmeerländer denken als an den winters düsteren Norden, und als ich
einmal früh an einem der Tage um Mittsommer, drei Uhr vielleicht – ich
kann nicht mehr zurückverfolgen, von welchem Fest ich kam, und ver-
mutlich wollte ich hinunter zur U-Bahn, der erste Zug in Richtung Nacka,
den Rest der Nacht im eigenen Bett verschlafen –, als ich hoch oben auf
der Straße am Granitabhang von Södermalm, von Katarinaberget also,
nach Slussen und zur der Altstadt hinunter ging, der Blick weit über
das Gedränge der Häuser auf den Inseln, auf den Buckeln landeinwärts,
Kirchtürme, Brücken, die scheußlichen drei Kronen, golden auf der
Turmspitze des Stadthauses, wo die Nobelpreise überreicht werden, die
Reformarchitektur der Vierziger- und Fünfzigerjahre hob sich in großen
Blöcken ab, und die berühmten fünf Glashochhäuser, Hötorget, wo man
in den Sechzigern angefangen hat, die Bebauung des 19. Jahrhunderts
abzureißen, große Quartiere sind für die monströsen Klötze der Park-
häuser, Geschäftsbauten, Bankresidenzen niedergemacht, an den Kais
die vielen ruhenden Schiffe, der Großsegler *af Chapman* gegenüber dem
Schloss, Jugendherberge, und überall die Stromarme, deren Wasser
schon in der frühen Sonne schimmerten, die in meinem Rücken aufstieg,
die Häuser am Altstadtkai mit einem glühenden Rot eingefärbt, die
Möwen schneeige Flocken, und über der Szenerie der Himmel nach Westen von einer nahezu weißen Durchsichtigkeit, ein Blau kaum zu ahnen,
eine beinahe schmerzhafte Klarheit über allem, da, als ich die Augen
nicht weit genug öffnen konnte, um all das mit dem trunken machenden
Licht ganz wahrzunehmen, musste ich mich festhalten an dem Eisen-
geländer, das auf der Begrenzungsmauer neben dem Gehweg entlang
läuft, ich wähnte mich wegzudriften, angehoben von einer Euphorie, einer
Begeisterung über mein Dasein in diesen Augenblicken, wegzuschweben
über den Felsabsturz und über das leuchtende Wasser hin in eine Leich-
tigkeit, mit der ich in das glasklare Licht überm Horizont eingehen
konnte.

Als ich vor Jahren zum ersten Mal an diesem Text schrieb, und auch später, sah ich mich erinnert an die Lektüren, die ich vor langer Zeit für ein Romanprojekt gebraucht hatte, Forschungsberichte zur alten Kultur nordwestamerikanischer Indianer, zu ihren Mythen und Welterklärungen, ihrem Götterpersonal, ihren Vorstellungen von der belebten Umgebung, die wir Natur nennen – die Kwakiutl, die wie ihre Nachbarn, die Nootka, am Sund westlich und nordwestlich von Vancouver lebten, waren sich sicher, dass die Lachse, von denen ihr Überleben abhing, eigentlich Menschen seien, Lachsmenschen, die sich einmal im Jahr in die Lachsgestalt kleideten, damit einige von ihnen gefangen und gegessen werden konnten, weshalb man auch die ersten Lachse im Herbst mit Zeremonien begrüßen musste, und man hatte peinlich genau darauf zu achten, alle Gräten wieder feierlich dem Fluss zu übergeben, damit nicht im nächsten Jahr einigen Lachsmenschen Gliedmaßen oder gar der halbe Rumpf fehlten, die Lachse also kamen zu Besuch, wie Menschen zu Besuch kommen, sie boten sich an, damit die Clans der Kwakiutl getrocknetes Lachsfleisch für den ganzen Winter haben würden, aber wenn sie gelaicht hatten, dann kehrten die überlebenden und die toten Lachse, auch die verspeisten, deren Gräten vom Fluss in den Ozean zurück getragen worden waren, in ihre untermeerischen Paläste zurück, gläserne Paläste in der fernen See, hinter dem Horizont, sie wurden wieder vollständige Lachsmenschen, und dort lebten sie bis zur nächsten Wanderung, so wie die Menschen leben.

Die Vorstellung von den gläsernen Häusern tief unter dem Meeresspiegel schien mir, wenn ich diesen völlig durchscheinenden Himmel im hohen Norden sah, sehr plausibel: Es war das ins Endlose reichende, wasserklare Licht, das hinter dem Horizont aus den Palästen heraufscheint. Man muss nicht an die indianischen Mythen glauben, damit ihre Bilder noch zu uns sprechen können.

To Design Is to Transgress: Toward an Understanding of Architectural Design

Achim Hahn

Architecture has an uncontested "seat" in the lives of people. From the practical standpoint, with respect to our day-to-day interaction with it, architecture constitutes itself, "unnoticed," through its thoughtful approach to dwelling, to designs, to building. Its counterpart is the expressive design of architecture since Vitruvius's "theoretical discoveries." This paper makes a first attempt to illuminate the connection between the practical constitution of our lived and built environments and the constitution of architecture by the architectural establishment.

1. Understanding and Designing

In German, the verb *entwerfen* (to project, to design) originally meant to let sink or fall, but is now rarely employed in this sense.—[1] We are more familiar with the meaning *shaping through planning*, e.g., *to weave, draw*, or *paint an image, to construct a geometric figure*. It is also used when something is designed in the figurative sense: something *takes shape, is formed*, also with recourse to one's own verbal competence to determine something *in broad strokes with words, to write, to describe*, as well as *to create something new, to plan*. The stem *werfen* denotes a movement, namely to propel something toward a goal. The noun

1   See Grimm, Jacob and Wilhelm: *Deutsches Wörterbuch*. Digitalized version at the Trier Center for Digital Humanities' digital database, 01/21 version, https://www.woerterbuch-netz.de/DWB (accessed February 20, 2021)

197

Entwurf (the project, the design) points to something in the future, a goal (*telos*). Ultimately, all design is anticipative. A person who designs is planning and anticipating what is to come. What the intention and anticipation make reference to must be identified prior to the actual design. In other words, the designer must become conscious of things past. Only then can they determine the future goal of the design. Designing itself is an action in the present and takes the future into account. Insofar, attaining the objective always lies prior to the act of designing. When designing, one is always already ahead of oneself. To a certain degree it can justifiably be claimed that designing also requires the ability to make reference to something ahead of us, to a primary design, to a design for living.

Designing draws on options among which human beings find themselves. The world and its conditions of orientation are givens. It is only in the world we have accessed and interpreted that we design our lives and go about setting them up. How that life is to be led and shaped is not programmed in detail. One can make choices and, through one's own decisions, design a particular future for oneself. Not making choices is of course also a possibility and requires active engagement. A person seizes the opportunity to study architecture and later discovers, within this field, the option to work as structural engineer or to design buildings. In their subsequent architectural work, they also have opportunities to orient themselves to one "school of architecture" or another, or to rely completely on their intuition. Seizing opportunities that life offers is always predicated on an understanding. There is an understanding about dealing with options by developing a sense of what suits oneself. One individual, for instance, has done well to change course to study architectural design. This understanding as being able to deal with options is a prerequisite to leading one's life. Of course, I am free to choose a different option, e.g., to study medicine. Life as a whole lends itself to design in the widest sense: it has to be led *somehow*. It is important to see that the options that are available to me are options in the world in which I live and with which I am familiar. Options also structure my social and material living environment and my dealings with it; I must accept them as such. They happen to me without planning. That they concern me, make me concerned, shows that I have taken them to be "mine." My ability becomes evident in the active seizure as practical implementation. I carry out the necessary concrete steps. But to do that I must already have regarded the options as mine. In this way, humans constitutes their lives not as autarch subjects, but rather in their responses to the experience or the facultative nature of life itself. We lead our lives always within the framework of the options that we have already seized. Being-in-the-world lends itself to this processual under-standing of and dealing with life in a familiar way.

This naïve being-familiar-with the things in our day-to-day environment (the German word "Zeug"—trans-lated here as tool or equipment—has a wide variety of applications, e.g., *Werk-Zeug* [work tool] or *Wohn-Zeug* [dwelling equipment]) characterizes our life practice. To master life, we must have a fixed image of it, of what the significance of the utilizable-things that surround us is, because, as a rule, this mastering concerns goods re-quired for survival. We have an understanding of how something can be of use. A house exists in order to be lived in. I ratify its "in-order-to"—*for-the-sake-of-which* buildings are erected to begin with—with every single perception of a house. By way of a particular chair, I always and necessarily apprehend its chair-likeness. That is why Heidegger emphasized "understanding" as the main mode of man's being-in-the-world.—[2] "But it is in dealing with the things that we understand, from the very outset, what something like a tool or things for use generally mean. We do not develop this understanding only in the course of use. On the contrary, we must already understand ahead of time something like tool and tool-character, in order to set about using a certain

2   See Gethmann, Carl Friedrich: *Verstehen und Auslegung: Das Methoden-problem in der Philosophie Martin Heideggers*. Bonn 1974

3   Heidegger, Martin: *Phenomenological Interpretation of Kant's Critique of Pure Reason.* Trans. Emad, Parvis / May, Kenneth. Indianapolis 1997, p. 16

4   This can be revisited in the attempt at reconstruction of the lifeworld of the "Ritter family," whose living situation suddenly became uncertain. See Achim Hahn: "Suburbane Räume 'als' Lebensräume" (2012). In: Hahn, Achim: *Architektur und Lebenspraxis: Für eine phänomenologisch-hermeneutische Architekturtheorie.* Bielefeld 2017, pp. 223–40

5   Hahn, Achim: "Entwerfen, Planen und Entscheiden", pp. 161–86, pp. 178–84

6   Hahn, Achim: "Das Entwerfen als wissenschaftliches Handeln der besonderen Art," pp. 127–41

tool."—[3] We have an understanding of what it is to dwell. Otherwise, we wouldn't know what to do with dwelling-equipment, the dwelling-things. In our dealings with the dwelling-things—[4] we carry out a processual, enduringly nonthematic "design" of living (and building). We are not conscious of the processual understanding of the lifeworld horizon of dwelling, and it does not at all trouble us in our daily lives. This horizon is undoubtedly a given. Not until we find ourselves in crisis situations, arising to the degree at which present housing threatens to collapse, do we become aware of the horizon and in this way become conscious of the being or the essence of dwelling-things. Not until then do we encounter our interpretations of dwelling and see that we have pursued a certain conception, namely, our design for dwelling, whose implementation is all of a sudden questionable and complicated. Here again there is never mention of *notional* explicitness or even *theoretical* cognition of designing being akin to how we lead our lives.

In acts of architectural design, the dwelling-equipment and the dwelling-things become explicit in their own way. Architects orient themselves within their horizon to the architectural design that the mode-of-thinking collective to which they are indebted has always carried out.—[5] This design of architecture, which anticipates its being and essence, is not thematized with respect to its origin and its justification. In practical, day-to-day design behavior, this is solely a matter of implementing the familiarity that the architect's backdrop of certainties offers, with respect to the concrete case at hand. Hence, only to the extent a design is implemented must it verify its aptness, in order to prove to be comparable to a "concrete theory" which has yet to show its suitability as a means of achieving life goals.—[6]

2. The "Poietic" Potential of Designing

Only human beings can make a project of themselves.—[7]
Only they, as *Homo symbolicus* (Ernst Cassirer), as *Homo pictor* (Hans Jonas), have the capacity to make themselves *images*. Designing presupposes and implements this "image-making capability."—[8] Yet it is initially irrelevant whether the "image" is produced verbally or in a drawing or in three dimensions. What counts here is that the capacity to conceptualize and the faculty of imagination are at work. Particularly the disciplines of philosophy and philosophical anthropology have considered and expanded upon this capability and this artistic force. Therefore, on the following pages I will take a closer look at philosophical positions that will help us understand architectural design in its particularity and distinguish it from other types of design.

Kant argued that reason only comprehends "what it brings forth itself according to its design."—[9] It draws on its options, for example, by dictating to nature which "questions" it must answer. And in doing so, it draws on "previously designed plan," which is to be rigorously correlated with one's own observations. The plan anticipates the being of the object that it has yet to design.

The term *poietical reason*, which the philosopher Georg Picht (1913–82) mentions when he compares a person's design actions with other human dispositions, is, in connection with Kant's discoveries, also of interest. Here a third kind of reason is consciously positioned next to theoretical and practical forms. "But the most uncanny and profound of all human abilities, namely, the ability to bring forth something which had previously not existed, even to create an artificial world, has thus far not been comprehended as an original gestalt of man's reasoning."—[10] In this context, designing is one of the activities that is subsumed under Aristotle's heading "poiesis." Generally speaking, "poiesis" denotes human actions which are oriented toward a goal or purpose and

[7] In French *projet* denotes plan, proposition, project, design, construction document; *projeter* denotes to throw, to hurl, to spray; to project, to plan, to design; to intend to, to decide to.

[8] See Jonas, Hans: "Homo Pictor: Von der Freiheit des Bildens" (1961). In: Jonas, Hans: *Das Prinzip Leben: Ansätze zu einer philosophischen Biologie*. Frankfurt am Main, 1994, pp. 265–301

[9] Kant, Immanuel: *Kritik der reinen Vernunft: Werke in sechs Bänden*, Weischedel, Wilhelm (ed.), vol. II, sixth edition. Darmstadt 2005, p. 23

[10] Picht, Georg: "Die Kunst des Denkens." In: Georg Picht: *Das richtige Maß finden. Der Weg des Menschen ins 21. Jahrhundert*. Stuttgart 2001, p. 29 The following English renditions of Picht's German text are offered in the interest of readability. We gladly defer to the translations of the forthcoming publication on his philosophical oeuvre.–Trans.

which, when appropriate means are employed, lead to an autonomous work that had not previously existed. Poiesis is the "art of bringing forth and producing." Here, "art" signifies that an acquired skill is a prerequisite for all created works. Without a doubt, "technical ability" presupposes a person's knowledge-based objective performance of reason. Picht now criticizes that the inner connection of the three Aristotelian fundamental forms of cognition—theory, practice, and art—has been lost. With his critique of the faculty of imagination, Picht argues, it is Kant alone who recognizes the "transcendental capacity that is the root of all creating."—[11] This capacity is interpreted by Picht as "designing." He alludes to Heidegger's terms *Entwerfen* and *Entwurf*, which he uses to construe human self-determination of being-in-the-world as understanding. Without engaging more closely with Heidegger's reasoning, Picht posits the "design" as the "basic form of all creating, all planning, and all producing."—[12] For him, the crux is letting the design—next to theory and practice—be considered an autonomous form of reason. "Designing is that original capability that enables people to produce and to plan, to build houses, to found cities, to establish nations, and to produce that artificial world that makes it possible for them to live in a hostile natural world."—[13] So what does that have to do with designing on the whole? It corresponds to an image that one forms of something that lies in the future. On the one hand, it should bear a resemblance to what we are familiar with; and on the other, it should be something new. How is that possible?

3. The House and the House-Like

Here, the *ontological* inquiry to which Eugen Fink referred comes into play, and which I will elaborate later. In a design, we determine the manner or *genus* of things. We know what a spoon is, what a cup is, what a chair is. If we

11 Ibid., p. 33

12 Ibid., p. 32

13 Ibid.

regard a new something as a chair or as a spoon or as a cup, then we exceed that which is purely optically visible, to arrive at the optically nonvisible, yet coperceived: being chair-like, spoon-like, cup-like. We transcend the individual entity in its manner of being, which must therefore already be familiar to us. We always already understand the individual-thing in its essential and characteristic way and gestalt. But it must be asked what it is that characterizes "a way." What is meant by "chair-like"? Is this a matter of properties that are connected with all chairs, or of options of usage—of the "place" of being chair-like, house-like, in the lives of people? The design seizes opportunities to determine the way something particular is represented. Here, too, the general only becomes clear by way of the specific. Because its details have to be read two-dimensionally, the architectural design of a building is a complete house in a manner different from the house that I grasp in its "involvement whole" (Heidegger), in which cases all of its "parts" can only be addressed against the backdrop of an overall impression in its familiar and well-coordinated meaning.

Such anticipations are necessary preemptions of our perception. To perceive something as a "house" and speak to it as such only succeeds in the everyday insofar as I am already familiar with houses in their typical form. "Typical" means that I have learned—by way of examples and counterexamples—to distinguish houses from garages and in the meantime have become capable of ascertaining certain forms as "a house," such that people in the linguistic and cultural community to which I belong will not contradict me. In the understanding of what is house-like about this house, I also constitute my own world. The world is not a container holding people and things. I understand world to be the horizon or orientational and behavioral options within whose open borders human beings lead actively grasped and shaped lives.

4. The "Seat" of Architecture in the World of Human Beings

This brings us back to Picht. He thinks about the design of a house and asks: What must the architect know when he designs a building? In addition to the technical-manual knowledge, which is learned, and the knowledge of natural sciences, which can only be appropriated as factual knowledge, something essential remains to be taken into consideration: the house must fit in the world in which we are enmeshed with our living and dwelling. Picht writes: "A house represents the whole world from a particular location, and the design of a house is successful only if it fits properly into the world context in which the house has its place."—[14] That means, however, that the productive ability to design always also codesigns the "image" of the world in which one day the house is to be inserted. Every design always also anticipates a world horizon in which the design should fittingly "sit." We are again thinking of options which can lead to success or failure. Poietic reason, following Picht, is always conscious of the rediscovery as well as the potential for failure.

In his considerations, however, Picht omits the "basic form" of design, which Heidegger referred to as *Verstehen* (understanding). Following Heidegger human beings *constitute* their world by always already understanding the being of the entity (the being house-like of the concrete house). Yet his constitution is not due to a "functioning subjectivity" (Husserl); rather, it always already exists in the world I have accessed and is a self-evident aspect of my world view.—[15] Because I always already understand and know what's what in my world, the *constitution* of living, designing, and building remains concealed in the background.

The commonly held expectation of architecture is that it should solve the problems of building technology and design that are mentioned in the brief. "Poietic reason" thereby supposedly mediates skillfully between the pur-

14 Ibid., p. 34

15 See Gethmann, Carl Friedrich: *Dasein: Erkennen und Handeln: Heidegger im phänomenologischen Kontext*. Berlin 1993

pose and means of building. And purpose and goal assign the product (the appropriate means) its meaning, *for-the-sake-of-which* the architectural design is to be undertaken in the first place. Architecture is sustenance, i.e., it is never an end in itself, but has its special "seat" in our life practice and usage. That is the only place to seek out the aim of building. We can draw near to this "seat" by thinking of the dwelling as humanity's *basic condition*. Thus, an architectural design has always been preceded by the practical *implementation* of a dwelling's design as integral component of our orientation in the world. If architectural design is about the manner of being of architecture per se, its implementation in the practice of life (dwelling) is about a person's reliance on resources for his manner of being.

5. Conceptual Design of the "Being" of Things

In the previous sections we have arrived at an understanding of design that has not yet been taken into account in the discourse on architectural criticism and theory. We will now retrace how the being of the things is "prefamiliar" or "accessible" to us when we perceive a concrete thing. This primary "knowing" of things in their essence also has an influence on the "preontological" understanding of architecture, as the architect executes it when designing. Eugen Fink (1905–75) ascertains that humanity must contemplate ontological experience. For this experience leads to the realization of "what a thing is, or a quality, what the general is, or the particular, the one and the many, what persistence is and essence, what reality is and possibility, or the essence of truth."—[16] The philosophical domain of ontology has to do with the being of the entity: "when and where and how do we encounter this 'being as such'? Everywhere and nowhere. We do not ascertain it, we know it before all ascertation." Fink writes: "Understanding being is the originary form of

16 Fink, Eugen: "Zum Problem der ontologischen Erfahrung." In: *Actas Dei Primer Congreso Nacional De Filosoffa*. Univesidad Nacional De Cuyo, Mendoza, Argentina 1950, pp. 733–41, here p. 734

familiarity, in which we always already stand and in which we reside."—[17] We must, in other words, presuppose the all-encompassing prefamiliarity of the world as the latitude of the being of the entity." We must, in other words, always already know the things, animals, plants, people *as such* if we want to gain something for ourselves from the experiences with them. The situation is similar with respect to colors, scents, haptic sensations. The *Seiendsein* (entity-being) of surface qualities, fragrances, and sounds is also given. "All regional differences are subsumed under the shared basic structure of being a thing. The pre-familiarities or 'a priori' cognitions, i.e., the precursors to all de facto experience—in which our respective dealings with the entity already take place—passed through human existence in the manner of the self-evident and in this way, evade the 'test.' The self-evident, what has always been familiar and without dispute, is the most powerful tyrant on earth."—[18] It does not, however, suffice to observe oneself, to retreat into oneself. What is self-evident to us is always ahead of this self-reflection. Fink proposes ontological reflection in its place. Such reflection "is the thoughtful comprehension of the *Seinsgedanken* [the thought of being], which otherwise dominates us with the power of matter-of-factness."—[19] The philosopher Fink is concerned with four questions: inquiring "into the thingness, into the entity as a whole, into the extents of being, and into the truth." But these questions don't interest us in everyday life either. For: "we live in indifference toward 'what has always been familiar,' and this indifference is what characterizes the health and self-assurance of life."—[20] It is about more than conceptualizing something preterminological. "Philosophy thinks the being, to the extent it *designs* fundamental terms, which from then on form the framework of the world; [philosophy] is the design of the ontological fundamental idea." Fink makes a case for daring to design anew and again setting in motion the ontological thought which the Greeks still

17 Ibid., p. 735

18 Ibid.

19 Ibid., p. 736

20 Ibid., p. 738

mastered in exemplary fashion. "The naïveté in our lives is the stillstand of the design."—[21] The basic terminology handed down to us has eroded into foregone conclusions that characterize our day-to-day lives. The time has come to set this in motion again.

Fink then turns his attention to Kant, because the latter decisively recognized the "design character of a priori cognitions." The ontological terms determine "what the entity is, how it is layered in Was-sein (the being what) and Dass-sein (the fact that it is, its existence), in reality and potentiality."—[22] Fink elucidates how "design" is to be understood in this context, and what above all the terms "a priori" and "anticipation" mean in this context, in reference to architectural design. In the everyday understanding, design connotes both the act of designing and its product, what has been designed. And yet the relation to time is essentially.—[23] "Design is a manner of planning ahead, of forward-looking regulation, of establishing a provisional directive or arrangement" and thereby precede what is realized subsequently. The design predates the "actual matter": "the architect's plan anticipates the future reality of the house and prescribes the process of the realization in construction; the design anticipates a matter and places it from the beginning within a single law."—[24] Architects have latitude: seizing upon opportunities puts them in a position to design a building. Options cannot be found at random, they must be suitable, i.e., they are what makes the work possible, so that it is coherent in and of itself and in its surroundings. Time always enters in as qualitative factor in each person's life and his individual biography. Thus, architects' experiences and what is expected are present to them without mediation. Just how they go about this reveals their creativity.

21 Ibid.

22 Ibid., pp. 738 ff.

23 See Hahn: "Architektur" (as in note 4), pp. 201 ff.

24 Fink: "Zum Problem …" (as in note 16), p. 739

6. The "Theoretical" Design of Architecture

What can be learned from what has been said thus far regarding a philosophy-of-science reconstruction of the architectural-professional design occurrences? Georg Picht identifies the architectural act in the obligation to "poietically" design a world that we humans have pre-conceived. For Eugen Fink, architectural design is an "ontic model" insofar as it shows and makes visible the architect's relation to the materiality of the things re-presented in the design. That means that architects determine matter-of-factly and unquestioningly the being of all architectural elements such as building, window, wall, etc., and their dimensions. What is carried out "nonthematically" in architectural behavior (designing), according to Fink, can and should be consciously the-matized in philosophical design: "The 'design' of philoso-phy is processual-precursory (a priori), it makes the rules for the actual, it becomes temporal in a 'thought,' in a floor plan, it is, moreover, a behavior toward enabling possibili-ties and is a creative act."—[25] What is significant, however, about an architectural design in which, obviously without reflection and unquestioningly, something is anticipated that should not only fundamentally establish the fineness of the design, but also, beyond that, the "essence" of the house? This is not the place to elaborate upon how Fink continues to pursue the ontological experience of the philosopher. It should in the meantime have become clear where the theory-of-science work should begin. Its aim would be to explore what has come to be accepted as natural, whose recognized standard in everyday practical situations unquestioningly provides a basis for dealing with the things associated with dwelling, designing, and building. For buildings are only designed when the needy human senses a need and a motivation, and thereupon "knows" that and how he can get assistance. The design of architecture is not at the forefront. The lifeworld being never had to become conscious of its design character.

25 Ibid. Fink hereby makes reference to the "design" of a theory of sci-ence for the nascent science of architecture. See Berr, Karsten / Hahn, Achim (eds.): *Interdisziplinäre Architektur-Wissenschaft: Eine Einführung.* Wies-baden 2020

The architectural establishment and its mode-of-thinking collectives are another matter: unknowing and naïve, they have succeeded in putting in place their own design of the dwelling and building things.

If the *lifeworld* is about the here and now regarding a concrete matter, e. g., understanding dwelling, what good it is, and setting oneself up to deal with contingencies, *separate worlds*, e. g., the institutional architectural theory, distinguish themselves by disseminating general propositions about objects. Such separate worlds do have a basis in the lifeworld in that they naïvely submit to the abundance of references, e. g., what the "theoretician" himself has learned about architecture by dwelling in it and observing it. In their *theoretical* attitude—turning away from concrete life practice—they aim for an "aesthetic-normative" design of architecture, which reduces it to general properties/characteristics, regularities, and notional statements: *commodity, firmness, and delight.* These main terms (like others in the same tradition) are by no means attained through empirical research. If it were to be posited theoretically and irrevocably and considered with respect to the thoughtful intertwining of dwelling, designing, and building, as well as the technological practice adapted to it, one *subject*, namely architecture, could be isolated and its essence could be specified.

Architectural design is necessarily administered as a transgression of life practice and its potential meaning. Since Vitruvius, with the "aesthetic-normative" design of architecture, there has existed an adjustment of the behavior toward dwelling and building practice.—[26] Since then, going hand in hand with *theoretical* architectural education, architecture itself has consciously and deliberately been designed toward a certain make-up of the being, in the sense that architecture's *being* is "always already" discovered a priori. This disposition ignores the pretheoretical understanding of the "essence" of architecture. Vitruvianism—[27] and significant parts of modern architectural theory—[28] have, in addition, ever more

26 See, in addition to the previously cited literature, Hahn, Achim: "Proto-Architektur." In: Feldhusen, Sebastian et al. (eds.): *Theorie der Architektur: Zeitgenössische Positionen.* Basel 2017, pp. 299–338

27 See Germann, Georg: *Einführung in die Geschichte der Architekturtheorie,* >

209

> second edition. Darmstadt 1987

28 See Kruft, Hanno-Walter: *Geschichte der Architekturtheorie: Von der Antike bis zur Gegenwart*, fourth edition. Munich 1995

successfully limited their subject area, regulations, and fundamental concepts so that an explicit *retreat* to lifeworld experiences, to the oneness of dwelling, of designing, of building, appears entirely out of the question.

7. Conclusion and Outlook

It remains, however, to be examined whether the orientation to a scientific mindset has the potential to reconstruct both the lifeworld and the professional, a priori design. To do that, this transdisciplinary science of architecture would, however, first have to become conscious of its own design of science. It would indeed take a stand for architectural design that verifiably aligns its goal to the core convictions of life, within which time and again the practical-everyday dwelling, designing, and building must discover and put into effect its "place." This task will probably not be left to an operational architecture institution that cannot build up any distance to its own way of thinking, as it is a consequence of the design of theory that has come down to us. Thus, in the end a question arises that cannot be answered here: how would a *science of architecture* have to be set up so that a critical reflection on design and apprehension of architecture's being is possible?—[29]

29 Important references regarding the establishment of a science open to everyday practicality can be found in Heidegger 1977 (pp. 35–39) as well as in Gethmann 1993.

The Essence of the Analogy in Architecture—
And the Spirit of *città analoga*

Henrike and Tom Schoper

Analogy is once again, or, perhaps more to the point, *still*
a topic of discussion in the creative disciplines of architecture and landscape architecture. In the eternal quest for
a binding design method, there is an alternation between
analogous and rationalist tendencies in the thinking and
in the shaping of city, building, urban space, and landscape.
But in architecture and landscape architecture, designing
is an act of creation, which—depending on the designer's
approach—is not only fed by the reference to the desired
usable space, the necessary construction, and the visible
form shape; designing involves a correlation, in equal measure, of experience, interpretation, and intuition. And of
these three, it is the seemingly subjective intuition that
commands architects' inordinate respect regarding both
teach-ing the next generation at our architecture schools
and explaining the reasoning behind our own designs.
Who would point to intuition to substantiate a design?
Yet it would be impossible to create something characteristic from one's imagination without it. So just what is the
source of this guarded approach to subjective intuition?
It has its origins in the complexity of the virtually unlim-
ited influences to which we are exposed.

1. An Attempt to Take a Hermeneutic Look at Aldo Rossi's Thesis of the *città analoga*

Architecture, in the field of (an always unfulfilled) design theory, is one area in particular where the elusive term "analogy" came to be applied in the nineteen-seventies: namely, via the essay by Aldo Rossi (1931–97) *L'Architettura analoga* (1975),—[1] in addition to the collage entitled *La città analoga* that Aldo Rossi produced together with Eraldo Consolascio, Bruno Reichlin, and Fabio Reinhart and exhibited at the *Biennale di Venezia* 1976. In both text and image, Rossi undertook a counterproject to the widespread conception of architecture, city, and society in a time marked by rationalism, which at the time were determined by a predominant line of thought: by quantity (as a synonym for quality in the late phase of the economic boom years), by looking to the future (as opposed to the past, which was still obscured by the fascists' crimes, including, e.g., stilted folksiness), and by the unequivocalness of perception (instead of the ambiguity of superimposition as had already been proclaimed in the philosophical postmodern work of Jacques Derrida and Jean-François Lyotard). Aldo Rossi, rather unfairly described as the main protagonist of Italian *rationalismo*, comprehends architectural design as an "analogy" in Michel Foucault's sense of the term. During the twentieth century, Foucault was one of the first intellectuals to pay tribute to architectural design as an autonomous form of thought and to reinterpret it as the "space occupied by analogies ... really a space of radiation. Man is surrounded by it on every side; but, inversely, he transmits these resemblances back into the world from which he receives them. He is the great fulcrum of proportions—the centre upon which relations are concentrated and from which they are once again reflected."—[2] This mirroring of conceptual references reflects the histories of individual stories within the design of the landscape, city, and architecture, thus becoming the objective of landscape and architectural design.

1 Rossi, Aldo: "La arquitectura analoga." First printed in: *2c. Construcción de la ciudad*, 02 / 1975, pp. 8–11

2 Foucault, Michel: *The Order of Things*. London 1970, p. 26

2. Ruminating on Relics of Time

In the essay "L'architettura analoga" mentioned above, Rossi attempts to explain his notion of analogy—that "inexpressibility" of his designs and sketches—by referring to the psychoanalysts Sigmund Freud and C. G. Jung:

> In their correspondence … the latter defines the concept of analogy in the following way: "I have explained that 'logical' thought is what is expressed in words directed to the outside world in the form of discourse. 'Analogical' thought is sensed yet unreal, imagined yet silent; it is not a discourse but rather a rumination on relics of the past, an inward facing act. Logical thought is 'thinking in words.' Analogical thought is archaic, unexpressed, and practically inexpressible in words." I believe I have found in this definition a different sense of history conceived of not simply as fact, but rather as a series of things of *oggetti d'affezione* to be used by the memory or in a design.—3

A certain word used in the essay catches our attention: What exactly does ruminate mean? The phrase "rumination on relics of the past" (to be understood along the lines of "regurgitation" or continuous "contemplation")—which Rossi makes note of in one of his *quaderni azzurri*—originates in a March 1910 letter from C. G. Jung to Sigmund Freud. In the letter, Jung attempts to explain a necessary differentiation of the forms of thinking which are embodied in consciousness and subconsciousness.—4 In search of a justifiable alternative to the ostensible rationality of an architectural design, Rossi identifies in C. G. Jung's remarks a significant differentiation of forms of thought: thinking is indeed always bound to the logicality of language; but parallel to rational, purposeful thinking there exists another way of thinking which is prelingual and nonrational and which is—chiefly—expressed in dreams, in fantasies, and in irrationality. Rossi recognizes in this comparative and quasi contemporaneous "ruminating" the opportunity to produce differentiated relations in architecture: between the collective architectural knowledge as pertains to a rational catalogue of knowledge (*l'elenco*), the concrete place (*territorio*), integral observations

3   See note 1; English translation: "The Analogical Architecture." Translated by David Stewart, published in: *a+u. Architecture and Urbanism*, 65 / 1976, pp. 74–76. Revisited by Henrike and Tom Schoper in 2021. In Aldo Rossi's original text, this passage reads as follows: Nel carteggio Freud / Jung definisce il concetto di analogia nel seguente modo: "... Ho / spiegato la che il pensiero 'logico' è il pensiero espresso in parole, che s'indirizza all'esterno / come un discorso. Il pensiero 'analogico' o fantastico è sensibile, figurato e muto, non un / discorso ma un ruminare materiali del passato, un atto rivolto all'interno. Il 'pensiero logico è / pensare per parole.' Il pensiero 'analogico' è arcaico, e non espresso e praticamente / inesprimibile a parole." Cited from Rossi, Aldo: "L'architettura analoga." Rossi / Helfenstein-Archiv, gta, Zurich, 228-1-26-1, typoscript, p. 1

4   McGuire, William / Sauerländer, Wolfgang: *Sigmund Freud / C. G.* >

213

> *Jung: Briefwechsel*. Frankfurt am Main 1974, pp. 329ff. The correspondence between Freud and Jung began in April 1906 and lasted seven years. At the beginning, the connection was fruitful because they viewed each other as kindred spirits and allies in their confrontation with the medical establishment of their time. As the correspondence progressed, the differences between how they viewed the discipline (*große Seelenforscher*; literally: great researcher into the soul) turned out to be irreconcilable. Despite the tragic conclusion, in which Freud put an end to their friendship, both received impulses—in particular, creative impulses—from the correspondence. It should also be noted that as far as is known, Freud never showed interest in the thesis on logical and analogical thought; no response to the letter dated from March 2, 1910, was found.

5 Lyotard, Jean-François: "Note on the Meaning of 'Post-'" (1985). In: *The Postmodern Explained, Correspondence 1982–1985.* Minneapolis 1993, p. 77. >

(*osservazione*), one's own projects (*alcuni di miei progetti*), autobiographical allegories (*allegorie autobiografiche*), objects of affection (*oggetti d'affezione*) and—vitally—the conscious selection (*la scelta*) one makes from this trove.

Linking objectivity and subjectivity in this "analogous world" already anticipates that in the *ana-logos* mode, *logic* is partially switched off, at least here it doesn't have the status it has in the "normal" world. Indeed, it takes a transgression of classical logical interdependencies for the analogy to unfurl its true force, to develop its own conceptual space.

3. The *Ana-Logical* within the System of Analogy— A Deliberate Antagonism

The etymology of the term analogy (from the Greek ἀναλογία = analogía = "proportion") shows that it is in effect a *proportional* system—it puts things, images, and/or terms in a certain, not universally valid relation to each other and attempts to utilize the similarity of the elements to arrive at a specific, particular, one could even say, willful conclusions. The ways of the analogy are, as it were, free and pointedly open, as long as the things/images/terms possess a certain similarity—a comparability—to one another. The essence of the analogy is based on the principle of reiteration, the reconsideration of once found and further accompanying topics with a comprehensible or simply subjective connection among and to each other: the goal is not what is "new" per se, not the "unprecedented," but rather that which results from reiteration and the subjective alienation of familiar elements. Jean-François Lyotard describes this phenomenon of reiteration with reference to psychoanalysis and the interpretation of dreams "as quoting elements from past architectures in the 'new' architecture" and as a "use of diurnal residues left over from life past."—[5] Like in a comparable "procedure in 'ana-': analysis, anamnesis, anagonia and anamorphosis that elaborates an 'initial forgetting,'"—6 working with the analogy requires quoting and reiterating modes which as a consequence—put in another context—bring about new relations and produce new wholes. The "*differend*"—7—not tenable from a purely logical viewpoint between the original content and the presented intention—is consciously countenanced here with the goal of an analogue linkage of similarities.

Lyotard uses the terms "cloud" or "archipelago"—these, too, analogies—in an attempt to present their hidden content to us in the form of a metaphor: the "cloud" with the elusive properties, continually changing, of the difficult-to-describe world of forms, in its interpretation subject to the ingenuity of the observer; the "archipelago" in contrast as a realm of islands, in which the properties *similarity* and *proximity* already suffice to reveal a world of comparables: the different types of discourse, e. g., within the framework of a design, correspond to individual islands, and it takes an experienced captain who can see to it that there is exchange among them and to this end can draw on the communication medium "sea." An extremely fitting "image" chosen by Lyotard, who, in his philosophy delves deeply into the problem of "dispersal between genres of discourse."—8

4. "Continuously Redesigning the Same Subject Matter"

But in our world or architecture, how does Rossi deal with the mode of analogy and the link between the individual islands of inspiration? How can the analogy be represented? For designing architects, the disarming answer is: by means of a drawing, better still, a collage, by processing the same subject matter—in Rossi's case, these are the "manically amassed drawings,"—9 his seemingly unvarying sketches, his constant repetition. In his *Scientific Autobiography* (first edition, in Italian: 1981) Rossi writes: "The compulsion to repeat may manifest a lack of hope, but it

> The term "diurnal residue" refers directly to Sigmund Freud's notion of memory and his thesis asserting that in every dream "we may find some reference to the experiences of the preceding day."

6 Ibid., p. 80

7 The term *differend* has its origins in Jean-François Lyotard's eponymous masterwork (Fr.: *Le différend*, 1983). Lyotard—though not directly as commentary on the analogy discussions of the late twentieth century, but very much as commentary on the difficulty of the era's discourse—introduces differend to diagnose the irreconcilability of the genres of discourse in the modern world with respect to terminology and outcome; he makes explicit reference to the "logical" systems our world is made up of and which hold it together—and pursuant to the differend principle—the conflict between the systems of discourse—do not presently exist.

8 Welsch, Wolfgang: *Unsere postmoderne Moderne*. Weinheim 1991, p. 259

9 Forster, Kurt W.: "Ein Mann ging kürzlich hier vorüber …" In: Becker, Annette: (ed.): *Aldo Rossi: Die Suche nach dem Glück. Frühe Zeichnungen und Entwürfe*. Munich 2003, pp. 32–41, here p. 38

10 Rossi, Aldo: *A Scientific Autobiography*. Chicago 1981, p. 54

seems to me that to make the same thing over and over in order to arrive at different results is more than an exercise; it is the unique freedom to discover."—[10] This is a freedom which arises from the reiteration mode—a paradox that should not be unfamiliar to designers of landscape and architecture.

In other words, it is not the built oeuvre that is primarily capable of unleashing the analogy and its crossreferences and comparisons, but rather the artistic externalizations in the form of sketches or indeed a collage like *La cittá analoga*. The strategic goal in the mode of design in our day-to-day affairs and planning is not only to portray space-defining design factors with respect to economic, ecological, infrastructural, traffic-related, and climatic factors, but also to take into account the (sometimes) concealed and thereby unseen history of a place in its sociological, cultural, urban, as well as ideational attestation. Not until these factors are represented in their entirety in a deliberate superimposition as a collage can we perceive the great complexity of the city as, in each case, a specific "territorio."

Attestations of the most divergent origin can and should be accommodated in the collage: the sequentiality of history as temporal, numerical, and textural succession of occurrences meets up with a collage's simultaneity of perception as a representation of images, drawings, texts, signs, etc.—such as in *La cittá analoga*. The result is not to be understood as the recognizable imitation of something existing or something in the future, but as an "imaging procedure" to enable us to become conscious of the complexity of man's cultural space.

5. The Inner Map, to Be Detected and Deciphered: "una geografia private"

Working in the analogy mode—or, in other words, architectural design in the spirit of analogy—involves directing one's gaze to something that is not visible: an inner map which one can intuit but not perceive concretely. What is the significance of this comparison? A map is a depiction of geography, of a given swath of land—it is not the same as this geographical segment of the world; it is both reduced in size as well as an abstraction and a translation of the concrete terrain. And yet the modes of representation of a map are institutionalized to such a great degree that the observer knows how to read them and can find his way in the concrete geography based on the abstract map. The analogy as mode of designing is therefore comparable to a map—the analogy, be it a drawing or a collage, is not design, and certainly not architecture. What it constitutes is more akin to an aid on the path to the design. This "inner map," this "geografia privata,"—[11] is fed by one's own trove of experiences and one's own memory, which we can never escape—this is why designing in the mode of analogy involves profoundly subjective thinking. Underscoring this, in his text *L'architettura analoga*, Rossi quotes Walter Benjamin's work *Berliner Kindheit um Neunzehnhundert*: "Walter Benjamin's sentence: 'But I am disfigured by my similarity to everything around me here,' might be said to contain the thought underlying this essay. It also accompanies my architecture today."—[12] The Benjaminian passage is thus central to Rossi's design hypothesis envisioning a *cittá analoga*: the ambivalence of one's own memory, which is both a boundary and an infinite trove of material. The expression Benjamin employs—*Entstellt-Sein* (being disfigured)—is quite deliberately not positively connoted, for the free *vita activa* is not always the basis from which we act when we design: that which arises in our imagination must (first) be perceived in its essential involuntary subjectivity before we can act on it.

11 Rossi, Aldo: *Quaderni azzurri, #19: Architettura*. September 6, 1975/July 76, note dated November 1975, Milan–Los Angeles 1999, n.p.

12 Ibid. Walter Benjamin's quote is cited according to the translation in Rolleston, James: *Walter Benjamin: An Intellectual Biography*. Detroit 1991, p. 12

"Collage als Analogie," Aldo Rossi/Bruno Reichlin/Fabio
Reinhard/Eraldo Consolascio, *La città analoga* (panel), 1976

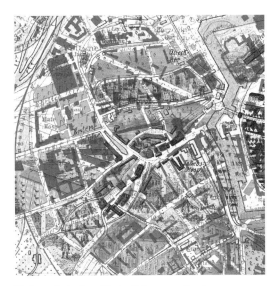

"Collage als Analyse," Luise Schumann, "Analoges
Dresden – Freiberger Platz," student design produced
in "RE-Vision Dresden, an advanced course" at the
TU Dresden, taught by the authors in summer 2021

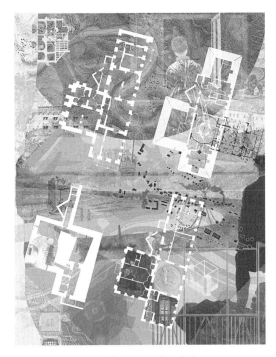

"Collage als Anamnese," references in a design
for Schloss Prossen, 2013–19, schoper.schoper
with Rosa L. Pakusch, *Un mondo prossiano*, 2019

6. The Analogue as Simultaneous Representative of Reality

Designing in terms of analogy—architectural work aided by the analogy—is not the equivalent of operating in vacuo. It is an activity that invokes a reality, and in it and on the basis of it, seeks to distill from infinite combinations of (just as infinite, as it were) things, found objects, impressions, anecdotes, and myths, something "other" and, of equal significance, something familiar. By this it is situated in an internal context with the fabric of that very reality in which the architectural design is to be inserted (for this is the very space of the analogy from which it also originates ...). Thus, in the sense and the spirit of the analogy, first the reality of a given context must be grasped. Only by presuming the reality of the context as sufficiently given and, in this givenness, as sufficiently reasonable, can we also engage concretely with this reality and formulate our thoughts on the new within this framework.

If we now refer to this context with reality in mind, we must remember that it is not "the" one reality at issue, but rather a compendium of what has been thought and of what exists—and this consists of four different forms and phenomena of reality: the anonymous, the real, the idealized, and the remembered. In Rossi's graphic chart of *La città analoga*, we reencounter these types of reality in four categories of the city: a) in the *topografia* as the earth (as ground) and *world* (as frame of man's activity); b) in the *città reale*, which, as existing city together with the topography, represents the framework in which the design thinking of the analogy may be integrated; c) in the *città ideale*, in which the ideal city is often conceived and dreamed, in which are found the variety of conceived, unrealized designs of cities, which in turn have nevertheless influenced the existing city in its development; and d) in the *città della memoria*, which contains both the destroyed, no longer physically extant forms of existence of the respective city, and, at the same time, the many invisible givens

that a city needs to support life (infrastructure, arrangement of circulation spaces, ownership constructs, etc.).
Upon reflecting on the forms of urban reality described
here, a cycle becomes visible, which indicates that the *cittá
analoga* itself represents the *momentum* of nonstasis, in
fact, of the dynamic change—which is part of the urban
fabric and therefore is in constant dialogue with the
many layers of history. And this perhaps is the reason for
the misunderstanding with regard to Rossi's notion of
the *cittá analoga*: it is *not*—the accusation often made
against Rossi—a romantic, backward-looking model for
contemplating the city, for thinking about the design of
architecture and landscape. But without memory, without
the view of the existing, of reality in its different dimensions, the new, which is brought into the discourse on
living with each other and among each other, will not find
a foothold in the context of history and the present. It
also reflects the main critique of modernism, which in the
nineteen-seventies had sparked Rossi's concept of *cittá
analoga*, and which still does not seem to have sufficiently
arrived in general thinking about architecture and the city.

7. The *cittá analoga* Situated between Architectural Strategy, Myth, and Subjectivity

More than a few accusations have been levelled at Rossi
and his concept of the *cittá analoga*: that he is hiding in
the realm of myths and out of touch with reality; that
with his subjective representations of the city and of
architecture, he has dedicated himself to nostalgia; that
this nostalgia as the symbol of postmodern architecture
would "ultimately lead to random games of interpretation
and a random assemblage of quotes."—[13] In short, the
recurring claim is that the result of the panel *La cittá
analoga* represents an all-too personal idea of the city,
and for this reason it is not suitable for further treatment
of architectural strategies. But is the superimposition

13 Puppi, Lionello: "Aldo
Rossi als Architekturtheo-
retiker und Kritiker." In:
Becker: 2003, pp. 56–67,
here p. 60

14 Franz Fühmann, quoted in: Schulze, Ingo: "Ich war begeisterter Dresdner." Deutsches Hygiene Museum (ed.): *Mythos Dresden*. Cologne 2006, pp. 19–27, here p. 20

15 Lampugnani, Vittorio Magnago: "Die Architektur der Stadt als poetische Wissenschaft." In: Becker: 2003, pp. 48–55, here p. 51

16 Ibid.

17 Ibid.

of layers of history synonymous with "arbitrariness," and myth with "nostalgia"—or is a myth perhaps more akin to what is "scientifically inexplicable about things"?—[14]

Our aim here is not to present the entire discourse surrounding this inquiry. But we would like to bring into play a possibly mediating term coined by Vittorio Magnago Lampugnani. According to Lampugnani, Rossi employed the *cittá analoga*—both in its underlying architectural principle and in architectural collage—to establish a "poetic science of architecture."—[15] Architecture has always struggled with the question of whether it is an engineering science or an artistic discipline. With reference to the notion of myth, Rossi found a possible answer: by expanding architecture as an engineering science to include the element of poetry aided by analogy. He argued, namely, that "the analogy as aid … releases typology from its history and its obligations, and makes it available to us thanks to the abstration gained thereby."—[16] The comparative analogy, he continued, establishes a connection "between analysis and design, between the investigation of the existing and the invention of the new."—[17] In *L'architettura della cittá* (1966), Rossi had still explicitly relied on typology as the "indeterminate constant in architecture." The changeability of architecture and its function, even while retaining its urban habitus, was considered the causal essence of architecture and the desire for permanence of the city. Ten years later, with his image of *La cittá analoga*, Rossi argues much more freely: his focus is no longer on the typology and its transformation, but on the inevitable change of the city in its form and being, against the background of its history. Thus, the analogy in its dual character of "absent presence" does not necessarily lead to the all-too personal theme involving a pictorial treatment of quotes, but rather, thanks to its abstraction, to a free approach to givens, which are now no longer tied to their historical form or their ancestral typology—an aspect that has now long been part of design practice and which has also exerted renewed influence on the teaching of design in the reciprocal opening of typology and function.

8. Where Are the Children of the Analogous City?

It is thus a bit astonishing that the analogy as way of thinking (which Rossi did not, of course, invent) and the collage as medium (which Rossi also did not invent) have
not become more widespread in architectural debate with
respect to designing against the backdrop of history
that we encounter nearly everywhere. Not long after the
presentation of *La città analoga* at the *Biennale di Venezia*
in 1976, this notion hit something of a dead end. Or as
Kurt W. Forster writes: "caught in a deep slumber, Aldo's
architecture today waits for the moment of awakening."—18 18 Forster: 2003, p. 38
The explanation might have to do with the fact that, on
account of their strong ties to Rossi's personality, the
collage and drawing as the main testimonies to this way
of thinking could not be readily disseminated by others.
And aside from less concrete references by architects such
as Herzog & de Meuron in their early years and the programmatic title of *Analoge Architektur* by Miroslav Šik
(who, however, had also incorporated other influences in his
design theory), neither the societal development (one only
need think of the fall of the Berlin Wall and the immense
potential that had opened up for cities such as Berlin,
Dresden, and Leipzig, as well as Prague, Budapest, etc.),
nor the development of architectural design techniques by
means of the computer and its image-producing programs
had helped the concept of *città analoga* out of its dead end.

The never-tiring critics of Rossi's ideas might detect
in it the limits of the *città analoga's* world of ideas. We—as
the authors of this article and as architects who fervidly engage with existing buildings and urban fabric—would like
to counter that building booms have not exactly been periods in which reflecting on architecture has flourished …
Our obligation to our cities gives cause to once again look
to the analogy as a medium of design and to propagate it
for architecture. For the analogy is not the mode of a retro-
spective way of thinking about the design of architecture
and landscape architecture: it is a method to find the new

by way of the familiar—and that is what humans look for in their designed environment: elements that are peculiar, that are different, that provoke confrontation—and which we can nonetheless name.

9. The *città analoga* as a Current Tool in Architecture, Landscape architecture, and City Planning?

From our remarks it becomes clear: thinking in terms of analogy is a mode of architectural thinking in conflict with the building sector's quantitative orientation, in conflict with the construction industry's quantitative orientation. For, of course, numbers—both with respect to surface area and returns—have no place in the mode of analogy. Nonetheless, it appears all the more important to situate the discourse on analogy and on the *città analoga* in the real world and make it implementable. For example, cities and city planning departments should no longer simply accept the wishes and ambitions of individuals, be they clients, investors, or private initiatives, but should instead make decisions based on the character of the respective city, which is always, on account of its own history, autonomous.

Accordingly, why shouldn't every architectural design— regardless of which city—be required early on, e.g., in the permit application, to explain its specific—analogue— stance toward the city and the site or its open spaces? In other words, *rationally* and *contextually* and *historically*. The analogue mode is not a matter of rehashing history— but conversely, "artificial authorship … is no excuse for a lack of historical awareness."—[19] It should instead be a matter of finding, from history and from stories, an autonomous sort of architectural response to the issues of completion, redensification, space-making of the city, the *locus*, or the landscape.

Along these same lines one can view the rationale behind the analogy in architecture and the idea of a *città analoga* as both an architecture-political instrument against the

19 Kuehn, Wilfried: "Aldologien." In: *Arch+*, 07/2017, pp. 47–53, here p. 53

international style of late modernism (from which Rossi may have formulated his arguments) and as a reasoning against the increasingly tiresome uniformity of cities in the early twenty-first century. Because following the repeated stock market crashes, architecture in the form of real estate has proven itself able to withstand crisis, our cities must now pay the societal price for the urge of individuals to secure yields: buildings (here we consciously avoid the word architecture) that pay no heed to the uniqueness of cities and cultural landscapes but are instead dedicated to profit maximization as the repetition of something that has already worked in this spot—by which we mean: what can be rented out or sold. Thus, nowadays *città analoga* denotes a critical engagement with the sort of building that fosters yields, not something to identify with in the places where it occurs.

So let us again attempt to find a way back to the independence of the city, the urban and the landscape space, to the autonomy of architecture and landscape architecture, beyond styles and fashions, beyond economic expectations and yields—the analogical mode, which is capable of touching so many layers of perception, could offer a path toward this goal in the design of (landscape) architecture.

Remnants of wallpaper dating from the nineteenth century on the living room wall
of a 700-year-old wood house, Steinen (CH)

Carpet of Memory:
Messages from Monuments

Nott Caviezel

Monument preservationists like to use metaphors to illustrate and substantiate the relevance of what they do. Symbols that expand upon what the subject matter of the monument is, that explain essence, character, and potential and endow it with more clarity, can definitely be helpful. In a sense, metaphors are vivid placeholders that, with the transferal of the actual context of meaning to something else, allow considerable leeway for different perceptions and interpretations.

Even in the earliest phases of modern historiography, for example, there is mention of the monument as a document which certifies its authenticity and, in association with the archive, also gives sustenance to the conception of the monument as a reservoir of memory. It was historians during the second half of the nineteenth century—first and foremost Johann Gustav Droysen (1808–84), later also Jakob Burckhardt (1818–97) and Ernst Bernheim (1850–1942)—who, in their theory and teaching, testified to material artifacts' value as a source, similar to that of the document.—[1] In 1882, the historian Moritz Thausing (1838–84) even mentioned, in reference to the restoration of Vienna's St. Stephen's Cathedral (of which he was critical), the monument as the "most venerable of all documents."—[2] The essence of records as historical documents, which possess an authenticity certifying a message from the past, fit quite well into the intended monument-

1 Warnke-De Nobili, Stephanie: "Die Materialität historischer Quellen und der historischen Zeugniswert von Denkmalen; ein quellenkundlicher Streifzug." In: Meier, Hans-Rudolf / Scheurmann, Ingrid / Sonne, Wolfgang: Werte: *Begründungen der Denkmalpflege in* >

> *Geschichte und Gegen-*
wart. Berlin 2013,
pp. 102–111

2   Published in the *Neue*
Freie Presse, April 26, 1882,
p. 3, quoted in Mahringer,
Paul: "Zwischen dem Spie-
gelbilde: Lebensfähige
Denkmale und StoryTelling
in der Denkmalpflege." In:
ÖZKD LXXI. 2017, 2/3,
pp. 171–74

preservationist shift in paradigm at the threshold to the twentieth century: away from the stylistically pure restoration in the tradition of the Frenchman Eugène Emmanuel Viollet-le-Duc (1814–79) and toward a monument preservation that takes into account as many layers of time as possible. This "accrued" state of the monument, which is reminiscent of the natural growth of a plant, including the change that occurs over the course of its life, actually contradicts the immutable value of the monument as document. But the record—which played a role in the auxiliary sciences of history and in the legal context when efforts were underway around 1900 to establish monument preservation as a scholarly discipline—was a welcome metaphor. Though no longer used as often, it has standing to this day, namely as an explanatory illustration of genuineness.

A related conception of the monument suggests reading monuments like a book. This notion is less strictly oriented to the semantic level of evidence, and more so to achieving the greatest possible readings, and ultimately the richness of history and of the stories that a book, or a monument understood as a book, can share with us. The existence of such layers of time, with their vestiges in monuments and in historic buildings in the most general sense, demonstratively stands for the becoming and dissipating of things, particularly in our time. In Germany, it has even become respectable—without necessity—to reconstruct buildings that disappeared long ago, reflecting interests that go over and beyond any sort of authenticity fetishism. Monument preservation has thus become a crucial test, revealing such reconstructions to be new buildings without a past and not acts of historic conservation.

An open book that is worth reading also fits as a metaphor for the landscape, as stratigraphy concretely narrating history's long duration, its layers of time. Tilmann Breuer (*1931), an art historian and long-standing art cataloguer at the Bayerisches Landesamt für Denkmalpflege (Bavarian State Office for Monument Protection), spoke of the cultural landscape as a boundless book of history.—[3] Reading the landscape is a metaphor that has a correlation in deciphering monuments. Both require a certain effort, as well as knowledge and experience. The rational analysis seeking to decipher what is visible and extant is one approach. The perception of the environment is, however, to a great extent also borne by subjective sentiments, which influence our attitude toward life, sometimes flaring as special moments, sometimes as lasting impressions that linger in memory. Subjective atmospheres evoke emotions, not seldom touching our souls. For example, when perched at a high elevation, we can survey the landscape: the ancient walls we see remind us of times past and the temporality of all things and of our own existence. In such moments, nothing is read and nothing analyzed, just felt and experienced, beneficial to the senses, atmospheres in the analogue world.

was alles wächst—how everything grows!

Atmosphere is a key concept in the systematic approach to the values of monuments that Alois Riegl (1858–1905) elucidated in his renowned text (1903) on modern historic preservation.—[4] Riegl links the atmosphere that a monument can create to the *Alterswert* (age value)—the relationship between age and value—which for its part is intrinsically related to the evolved state of the monument. To a special degree, with his notion of *Alterswert*, Riegl emphasizes the monument's proximity to nature: "the evidence of the passage of time has a calming effect on human beings as witnesses to the laws of nature, which all human works are certainly and unerringly subject to."—[5] In a text that appeared two years later, Riegl takes this idea a step further, seeing "the modern cult of monuments of increasingly being compelled to view the monument not as a work of human beings, but as a work of nature."—[6] Even before the turn of the century, this point of view, which definitely sought to have consequences for

3   Breuer, Tilmann: "Ergebnisse, Probleme und Desiderate der Denkmalerfassung auf dem Lande." In: *Bauen und Bewahren auf dem Lande*, documentation of the seventh press tour of the Deutsches Nationalkomitee für Denkmalschutz in association with the Bayerisches Landesamt für Denkmalpflege, September 23–24, 1981. Bonn 1981, pp. 16–17, esp. p. 17

4   Riegl, Alois: *Der moderne Denkmalkultus, sein Wesen und seine Entstehung.* Vienna 1903. Printed with other important texts in: *Konservieren, nicht restaurieren: Streitschriften zur Denkmalpflege um 1900.* Bauwelt Fundamente 80. Braunschweig / Wiesbaden 1988, pp. 43–87

5   Ibid., p. 57.

6   Riegl, Alois: "Neue Strömungen in der Denkmalpflege." In: Dvořák, >

> Max / Kubitschek,
Wilhelm/Riegel, Alois (eds.):
Mitteilungen der k.k. Zen-
tralkommission für Erfor-
schung und Erhaltung der
Kunst- und historischen
Denkmale, third series,
vol. 4, Vienna 1905. Printed in: *Konservieren, nicht*
restaurieren: Streitschriften
zur Denkmalpflege um 1900.
Bauwelt Fundamente 80,
Braunschweig/Wiesbaden
1988, pp. 104–19

7   Quoted in Lehne,
Andreas: "Denkmalschutz –
Landschaftsschutz: Zwei
Seiten derselben Medaille?"
In: *Denkmal heute*. 1 / 2014,
pp. 28–31

8   See note 3, p. 48

monument preservation, had appeared on the horizon.
When Riegl authored the charter of the K.k. Central-
Commission zur Erforschung und Erhaltung der
Baudenkmale in 1899, he stated that "conservators should
take a stand not only for conservation of monuments
and groups of monuments, but also for 'squares, vedutas,
indeed entire townscapes,' and moreover '[it is] always
[necessary to] take care that the landscape element, which
plays a major role in such overall images, … always be
retained to the greatest possible extent.'"—[7] It is quite
logical to think that a landscape and the built structures
within it interdependently belong together, and the beginning of the twentieth century saw the emergence of a
preservation movement, the *Heimatschutzbewegung*, that
actively supported this holistic viewpoint. Nevertheless,
historic preservation and nature conservation drifted
apart. By the interwar period, they already had become
separate administrative and legal entities. This distinction between areas that actually belong together is one
of the reasons we presently have such a hard time with
a conservationist approach to the cultural landscape. The
appropriate parameters are even often lacking, though
this is precisely what would be needed to attain the
wholeness of the cultural landscape with a spatial(-geo-
graphical) and a temporal(-historical) dimension that,
both in rural and in urban areas, comprises all functions
that regulate space.

In places that have evolved over time, where surfaces
bear evidence of the passage of time and a patina has accrued, concrete earthly existence becomes manifest. The
Alterswert as clear proof of "the notion of the nomological
cycle of becoming and decaying, of the emergence of the
particular from the general and its inevitable gradual dis-
sipation back to the general," does not imply stillstand,
but rather movement and change.—[8] The natural, living
landscape with its topography and vegetation, as well as
the landscape that has been shaped over the course of
centuries and millennia, reveal this inexorable processes

of change, onto which we humans also have inscribed ourselves. This existential and conciliatory insight demands respect and care from us humans for both the monument and the landscape, considering that, if we gauge it by Fernand Braudel's historic "longue durée," the "languidly flowing history," our own lifetimes are the equivalent of not much more than the blink of an eye.—[9]

9   Braudel, Fernand: *La Méditerranée et le monde méditerranéen à l'époque de Philippe II*, Paris 1949. English edition: *The Mediterranean and the Mediterranean World in the Age of Philip II*. 3 vols., Berkeley 1995

unheile Eile—fateful haste

Historic preservation is a calm affair. It requires time and patience, because the subject matter, the places, and the objects with which it must engage did not come into existence overnight. Before any random construction measures are implemented, the variety of existing *Denkmalwerte* [*values of the monument*] at and in historic buildings should be examined, as should the materiality, so that one can allow the particularity of a site's aesthetic expression and spiritual message, its characteristic atmosphere, to have their effect: Can I recognize different layers of history? How are they to be interpreted and evaluated? Where are interventions necessary and how should they be carried out without compromising the *Alterswert* in the process? What is patina and what is dirt? These are some of the questions that arise when the aim is to retain and refurbish a historic building, and repairing it has priority over its oftentimes violent renewal. These questions can also be asked in reference to the landscape. Recklessly dismantling or removing what has evolved over time is generally to be avoided, for what is gone is gone and cannot be recreated. When in doubt, "in dubio pro reo."

To this day, the urge to sacrifice, to our frequently short-term needs, what has been handed down to successive generations remains unabated. The rampant growth, often exorbitantly far-reaching and eating into the monotonous landscape made up of infrastructures and buildings,

231

is confronted with alternatives that, carelessly applied, can be just as destructive and oppressive. If we want to put an end to wasteful land use and the increase in impervious surfaces, a logical response would be to find new ways to use and convert the building stock. This, however, puts pressure exceeding anything experienced thus far on historic settlements and buildings, because historic buildings cannot accommodate every type of subsequent use. In retrospect, during the period of time spanning from the postwar era to the present day, the exhaustion and destruction of the landscape makes clear what can happen to the historic building stock when the concept for the use and of the subsequent reuse is rashly put together and based solely on economic considerations. But paying heed to ecological sustainability and careful consumption of resources cannot offset cultural sustainability, a criterion that reaches far back in time and simultaneously embodies both the present day and a view to the future, yet tends to be forgotten. When it is a matter of preserving the existing atmosphere, even clever and meaningful contextually attuned interventions and additions, which of course can be reconciled with the notion of repair, demand that those involved have a pronounced consciousness of the value of "the existing" would be something like "the activity of existing."

It goes without saying that the opportunity to gain access to the actual historic building stock is an absolute prerequisite. Ultimately, what is needed is the continuation of a—sometimes lost—culture of nurturing that had devoted itself to historic (monument) preservation. If nature conservancy and historic preservation were to reach out to each other more often, it would be a step in the right direction. Not least of all, the kinship of biodiversity, on the one hand, and cultural diversity, on the other, would offer a common thread that here and there would carry along with it a basically similar motivation for preservation and maintenance. The care and maintenance of the landscape, which by its very nature must take longer periods of time into account, and measures taken, as, for example, to plant trees, often takes generations until the intended effect is achieved. This too corresponds to an approach to historic preservation in the sense of cultural sustainability: the measures implemented for a monument imply long-term planning. Historic preservation will have a long-lasting effect "if [it keeps] as many options as possible open for future generations, both in terms of dealing with and understanding the object."—10

10 Swiss Federal Commission of Monument Preservation (ed.): *Guidelines for the Preservation of Built Heritage in Switzerland*. Zurich 2007, p. 89. https://www.research-collection.ethz.ch/handle/20.500.11850/81510

es promeniert—it promenades

One barely notices the fact that here and there, in every nook and cranny, whether in the mistreated landscape or in the building stock handed down to us, much is gradually disappearing, like an eroding mountain. Though these erosions might individually seem to be trivial, the insidious loss in its entirety is allowing what was once richness to transform into impoverishment. Or rather: many observers have noticed that the landscape is being encroached upon more and more by buildings, and that we are increasingly being confronted with perforated townscapes and meager, banal densifications that have no use for the aptness of an only seemingly shoddy historic existing building. Taking the time to leisurely explore our living environment—both macro and micro—might open our eyes and offer us a sensual experience.

In Bern, in the general vicinity of the Zentrum Paul Klee (1999–2005) designed by Renzo Piano (*1937), an unusual concept has been implemented. Instead of decreeing a new Paul-Klee-Strasse to honor the artist, the city named a total of eighteen streets and trails after the painter's works. The names of this essay's sections showcase a few of them. Others read, for example, *Gehobener Horizont (Elevated Horizon); Schreiten und Gleiten (Striding and Gliding); nur auf Umwegen (only circuitously); mehr Vogel (more bird); Wurm am Weg (A Worm by* *the Wayside); Monument im Fruchtland (Monument in a Fertile Country).* The paths lead along a small pond and across urban fields to the forest's edge and into the woods, and now and then the blue street signs appear in the landscape and the urban green, not only reminding us of Paul Klee and his oeuvre, but also pointing out the immediate benefit of the analogous experience of the landscape. With their odd wording they are irritating while also encouraging movement and contemplation; perhaps that is the answer to the work title and street named *warum zu Fuß? (Why on Foot?)*. The sound of the street named *Teppich der Erinnerung (Carpet of Memory)* is overarching, sweeping, and poetic. By invoking memory, Klee takes up a basic human need—which, like love, affection, and a feeling of security (once food, shelter, and clothing are secured) makes life worth living. Klee's *Teppich der Erinnerung* (work list of 1914, no. 193)—[11] is one of his earliest abstract paintings, which he began in 1914 and repeatedly painted over until 1921. By applying oil paint to an oil primer and a chalk primer on the canvas, Klee arrived at the appearance of a worn-out rug, a three-part allegory suited to both landscape and monument: the carpet as a memory spread out, through the repeated painting over of the layers of time, and in the appearance of worn-out carpet, the ageing and the age. Who knows if, in the selection of a title for his wonderful painting *Monument im Fruchtland*, Klee was aware that the word "monument" is rooted in the Latin "monere," "to warn or advise"—or whether he had in mind that the German word for warning or admonishing, "mahnen," is contained within the word "Mahnmal," itself another word for monument?

The proximity and the interpenetration of nature and art is revealed in all its facets. The frequently spiritual dimension in Paul Klee's works, which shows up, for instance, in his enigmatic titles, indicating a realm beyond the rational, in the depths of emotions, is also applicable in the discussion of the monument and its values. Riegl's

11 The exact location and bibliographical information for all of the works mentioned here can be accessed in the Paul Klee Zentrum collection's digital database: www.emuseum.zpk.org.

notion of atmosphere, as offered to us by monuments, as subjectively felt emotion, does not contradict the rational perception that monuments also call on us to contemplate. And so our perception of monuments, as well as that of landscapes, oscillates between its sensual-spiritual messages that we receive and its rational comprehensible material. In a speech given on January 27, 1905, in celebration of Kaiser Wilhelm II's birthday, the art historian Georg Dehio—who at the threshold the twentieth century was at the forefront of the discourse on the path to modern historic preservation—mentioned this special quality of the monument: its "spiritual-physical dual nature."—[12] Dehio notes that the physical nature of works of art situates them in the foreground of the predominant economic and legal systems, but that their "true essence" is nevertheless a spiritual one, although elsewhere it becomes clear that Dehio's use of the word *geistig* (scholarly, spiritual, intellectual) referred to the work's historical character. Dehio thereby promoted the aforementioned documentary value of a monument as its most important characteristic. Ultimately, however, his motivation to support historic preservation, which is based on the authenticity of the monument to be preserved, finds its complement in the more subjectively perceived dimension of the experience and effect of a monument. At the very beginning of his pamphlet against the continuation of the reconstruction of the Heidelberg Castle, he notes that ruins are not just witnesses to history, but are also, as a wonderful whole, "[interwoven] from ephemerality and eternity, from art, nature, and history, into one impression in a way that human intellect alone—or even the greatest artist—could never have accomplished."—[13] Ultimately, however, the overarching message is a plea for respectful treatment, or in Dehio's words: "Protecting monuments is not a matter of seeking pleasure, but rather an act of reverence."—[14] This fundamental attitude about how we approach our built heritage can also be transferred to a gratifying relationship between societies and landscapes.

12 Dehio, Georg: "Denkmalschutz und Denkmalpflege im neunzehnten Jahrhundert, Festrede an der Kaiser-Wilhelms-Universität zu Straßburg, den 27. Januar 1905." In: Dehio, Georg/Riegl, Alois: *Konservieren, nicht restaurieren. Streitschriften zur Denkmalpflege um 1900*, with a commentary by Marion Wohlleben and postscript by Georg Mörsch. Braunschweig, Wiesbaden 1988, pp. 88–103, esp. p. 92

13 Dehio, Georg: *Was wird aus dem Heidelberger Schloß werden?* Straßburg 1901. See xii., pp. 34–42, esp. p. 34

14 Ibid.

Prospectus for an Academy in the Countryside
A Dialogue

Jörn Köppler, Simon Strauß

Arbeit an Europa, a nonprofit organization, is planning
to convert a barn in Uckermark, Germany, into a venue
named European Storehouse. The aim is to create a
European academy: a public place where Europe's cultural abundance will be admired, discussed, and staged.
Particularly in light of the breakdown in trust in the
European Union as a purely institutional and functional
representative of European thought, it is crucial that ways
be found to engage self-confidently with the traditions
and potential of Europe's cultural dimension. For several
years, this nonprofit founded by young intellectuals has
been working toward that goal. It is guided by an idea
reflected in the paintings in Raffael's *Stanza della Segna-
tura* at the Vatican Museums—namely that Europe's
makeup is the result of the interplay of three trajectories:
religion, science, and art.

*The fieldstone barn, which is to serve as the European
Academy's base, was built around 1870 as part of a larger
farmstead. It had not been in use for several years following
its service as part of a collectivized farm during the East
German regime. Last year it was acquired by members of
the nonprofit organization and cleaned up. The historical
fabric of the building—which is situated on the village
square—is to be preserved and will thereby function as a
memento of the old farm ensemble. It is to be left intact to a*

great degree. A new wood structure only partially coming in contact with the historical structure will create a "house-within-a-house" that can be subdivided into different rooms.

Thus, it will not only symbolically but actually be a realization of the "storehouse" concept of Europe's history and substance: its culture, religion, science, and art. In this sense, the furnishing of the event space—which will be served by a kitchen, offices and restrooms—in the "store-house" is of central importance. In a subsequent construction phase, residential units for visiting scholars will be added as required. In the antique tradition, the building is to be framed and circumscribed by a garden with an inserted patio, bringing about a coherent whole. At specific points, the garden opens to the village square, incorporating the local life.

The idea of convening in a new space situated within old walls corresponds to Europe's fundamental idea: being both informed by history and oriented toward the future. The aim is to get the old group back together to continue the conversation and confidently head into the future. The existing building gives the nascent event space a foothold and a secure envelope: it is not by any means obsolete or in need of protection, but offers shelter from the elements and provides shade. In return, the cultural events and evening concerts, as well as civic meetings, visiting scholars' chats, and summer fêtes will put new life into these old walls.

Jörn Köppler An academy in the countryside whose mission is to reflect on Europe's cultural layout—on its art, science, and religion. What can the ideas signify—today, in the past, in terms of content, and architecturally?

My first thoughts on this (incidentally, I had them during a walk in the fields of Fahrland, our village near Potsdam), particularly on the spatial quality of such a place: images and moments appear in my mind's eye that I tie to this question and which I list here—in no special order—as a lead-in to our conversation:

field's edge
campfire
genius loci
stone walls as field boundaries
fountain
cloister
rain
"watering-can ... the water in it darkened by the shade
of a tree, and a water beetle" (Hugo von Hofmannsthal)
scarcity

Tusculum, Cicero—"When, therefore he [Apollo] says,
'know yourself,' he says this, 'Inform yourself of the
nature of your soul'"

a courtyard chestnut tree's gentling rustling leaves
and sun-dappled brickwork fervor, consolation

What do you think of these? Are there points of reference
that you can tie to the idea of an academy of European
thought in the countryside, in front of—historically speaking—the cities' gates?

S i m o n S t r a u ß Yes, especially Cicero's "know your
soul" strikes a chord. For, that's what such an academy
should be about: it should be a place where souls can
engage in conversation, and not where different intellects
talk past one another. Our greatest difficulty is still, after
all, how to find common ground. The most challenging
issues in our lives are not political, social, or discursive,
but have to do with the person vis-à-vis. How can we
approach each other in a way in which words are not only
spoken to boast about oneself, or don't fall on deaf ears,
but have an effect on us? When I think of an academy in
the countryside, I think first of all of time in abundance,
of a group that meets in a courtyard on whose edge a
fountain burbles and which is lined by an arcade. There
they sit in the morning, without a seating arrangement,

without a schedule. There is just this one question: What do you dream of?

And later the group takes a walk through the fields, down to the lake; along the way they pass by the remnants of stone walls which had been the foundations of something large and are now inhabited by lizards—the stones are warm, the sun's rays linger on the joints. One sits, one waits, one doesn't have plans. As Truman Capote put it, "I was eleven, then I was sixteen. Though no honors came my way, those were the lovely years." That could be the motto for the European Academy in the Countryside: the aimlessness, the roaming about, the walk across the fields, contemplating together, assessing, describing—those could very well be the mental characteristics that would suit your architectural associations ...

This "not having anything on the agenda," the unencumbered passage of time in summer, the midday heat, levitating, the aimlessness—indeed, I believe that moments tinged like this can be very important for the notion of an academy in the countryside: because they delineate the conception of a life other than the one that we presently permanently create in public discourse. Be it in the media, politics, commerce, science—wherever we look, we indulge in, how shall I put it, obsessions of perfectibility, in which notions of controllability of everything and everyone dominate the relationship between us and the world. In symbolic terms, human beings appear to have been reduced to functioning—to "performing" professionally and on a personal level, even in one's love for another person. What a pitiful thought! And what a paradoxical preliminary result of the project of Enlightenment, which set out to place contemplation above rampant materialism.

More paradoxical still, it seems that everything has already been described and criticized. Theodor W. Adorno and Max Horkheimer's *Dialectic of Enlightenment*, for example, has in my view said everything essential there is to say about it. Above all, the text mentioned the timely

point that pure rationality, seen in its entirety, as we adhere to it in our scientific and economic creeds, ultimately
converts into irrationality, because pure reasoning does
not—and cannot—know categories such as meaning,
morality, or "knowing your soul." Oh, yes, and then the
coronavirus comes along. The onset of the actual. The
great *memento mori*. And this is where, in my view, next
to suffering—or perhaps: through suffering?—a perspective lies. The possibility to shift the vantage point—toward entirely different realities and to try to discuss them.
Or even to shift it toward the educed reality, existent in
and of itself. And toward the solace contained in the words
you mentioned, a dream-like image of the light at the
field's edge—as an image of vitality, as a reminder of the
beauty of correlated lives.

Learning through suffering … Yes, perhaps. And yet, the
pandemic amounts first and foremost to a spiritual *cae-
sura*, a true break with all that is familiar and accommo-
dating. Of course, it is in some respects classic to dream of
an academy in the countryside in such times. The flight
from the city, which stands for all the frenzy, inexorability,
carelessness that put us at risk right now, to sparsely populated stretches of land where there is ample space and
time to allow us to consider the day from a remove and
see what remains of it if we take seriously what it could
be: a recurring preparation for death. Each day, to para-
phrase Montaigne, human beings experience an entire
lifetime in fast forward. They wake up, feel young, reach
their peak, become older, and die when the sun goes
down—in constant repetition. But we don't seem to recognize how valuable that is: this chance to prepare, to
rehearse our mortality with the help of the sun, clouds,
and light.

That is what an academy in the countryside should
(also) be about: taking the appropriate "spiritual-practical"
actions, as it were, to approach the fiery metaphysical
nucleus that nature keeps in readiness for us. And cor-

respondingly, such an academy should, I think, engage with an important concept that has withered away in what is becoming a small-minded world: beauty. But what does it mean when someone says something "is beautiful"? Is he not declaring that a thing or being in some inexplicable way stirred his blood, because there is something about it that has profundity? Because it cannot be achieved pragmatically, because it remains at the last instant impenetrable, does not announce itself, makes a silent appearance. But it makes a radical impression, tears down all struts and bulwarks. Beauty is found where there is no function to fulfill, and where it can move closer to the heart, not allowing any distance between the two. The time one spends with beauty is not clocked. A "time out," so to speak. One is on a detour, veering left and right of the straight line. There's no point in going on a quest for beauty, one must allow oneself to be caught and led. Not the confident self, the activist "I" is the focus, but rather the seeing recipient. Not the one who has always felt addressed, but the one who has long been waiting to be spoken to. Beauty reproves the ambitious, it protects the astonished.

In such an era, only the approximate can save us, the inwardly glowing—by which I mean beauty. We must build a casing, an open shelter for this thought, for this overarching conception—to protect its preciousness—not to privatize or musealize it, but to let it radiate for all who sense its liberating vastness. Not an easy task for architecture—but all the more significant, don't you think?

Oh, yes. This moment of beauty is, as I see it, perhaps the existential lynchpin of a way of building which, like Hofmannsthal's age-old "abstract words" that fall apart "in my mouth like putrid mushrooms," yet, at the moment one experiences beauty, can catch sight of a harrowing presence of the truth. That moment you so aptly described in which reality seems to become transparent, in the morning, in the light of dawn reflected on a table's weathered wood surface, in the light that shines through the leaves of a fruit tree, touched by the delicate shade provided by the crowns of the trees—this light of beauty seems, if only for a few moments, to connect us to the things and to reality and to say so much to us which we cannot distort instrumentally. In any case it seems to me that we have arrived at an almost infinitely fragile moment, for which I find no better description than as a feeling of fervor: as if we were looking wondrously for the blink of an eye at the truth, the basis and meaning of the actual. And how is it manifest? Serenely, inspired by vivacity through and through, gentle and complete—yes, full of delight. Affectionately consoling the finality of life.

In its significant works, architecture has indeed sought out this fragility, a manifestation of meaning, as you mentioned, to create a sheltering and mnemonic envelope. Like poetry in a metaphorical sense, it lends more time to such ephemeral moments and gives them a place in our lives. At the same time, for artistic work, in my view, there is another decisive concept in addition to beauty— the notion of *poiesis*. The concept, following its meaning in Classical Greek—"to bring forth" or "to let emerge"— holds that no human work can ever create the transcendence inherent to the moment of beauty on its own. Kant writes "that nature has produced it: this thought must accompany our intuition and reflection on beauty," by which he means, in short, that only the educed reality— and not the one that we have produced—can allow us to experience truth in the sense of transcendence. Or, as Augustine so tersely put it: "verum est id quod est" [truth is that which is]. Which brings us back to building in nature, the educed reality in the countryside, which in my view does not at all represent a flight from the city, rather a highly promising quest for this "which is." Because only from it, reflecting, might be derived "which is to *be done*." And that makes me think of Thoreau, who moved to the remote Walden Pond to build a hut with his own hands, because he expected this place in nature "to front only the essential facts of life, and see if I could not learn what it had to teach, and not, when I came to die, discover that I had not lived."

So how must architecture be constituted so that it satisfies this demand? Essentially, and the word essential is in all capitals here, it is quite simple from this vantage point: it should not be staged as a self-referential, obsessive work of purported artistic genius. It should instead be like the gestalt of the mighty Doric columns of the temple at Paestum, or the quiet alternation of column and pillar of a Romanesque cloister—built as a mnemonic, in other words, permanent reverberation of the ephemeral aspect of nature's beauty. And that ultimately is what architecture could tell us about: of such a precious moment of individual intersection of transcendence in the experience of beauty and the long, adventurous history of our shared narrative of import and meaning, starting out from these very moments: stories of water beetles, campfires, and burbling fountains in shady courtyards lined with quiet ambulatories...

... and with windows. They are, after all—in this sense— a building's poetic elements. Our protecting eyes to the world. Sometimes I think that there is nothing sadder for a building than having closed roller shutters. Nothing is colder, more unwelcoming, or lacking in atmosphere than barricaded windows. There are towns, particularly in the Uckermark, where the shutters are closed in the early afternoon: at 4:00 p.m. on the dot they rattle down heavily—metallic and guillotine-like—onto the windowsill. Then, late into the night, the bluish green light from the television screens flickers through the thin cracks between the slats. Unseen by the others, one prefers to look far into the distance instead of close up. Obstructing windows supposedly reduces heating costs—but this claim disregards the cost of keeping the TV running. Covering windows signifies more than doing without daylight and natural ventilation and suffocating in one's own hominess, more than disfiguring a façade. It is a violent act, coarse and abrupt. Spaces, even worlds that had freely streamed one into the other, though separated by glass, are now completely disconnected. At night when the streets are empty and the construction billboards blink lonesomely, if one runs out of thoughts and time passes agonizingly slowly, if one can't sleep and takes a walk in a dark city, a brightly lit window, even on the eighteenth floor of a dilapidated prefabricated apartment building, is some-times more consoling, calming, than a chat on the phone. Dark windows are like lifeless eyes, but when they glow, they come to life, are comforting: there is someone else who is awake, who is not asleep, who is sitting up there in his room and reading, perhaps pondering something, waiting for something, which one could gesture to or, in the most serious case, even approach.

And then there's looking out the window! Just peering out, without a plan or purpose, unrelated to forecasting the weather, unbridled. Doing nothing else. Sitting at the window and observing. Becoming a watchman: "Born to see. Summoned to watch." Holding one's breath, not looking at the clock, and certainly not at the phone. In the south, the old women lean out of their windows from dawn until dusk, they spend their time casting glances, and sometimes sentences and oranges as well. They look down with amusement at persons hurriedly passing by, what would he know about happiness and fate? Their windows are their sustenance, even organs with which they have become bound up. Through them they breathe and feel free. *Finestra aperta*: an open window is also an open heart.

An "open society" needs open windows—otherwise it will perish. When people in Europe speak of political unity and cultural fervency, I always also think of windows. They are the most beautiful symbol of our community, our connection across a street and beyond. As long as the nations leave their windows open, as long as we ob-serve each other expectantly, there will be a Europe—a beautiful Europe. When I dream of our academy in the countryside, I also dream of the many open windows, the wind coming through them, windows out of which people lean, cast glances at each other, become still. Basically, it doesn't really take much more than an open window to think deep thoughts. And a wafting fern just outside it.

Your words, your dream of a European academy, established in the metaphor and the concrete poesy of the window—they bring to mind the words "sanitorium of the soul," *psyches iatreion*, which are said to have been visible above the entrance to the library of antiquity, the Ramesseum in Thebes. For there is so much power, so much that is fortifying in the moment in which the introspective view comes in contact with the beaming exterior! It is, if I may say so, a lyrical moment; like the beginning of all poems, whose narrative would become the blueprint and measure of a window. Everything that we have said about beauty, the moments of fervor, the experience and memory of transcendence, translucence, can become architectural form here, can become that primary architectural element which indeed seems to be the embodiment of the poetic: because this form, the well-wrought window, only presents, presents, so to speak, from within itself, to you and to the actual exterior, letting it stay open, and does not lay siege to you and hold you prisoner like a screen bellowing "here I am." Are you familiar with the poem by Trakl, "A Winter Evening," which begins with the word: "When snow falls against the window,/Long sounds the evening bell"? Here too the memory of sitting at a window eating and watching time and life as the snow quietly falls to the earth. And the hope of being liberated from all the techno-mannerist decoration: designing windows which are commensurate with the here and now.

But now I'll take it a step further: first, the window, like the doors as delicate framing mediators, in front of them the landscape, gently rolling, the garden, the sandy paths upon which the scholars have place tables they have brought out from their ateliers to be used at dinner, for conversation, debate, and festivities. And arching above it all: the starry firmament. On the other side of the windows and doors, which are spanned by the old roof structure, stone bracketed corridors, in the semidarkness of the light from clerestory glazing which leads around the library and lecture hall at the building's core. Or is this space at the heart of the library, the "sanitorium of the soul"? At the center of the other fiery nucleus, in contrast to the metaphysics of nature—history?

Yes, perhaps the hall could be situated within the library, although books should never merely be bulwarks against the world around us. They must also be the gateway to thought, they should always receive enough light and claim their own space. So, as you describe the fabric of our academy—the lyrical concentration on the beginning, the framing opus of stone, which always also must be comprehended, the desks, the view up to the roof structure—all coalesces in the image of an auspicious educational establishment. In German the two words have a lot in common—*Bild* (image, conception) and *Bildung* (education, learning). Friedrich Schlegel was not the only one to make the connection: "To become a god, to be a man, to educate oneself—all these are different ways of expressing the same meaning."—[1] In other words, human beings are only made in the image of God if they educate themselves, and grasp their entire brief lifetimes as the one great chance to grow.

And what better place could there be than the countryside to understand the different connotations of growth? Seen historically, the important thinking in philosophy, religion, and art did not originate in cities, but rather outside the marketplace—it happened in the provinces. Today that has been forgotten. Everyone heads to the cities and hopes to be stimulated by them. But in the end, they all hid their desperate loneliness behind templates and masks. What are the major tendencies of our time, our continent?

1   Schlegel, Friedrich: "Fragmente." In: *Athenaeum. Eine Zeitschrift von August Wilhelm Schlegel und Friedrich Schlegel. Ersten Bandes Zweytes Stück*. Berlin 1798, p. 73 [English translation cited from Lukács, Georg: *Soul and Form*. New York 2009, p. 65]

There should be a European academy to answer such questions. Interacting with its environs: with nature, the "gently rolling countryside," yes, but also with the history of the old Feldstein walls which once stood in eastern Germany and were used cooperatively. At the time, they were a sign of the hope for a more equitable world of work. One gable still displays a line from the old anthem: "And Facing the Future …" We must not forget: these walls are not for all of time silent landmarks of days past, but also have something to tell about the people who thought, lived, and worked here, who died here in the hope that others will take up aspects of what they created—that's how human life is perpetuated. That is what our academy could be about: finding an equilibrium between hearing and seeing, reverence and recollection, on the one hand, and discussing and planning a process that does not lose sight of history, yet is squarely oriented to the future, on the other. In your architecture this equilibrium would be given expression—by gently embedding the present day in the foundation of what already exists.

According to Friedrich Nietzsche, beauty is always a promise of happiness. In other words, not yet happiness per se, but an intimation of it. In this sense, how "beautiful" it would be if we were to create a place together that carries this thought within it and connects it to the weathered lines embellishing the gable.

Appendix

FRANK BOEHM is an architect and curator. After receiving a stipend to explore "Research by Design" at the TU Eindhoven, he taught several courses as an instructor. From 2004 to 2009, he was professor of curating and exhibition design at the IUAV's Art Department. As an architect, since 2000 he has implemented his designs of spaces for art. From 2006 to 2013, in his capacity as a curator, he built up the collection of the Deutsche Bank in Italy. From 2014 to 2021, he was executive director and artistic director of the Stiftung Insel Hombroich, and since 2016, he has been a member of the board of directors. At Hombroich he has curated exhibitions on the work of Yuri Ancarani, Thomas Demand, Terunobu Fujimori, Per Kirkeby, Joanna Piotrowska, and Ursula Schulz-Dornburg. He regularly publishes essays on architecture and spatially specific artwork.

NOTT CAVIEZEL studied history of art and architecture, medieval history, and archeology in Freiburg (CH); in 1989 he completed a doctorate in Freiburg on the topic of "Gothic Hall Churches and Stufenhallen in Switzerland." He then spent three years as an assistant professor at the chair of art history at Freiburg and received additional training to become qualified as a director of archaeological fieldwork. From 1983 to 1986, he was codirector of the NFP 16, a federal research project on Methods for Conservation of Objects of Cultural Value. From 1987 to 1995, he was director of the Society of Art History in Switzerland; since 1995, he has pursued his own research projects and been engaged as an instructor at the universities of Bern and Lausanne, including being named to an interim professorship. From 2002 to 2011, he served as editor-in-chief of *werk, bauen + wohnen*. Since 2005, he has been a member of the Federal Commission for Monument Preservation (Eidgenössische Kommission für Denkmalpflege, EKD), of which he also served as president from 2009 to 2018. In 2012, he was appointed full professor and head of the department of Monument Preservation and Building within Existing Structures at the TU Vienna.

GÜNTER FIGAL lives and works as philosopher in Freiburg im Breisgau. He completed his doctorate on Adorno in 1976 and his postdoc work on Martin Heidegger in 1987 in Heidelberg. From 1989 to 2002, Figal was professor of philosophy at the Universität Tübingen, from 2002 to 2017 full professor of philosophy at the Universität in Freiburg im Breisgau. He has held numerous guest professorships, including at Kwansei Gakuin University in Nishinomiya, as holder of the Kardinal Mercier Chair at the University of Leuven, as Gadamer Distinguished Visiting Professor at Boston College, at the University of Turin as holder of the International Chair of Philosophy Jacques Derrida, at the Universität Salzburg, and at the East China Normal University in Shanghai. From 2003 until his resignation in 2015, he headed the Martin Heidegger Society. Since 2009, he has been editor of the Heidegger Forum series, which is published by Vittorio Klostermann, and since 1998, editor of the Philosophische Untersuchungen series, and since 2002 of the Internationale Jahrbuch für Hermeneutik. Since 2013, Figal has

also edited the first German-language Heidegger lexicon. He has published numerous texts, essays, and books. Since 2015, his manuscripts and correspondence have been administered and archived by the Deutsches Literaturarchiv in Marbach am Neckar.

LUDWIG FISCHER first studied biology, then German, Evangelical theology, and general rhetoric at the universities of Tübingen, Basel, and Zurich. In 1967, he completed a doctorate in rhetoric, and from 1968 to 1970 was an instructor in the fields German language and literature at the University of Stockholm. From 1971 to 1976, he worked as research assistant at the TU Berlin, where he completed his postdoc in 1976. From 1978 to 2004, he taught and researched as full professor of modern German literature and media culture at the Universität Hamburg. Fischer has published several books and numerous essays on German literature (primarily works completed after 1945), on poetics and aesthetics, and on social and media history. One focus of his work is the theory and history of social nature and its literary and medial transmission; within this focus, landscape theory and landscape aesthetics play an important role. Since becoming an emeritus professor, he has increasingly turned his attention to literary projects and to the theory and history of nature writing in the countries in which the German language is prevalent. He "moonlights" as an ambitious gardener.

TONY FRETTON is a principal with James McKinney and David Owen of Tony Fretton Architects. Buildings by the practice include the Lisson Gallery, Red House Chelsea, Fuglsang Kunstmuseum in Denmark, the British Embassy in Warsaw, Solid 11 in Amsterdam, and recently two apartment towers in Antwerp and the City Hall of Deinze in Belgium. Fretton has held the chair of architectural design-interiors at the Technical University of Delft (1999–2013), as well as visiting professorships at the Harvard GSD (2005–06), ETH Zurich (2011–12), AHO Norway (2015–16), University of Navarre, Spain (2016), and ETSAB Barcelona (2017–18). He is currently master of Diploma Unit 2 at the London Metropolitan University School of Art, Architecture and Design and visiting professor at University of East London. His sketch books have been collected by the Victoria and Albert Museum, and his models and drawings by the Drawing Matter Trust. Fretton's *A.E.I.O.U: Articles Essays Interviews and Out-Takes* was published by Jap Sam Books in spring 2017.

CHRISTOPHE GIROT received a dual master's degree in architecture and landscape architecture from UC Berkeley. From 1989 to 1999 he held the chair of design at the Versailles School of Landscape Architecture. Since 2001 he has been a full professor of landscape architecture at the ETH Department of Architecture in Zurich, where he also served as dean (2017–21). At the ETH he founded the Institute of Landscape Architecture (ILA) with Professor Günther Vogt in 2005, and then cofounded the Landscape Visualization and Modeling Laboratory

(LVML) with Professor Adrienne Grêt-Regamey in 2010; he also founded the new Institute of Landscape and Urban Studies (LUS) in 2019. Together with Professors Günther Vogt and Teresa Galí-Izard, he launched the first masters of science in landscape architecture at the ETH. His teaching and research interests span new topological methods in landscape design, landscape perception and analysis through new media, and contemporary theory and history of landscape architecture. His professional practice focuses on large-scale landscape projects such as the Alptransit Deposit in Sigirino Ticino or the Third Rhône River Correction in the Canton of Valais. His most recent publications *The Course of Landscape Architecture* and *Thinking the Contemporary Landscape* seek to establish both past and current trends in landscape history and theory.

ACHIM HAHN is a habilitated sociologist and architectural scientist. He has been a senior professor of architectural theory at the TU Dresden since 2018. His current field of research is the scientific theory for a science of architecture. His most recent books include: *Architektur und Lebenspraxis: Für eine phänomenologisch-hermeneutische Architekturtheorie* (Bielefeld 2017) as well as—with coeditor Karsten Berr—*Interdisziplinäre Architekturwissenschaft: Eine Einführung* (Wiesbaden 2020).

ALBERT KIRCHENGAST is an architecture theorist. He completed his doctorate at the ETH Zurich, where he taught and researched for ten years at the gta and then at the ILA. He was a visiting scholar at the IWM in Vienna, the CCA in Montreal, and the Harvard GSD. From 2018 to 2021 he was a senior scholar at the Kunsthistorisches Institut Florenz, Max-Planck-Institut, and in 2019/20 he was guest professor at the TU Vienna. He has published numerous articles in newspapers and in professional journals, as well as several books, including a monograph entitled *Das unvollständige Haus: Mies van der Rohe und die Landschaft* (2019) and *Franz Riepl baut auf dem Land. Eine Architektur des Selbstverständlichen* (2018) which received the DAM Architecture Book Award, and *Landschaft im Gespräch* (2015). He presently teaches at universities in Germany and Austria and is visiting lecturer at the LUS (ETH Zurich).

JÖRN KÖPPLER is an architect. He and his wife Annette Köppler-Türk are principals of Köppler Türk Architekten in Potsdam; their work is situated primarily in the residential sector. He studied at the TU Berlin and was university assistant at the Institut für Architekturtheorie und Baukunst, TU Graz, where he completed his doctorate in 2007. Since 2001 he has taught architecture; the focus of his research is the architecture of modernism, its possible meaning, and its translation into built form. His texts appear regularly in the *FAZ*, *taz*, *Bauwelt*, and other publications. He has written the books *Sinn und Krise moderner Architektur: Zeitgenössisches Bauen zwischen Schönheitserfahrung und Rationalitätsglauben* (2010) and *Die Poetik des Bauens* (2016), which sums up his research fellowship at the Villa Massimo in Rome.

LARA MEHLING is a German-American landscape architect and historian currently based in Zurich, Switzerland. After receiving a BA in environmental humanities and completing her master of landscape architecture at the Harvard University Graduate School of Design in 2015, Lara joined the Institute of Landscape and Urban Studies at the ETH Zurich as a research and teaching associate. She has previously worked at landscape architecture firms Studio Vulkan and Vogt Landschaftsarchitekten and is currently working on a dissertation in landscape history while teaching design and pursuing the topic of landscape ornament in installations, exhibitions, and workshops through the design/research platform After Apricots, which she cofounded in Zurich and Istanbul in 2017.

FLORIAN NAGLER is an architect and head of the department of design and tectonics at the TU Munich. After studying art history and completing an apprenticeship as carpenter, he studied architecture at the Universität Kaiserslautern. Following a stint at Mahler Günster Fuchs he opened his own office in Stuttgart in 1996. He and his wife Barbara Nagler have also operated an office in Munich since 2001; their work has received several prizes. In 2000, prior to being appointed professor at the TU Munich, he served as interim professor at the BU Wuppertal, and held a guest professor at the Royal Danish Academy in Copenhagen and at the Hochschule für Technik Stuttgart. Nagler is a member of the Academy of Arts in Berlin and the Bavarian Academy of Fine Arts in Munich. Since 2012, he has headed the research project "Einfach Bauen" which received funding from Future Building, an initiative of the German Federal Institute for Research on Building, Urban Affairs and Spatial Development. The project is set up in several phases. The hands-on research engages with the fundamental issue of "how to erect buildings that are robust, durable, and low-tech without having to relinquish user satisfaction or the value of beauty."

DUNJA RICHTER is a landscape architect and garden historian. She received a master's degree from the Dresden University of Technology and PhD on the Zurich Botanical Garden's plant trade during the nineteenth century from the ETH Zurich. Before joining the Institute of Landscape Architecture at the ETH Zurich in 2009, she was employed at the Department for the Preservation of Gardens at the State of Hessen's garden and castle authority and as project manager at Zurich's municipal city planning authority. At present she works as a senior researcher at the Institute of Landscape and Urban Studies (LUS) and has been program coordinator for the two-year master's degree program Master of Science ETH in landscape architecture. Her research and teaching focuses on the history of garden design and landscape architecture, with a concentration on exchange processes, as well as on the meanings and uses of plants in the context of a growing globalization.

ANJA RONACHER studied photography at the Royal College of Art in London and the Estonian Academy of Arts in Tallinn, as well as scenography at the University of Applied Arts in Vienna. Her photographs of objects, often artifacts found in museums, are filled with darkness. They have been explored as symbols and for their ritual and spiritual purpose (masks for the death cult, men of sorrows, burial objects). The dark creates a space in and of itself while also referring to what lies beneath. The images collude with and reveal a greater darkness that surrounds and, ultimately, is within and behind human consciousness. Most recently, Anja Ronacher's work was exhibited in a solo show at Krinzinger Projekte, Vienna, at Leto, Warsaw, and in group exhibitions at the Lithuanian National Museum of Art and the Sharjah Art Foundation in the United Arab Emirates. She lives and works in Vienna, Austria.

HENRIKE SCHOPER first completed an apprenticeship as textile printer. From 1987 to 1989, she studied cultural economy in East Berlin. In 1991, Schoper enrolled in the architecture program at the TU Munich. Three years later she transferred to the HdK Berlin, where she graduated in 1998 and was awarded the Max Taut Prize. She worked at a variety of architecture firms in Basel and Berlin before founding an office in 2000 with Tom Schoper. In 2007, she took a position as a research assistant at the Chair of Public Buildings and Design at the TU Dresden, and began her dissertation on Aldo Rossi's città analoga theory in 2012, receiving her doctorate in 2017. Through their design work and in essays for magazines and newspapers, she and Tom Schoper inquire into the potential of the building stock.

TOM SCHOPER studied architecture from 1987 to 1994 at the TU Munich and ETH Zurich. From 1994 to 2000 he acquired a wide range of practical experience as an employee of Professor Benedict Tonon in Berlin. Next, he and Henrike Schoper set up an office together and named it schoper.schoper. In 2004, he took a position as research assistant at the Chair of Architectural Delineation, TU Dresden, where he completed his doctorate on "The Identity of Architecture" in 2009. His compilation of interviews on architecture theory is entitled *Ein Haus: Werk–Ding–Zeug?* (2016); in the book, five architects grapple with the question of the background of architectural design. In addition to his design work, he is often invited to be a guest juror and hold lectures at universities in Germany and abroad. From 2019 to 2021, he served as interim professor of design and interiors at the TU Darmstadt.

SIMON STRAUSS studied classics and history in Basel, Poitiers, and Cambridge. In 2017, he completed his postdoc at the Humboldt-Universität in Berlin with a work on the conceptions of ancient Roman society. He lives in Berlin and Frankfurt am Main. Since 2016 he has been working at the *Feuilleton* of the *Frankfurter Allgemeine Zeitung*. In 2017 he made his literary debut *Sieben Nächte*; two years later his second novel, entitled *Römische Tage*, appeared. In 2020, he edited *Spielplan-Änderung!* In the

book, thirty authors each describe a little-known play which they propose should be added to the repertoire of German-language theaters. He is a charter member of the nonprofit organization *Arbeit an Europa e.V.* and initiator of the European Archive of Voices. Strauß is a member of the Bavarian Academy of the Fine Arts and of the Department of Performing Arts.

KLAUS ZWERGER was associate professor at the University of Technology in Vienna. As of autumn 2021 he is professor at SEU in Nanjing. Three long-term scholarships at Todai and a guest professorship at Hosei University provided ample opportunity to become familiar with Japan. Extensive field research in China, Europe, and Southeast Asia resulted in several lecture series, numerous seminars, and workshops in China and Europe. Working as a joiner and carpenter he has collected experience with the nuances of wood. His scientific research is focused on historic wood architecture. He specializes in comparing East Asian and European building traditions and publishes widely on this topic. Two noteworthy publications are *Wood and Wood Joints: Building Traditions in Europe, Japan and China*—a seminal work, which is currently being translated into Chinese—and *Cereal Drying Racks: Culture and Typology of Wood Buildings in Europe and East Asia* (2020).

© 2022 by jovis Verlag GmbH
Texts by kind permission of the authors.
Pictures by kind permission of the photographers / holders of the picture rights.
All rights reserved.

Editing and Layout: Albert Kirchengast
Translation (German to English): Elise Feiersinger
Copyediting: Michael Thomas Taylor

Graphic design: Willi Schmid & Radim Peško
Typefaces: Landscript Condensed (radimpesko.com), DeVinne
Paper: Fedrigoni, Constellation SNOW E.07, $350\,\mathrm{g/m^2}$ and Mondi Offset, $120\,\mathrm{g/m^2}$
Lithography: Bild 1 Druck, Berlin
Printed in the European Union.

Bibliographic information published by the Deutsche Nationalbibliothek
The Deutsche Nationalbibliothek lists this publication in the Deutsche
Nationalbibliografie; detailed bibliographic data are available on the Internet at
http://dnb.d-nb.de

jovis Verlag GmbH
Lützowstraße 33
10785 Berlin

www.jovis.de

ISBN 978-3-86859-541-3